Harry "Bucky" Lew

Harry "Bucky" Lew
A Biography of Basketball's First Black Professional

CHRIS BOUCHER

Foreword by Douglas Stark

McFarland & Company, Inc., Publishers
Jefferson, North Carolina

ISBN (print) 978-1-4766-9784-0
ISBN (ebook) 978-1-4766-5795-0

Library of Congress cataloging data are available

© 2026 Chris Boucher. All rights reserved

No part of this book may be reproduced or transmitted in any form or by any means, electronic or mechanical, including photocopying or recording, or by any information storage and retrieval system, without permission in writing from the publisher.

Front cover image: Bucky Lew during his 1900–01 Lowell YMCA playing days (courtesy of the Center for Lowell History, University of Massachusetts Lowell)

Printed in the United States of America

McFarland & Company, Inc., Publishers
Box 611, Jefferson, North Carolina 28640
www.mcfarlandpub.com

For the Lews

Table of Contents

Foreword by Douglas Stark	1
Preface	5
1. A Career on the Precipice	7
2. Gateway City	16
3. Other Options	23
4. A New Hope	35
5. Relapse	41
6. Problematic Professionalism	48
7. Opening Night	56
8. Basketball's Dead Ball Era	64
9. Star Turn	71
10. Face of the Franchise	80
11. Over to Haverhill	91
12. Injuries and Indignities	100
13. Near Misses	107
14. From Allyship to a Championship	119
15. Home Again	128
16. Franchise Owner	136
17. Back to School	147
18. All Things Considered	155

Table of Contents

19. Partnerships 162
20. Lew Circles the Bases 173

Chapter Notes 183
Bibliography 201
Index 203

Foreword

by Douglas Stark

LATE IN LIFE, HARRY (BUCKY) LEW sat for an exclusive interview with Gerry Finn of the *Springfield Union*, in Springfield, Massachusetts, where Bucky and his family relocated several decades earlier.

The interview conducted in 1958 might be the only surviving interview Lew ever gave regarding his life. It might also be the only interview for which he sat. As a Springfield resident, Lew was now living a short distance from the birthplace of basketball, which occurred in 1891 at the International YMCA Training School (now Springfield College) when Dr. James Naismith created an indoor game for the city's young men to play during winter. It would be another decade until the Naismith Basketball Hall of Fame officially opened its doors to the public, five years after Lew's death in 1963.

Likewise in 1958, Bill Russell was in his second year with the Boston Celtics, having led the team to the 1957 NBA Championship, their first, as the only Black player on the roster. In the same building, the old Boston Garden, in January 1958, the Boston Bruins integrated professional hockey by signing Willie O'Ree. Progress was being made, slowly, but it would be another year, until 1959, when the Boston Red Sox would become the last Major League Baseball team to integrate when they promoted Elijah (Pumpsie) Green.

Those pioneers possibly never heard of Lew or his role as the first Black professional basketball player. His accomplishments occurred half a century earlier, at a time when the game of basketball was a decade old and the professional game had started four years earlier. Basketball was still a crude game and travel was by train, games were played in armories, and some baskets had no backboards. Players were considered cagers as they played inside a court surrounded by chicken wire to prevent unruly fans from interfering with the game.

When Lew sat with Finn, he was open about his role in the game

Foreword by Douglas Stark

and the challenges he faced. A native of Lowell, Massachusetts, Lew played basketball at the YMCA and was looking to continue playing basketball when he joined Lowell of the New England Basketball League in 1902. "I can almost see the faces of those Marlboro [sic] players when I got into the game ... some of the local papers put the pressure on by demanding that they give this little Negro from around the corner a chance to play."

Lew went on to discuss the obstacles he had to overcome: "all those things you read about Jackie Robinson, the abuse, name calling, extra effort to put him down ... they're all true. I got the same treatment and even worse. Basketball was a rough game back then. I took the bumps, the elbows in the gut, knees here and everything else that went with it. But I gave it right back. It was rough but worth it. Once they knew I could take it, I had it made. Some of those same old boys who gave the hardest licks turned out to be my best friends in the years that followed."

For decades, Lew's accomplishments have largely been forgotten, relegated to the dustbin of history, until here vividly portrayed by the diligent work of Chris Boucher, a Lowell native, who has methodically reconstructed the story of Lew, including his family's history of pioneering work on behalf of abolitionism, fighting in the American Revolution and Civil War, and being part of the Underground Railroad. Set within the context of his own family, extending back generations, Lew's pioneering role in breaking basketball's color barrier is as impressive and noteworthy as his family's generational pioneering work.

And yet, Lew's accomplishment is even more impressive when considered within the larger context of his time and the world of sports during his generation.

His journey presents interesting points of intersection that indicate how impactful his accomplishments were while shedding light on the period of Jim Crowism and how it impacted his achievements. It also highlights the successes that Black athletes in Massachusetts had at the turn of the 20th century.

During the Jim Crow Era of the late 19th century and first half of the 20th century, Black athletes challenged racial segregation in a variety of sports. Resistance expressed itself in either creating all–Black teams to strengthen community solidarity or integrating local sports to achieve wider legitimacy and recognition.

Early Massachusetts Black athletes achieving recognition and fame included Frenchy Johnson, a former slave who rowed on the Charles River in the 1870s; Frank Hart, who excelled at pedestrianism, a popular

Foreword by Douglas Stark

sport at the time; William Henry Lewis, a football player at what is now the University of Massachusetts Amherst; cyclist Kittie Knox, who challenged both racial and gender stereotypes; and Clarence Matthews, a Harvard-educated baseball player who was reputed to be considered to break baseball's color barrier decades before Jackie Robinson.

Another early champion, Major Taylor, having relocated to Worcester from Indianapolis, was the first African American sports champion. His fame was international and, as we learn, Lew also competed in cycling in 1901, thus his name mentioned in the local newspaper: "Harry Lew, the Major Taylor of this city, is a little wonder and the race going people of this community will have a chance to see a star in the different events of the season."

Another of Lew's contemporaries was Louis Sockalexis, the first Native American professional baseball player. A member of the Penobscot tribe in Maine, Sockalexis played for three years with the Cleveland Spiders from 1897 to 1899. By 1902–03, when Lew was beginning his professional career, Sockalexis played for the Lowell Tigers, a minor league baseball team. Lew also played baseball in 1903 and there is a possibility that their paths crossed on the baseball diamond.

Lew was part of a small group of pioneering athletes in Lowell and the greater Boston area seeking to integrate sports and carve their own role.

Not only is Lew's story important from the perspective of his contemporaries in the early 20th century, but it is also instructive in his role as a player, coach, manager, owner, and referee. Not only did Lew become the first Black professional basketball player in 1902, that same year he also became the first Black basketball head coach of an integrated team. He conquered two firsts in that same year, both before the age of 20.

From a basketball perspective, his efforts predated Edwin Henderson's work to introduce basketball to African Americans in Washington, D.C., in 1904. It wasn't until 1906 that Bob Douglas, a Caribbean immigrant, first saw the game of basketball being played in New York, a moment that would forever change his life as he eventually founded and owned the New York Renaissance, arguably basketball's most successful all–Black basketball team.

But Lew's status as a "first" should also be considered within the larger context. As historians David K. Wiggins and Ryan A. Swanson note, by competing, Black athletes forged "opportunities to display black self-help, race pride, business acumen, and organizational

Foreword by Douglas Stark

abilities." Much attention, and deservedly so, has been given to Cumberland Posey, who played, owned, and managed baseball's Homestead Grays and was regarded as one of basketball's best Black players during the 1910s. He was a forerunner to baseball's Rube Foster and basketball's Bob Douglas in terms of Black team ownership and Black enterprise.

Lew was a Black businessperson involved in all aspects of basketball a decade earlier. He played, coached, refereed, managed, and owned teams that traveled throughout New England spreading the word of basketball while promoting equal rights and racial uplift. He owned and managed white teams, a stark difference from Posey, Foster, and Douglas.

His good name and reputation were cited by Fred Dobens, a newspaper editor in Nashua, New Hampshire, when the Brooklyn Dodgers approached him as they were considering integrating their Nashua Dodgers farm team in 1948. Lew first played in Nashua in 1902 and thereafter for 20 years. Dobens' high school team played halftime games when Lew was in town. He remembered Lew well and put in a good word when the Dodgers called.

While it is unknown if Walter Brown, owner of the Boston Celtics, knew of Lew, what is known is that it was almost 50 years after Lew first debuted until the Celtics drafted Chuck Cooper in 1950.

As indicated, Lew's accomplishments in the first 25 years of the 20th century are remarkable and his story comes to life in this wonderful work by Boucher. His story gives greater insight into this period and the role Black athletes carved out in their communities.

Sadly, Lew still seems to be a forgotten figure, missing from the pantheon of heroes and influential figures in the Naismith Basketball Hall of Fame. Other pioneering firsts in other sports, baseball's Bud Fowler and football's Fritz Pollard, have been given their rightful place within their sport's shrines.

Toward the end of his article, Gerry Finn makes a passionate plea for Lew. "When they're handing out memberships to the Basketball Hall of Fame, how about a vote from Bucky Lew? Is there anyone in the hall who can say he doesn't deserve it?"

Finally, Lew's story is public, no longer forgotten, and no less timely.

Douglas Stark is a museum professional who has worked in sports museums, including the Tennis Hall of Fame, USGA Museum, and Naismith Basketball Hall of Fame. His career has focused on making history more engaging, relevant, and accessible to a diverse audience. He has also written several books about basketball history.

Preface

THIS BOOK IS ABOUT THE BASKETBALL LIFE and major league legacy of Harry "Bucky" Lew, basketball's first Black professional and the man who integrated every one of its key roles—player, coach, manager, referee, and even franchise owner. All over a century ago!

Despite his incredible achievements, all well documented in the newspapers of the day, Lew has been largely forgotten. Why? There are many reasons, but the most important is the mistaken impression that Lew was "one-and-done"—that he had no influence on the full integration of major league sports that came a generation later.

This is wrong. Lew had a *direct* influence on it. When the Dodgers were trying to build an integrated farm team in the United States at the same time that Jackie Robinson started in Canada, they struggled to find a welcoming city until they reached Fred Dobens, a newspaper editor in Nashua, New Hampshire. He assured them that Black players would be welcome there.

How did Dobens know? When he was a high schooler, his basketball team played at halftime of Lew's games in his city. Dobens saw firsthand the love local fans, the press, and his peers

Photograph of Harry "Bucky" Lew from the 1904 *Lowell Daily Courier*. Lowell newspapers used this photograph or an illustrated version of it throughout Lew's lengthy career. Lew disliked having his picture taken and avoided having a photograph taken when he could (NewspaperArchive).

Preface

held for the man. The Dodgers' first Black players were treated the same way.

Roy Campanella and Don Newcombe were as successful in Nashua as Jackie Robinson was in Montreal. And once the Dodgers integrated their organization, all of major league sports followed in relatively short order. Lew's example set it all in motion and this is his true legacy.

This book is the first full-length, nonfiction treatment of Lew's career. (I also authored a fictional, young adult version of his story in 2023.) Much of this work covers Lew's time in the New England Basketball League. Recognized as a major league of its day, the NEBL gave Lew his start as a pro and provided the setting for many of his most dramatic moments. Of course, Lew continued to make history over his full 25-year career, and each and every one of his many milestones over that time is also thoroughly chronicled.

In my research, I had help from a long list of people. These include Wendy Johnson, Lew's granddaughter, whose many memories of her grandfather grounded the book in reality and brought it to life in front of me; the late Gerard O'Connor, Professor Emeritus of English at the University of Massachusetts Lowell, whose father played with Lew and remembered him fondly; and Douglas Stark, an author whose work on early basketball captivated me and inspired me to look deeper into the history of the game in my own neighborhood. Others who provided helpful context include authors Murry Nelson, Charlie Bevis, Chaz Scoggins, and Ed Rice as well as historians Martha Mayo, Tony Sampas, and Carisa Kolias from the Center for Lowell History at University of Massachusetts Lowell. And, of course, my wife, Erica, for her careful proofreading and moral support!

I further drew on the firsthand accounts of Lew's games from the newspapers of the day, including the *Lowell Sun*, *Lowell Daily Courier*, *Lowell Courier-Citizen*, *Nashua Sentinel*, *Boston Globe*, and other area papers. Most of these were available in a digital format via a subscription to NewspaperArchive from Lowell's Pollard Memorial Library so I owe special thanks to that institution. Newspapers.com was also particularly helpful.

Finally, I referred early and often to the *Pro Basketball Encyclopedia* created by basketball historian William Himmelman. The Web site provides a wealth of information on the early game, and while its data on Lew does have some gaps, I would have been lost without it!

Chapter 1

A Career on the Precipice

On one early May evening in 1902, the future of basketball superstar Harry "Bucky" Lew seemed far from assured. Despite the celebration at the Young Men's Christian Association—a banquet thrown to honor the Lowell, Massachusetts, team he led to an amateur championship—no one could blame the 18-year-old for having serious doubts about his pro basketball dreams. Jim Crow dominated most of the country, segregating Blacks and whites into separate and unequal ways of life. And it might even deny him a chance to go pro.

"That was Bucky Lew"

Lew was born and raised roughly 75 miles from Springfield, where James Naismith had invented basketball the previous decade, and the emerging sport was as popular in Lowell as it was anywhere in the world. The city had an active amateur basketball scene, with YMCA, high school, and college teams, and it was also well represented in the pros. Lowell's two teams in the New England Basketball League led the league in attendance.[1]

The birthplace of the industrial revolution in the United States continued to grow as mill agents lured waves of immigrants to the gateway city with the promise of work for anyone willing to work hard. Irish, French Canadians, and many others answered the call, and they made up most of the city's population—and its basketball players.

Lew's YMCA team finished with a record of 20 wins and seven losses that year. It dominated the YMCA's "triangle league," which included Ys in neighboring cities from Massachusetts and New Hampshire, and the team won more than its share of games against high school and college teams, too.

The banquet was a big enough event that the city's largest newspaper, the *Lowell Sun*, covered it that night. The *Sun* reporter described an overflowing buffet of oysters, lobster, turkey, ice cream, jellies, and cakes. Speeches were also on the menu, and as the attendees feasted, the basketball coach and physical education instructor, Victor Meister, praised the team for its record and sportsmanship.

Meister likely only added to the drama when he noted that the team's success came despite an early obstacle: "We were somewhat handicapped the first of the season by the loss of two of our players, Field and Lynch, who left us to join the ranks of the professionals."[2] As Meister made clear, a pipeline from the YMCA to the pros was in place. All things being equal, Lew's shot should come next. But he hadn't received an invitation to join any of the NEBL's eight teams.

As a Black player, Lew was different from his former teammates

Bucky Lew with his 1900–1901 Lowell YMCA teammates. Lew is standing in the back row alongside coach Victor Meister. Skip Field, Walter Muzzey, and Robert Syme are in the middle row, from left. Ted Pearson and Dan Lynch are in the front row, from left. The shield at the bottom of the picture was awarded to the team for winning the YMCA's Merrimack Valley Championship (image courtesy Center for Lowell History, University of Massachusetts Lowell).

Chapter 1. A Career on the Precipice

who leveled up as well as nearly everyone else playing organized basketball at the time. Race hadn't been an issue for him as an amateur, because Lowell's YMCA, like its public schools, was integrated. Pro basketball, however, was a different story. While the pro game had been in existence for at least four years, no one had paid an African American to play yet.

Despite its owners recruiting players from all over New England as well as New York, New Jersey, and Pennsylvania, the NEBL was an all-white enterprise. The players that had jumped from the YMCA, Dan Lynch and Skip Field, enjoyed relative success last season, and if he were given a chance, Lew could expect the same. He just didn't know if he would be given that opportunity.

At least the reporters from his hometown papers were behind him. Another *Sun* story, which covered the team's victory over the Massachusetts Institute of Technology, said the budding rocket scientists concluded that Lew's team could play with anyone. "The M.I.T. boys were defeated ... which was a surprise.... In their opinion, if Lowell could beat them, she ought to be able to win from any amateur team in the State." And the reporter singled out one player as the leader of the team:

> One of the Lowell men ... at critical stages of the game was on hand with the sphere in his tight embrace to aid his fellows in piling up the score. That was Bucky Lew. He made nine points while his opponent was napping. As captain of this year's team, he has led all his fellows in fast and clean work and has been exceptionally successful in scoring.[3]

"Football, murder, and a house on fire"

Some of Lew's fans might prefer he not get that chance to go pro—out of concern for his own safety. Early pro basketball was a very violent game. One reporter, witnessing a game for the first time, described it as a combustible mix:

> Did you see Saturday's football game between Dartmouth and Brown? Yes? Well, that was no more exciting than the basket ball as it was played last night by the P.A.C. of Lowell and the Marlboros of Marlboro town. It was the first game of the season [and] a party of newspaperman saw the contest. It was the first glimpse of the real thing for most of the party and it proved so altogether and unexpectedly fast and furious that they were almost swept of their feet. Basketball, in short, combines all the exciting elements of boxing, wrestling ... football, murder, and a house on fire.[4]

Harry "Bucky" Lew

Even early promoters of the game had serious concerns. George Hepbron, head of the Amateur Athletic Union, warned of its risks in his early instruction manual, *How to Play Basket Ball*. He wrote, "There is not a game that offers the opportunity for rough playing, and which is more exciting to the temper, than basket ball."[5] He also maintained that "in no game, not even foot ball, is there so much chance for underhand, dirty work."[6]

Fistfights were common. Another local paper, the *Lowell Courier-Citizen*, reported on one such exchange with the headline "Two Teeth Gone from Tighe's Set—Devlin's Blow Loosens Ivories." According to the story, after his opponent tore the ball away from him, "Devlin seemed to lose his head for a moment; his fist shot out and met Tighe's mouth, knocking a bit off two of the PAC man's teeth. Tighe was sent into dreamland."[7]

The frequency of fights was bad enough, and the fact that some of the players were also pro boxers made it worse. With trained pugilists behind them, punches could lead to serious damage. The previous August, one of Lowell's basketball players was killed in the ring.

According to the *Sun*, in the "Fatal Boxing Bout," John Dion was knocked out in the ninth round of what was supposed to be a 20-round fight. After a right-left-right combination, the final blow landed "on the point of the jaw and Dion went down like a log." Medical staff at ringside were unable to revive him and so were doctors at St. John's Hospital, where he died a few hours later.[8]

Since boxing was illegal in Massachusetts, the opposing fighter, referee, and owner of the club that hosted the match were arrested by police and subject to a grand jury inquiry. All involved were ultimately cleared of any wrongdoing, however. Boxing was permitted for exhibition purposes between members of a sporting club, and the fighters were members, for the night anyway. The men were released without charges, their cause apparently helped by the coroner's conclusion that the cause of death was Dion's head hitting the floor and not a direct punch.

While the fatal fight occurred during a boxing match and not a basketball game, Dion had appeared on the rosters of both of Lowell's pro teams that year and the referee, William Kelliher, played pro ball too.

"It's great sport being an Indian"

One ray of hope for Lew's pro dreams was the appearance of Louis Sockalexis in the city that spring. Sock had made history as major

Chapter 1. A Career on the Precipice

league baseball's first Native American player five years before and he was attempting to revive his career in Lowell. But the scrutiny that came with his early success presented another set of concerns.

Sock played for Cleveland in 1897. In an era before official nicknames, the team Sock joined had been known as the Spiders, but after his hot start and the fan attention that followed, the press quickly re-named them the Indians. (Cleveland's team is known as the Guardians today.)

Almost halfway through his rookie season, Sock was among the league leaders in many offensive categories. According to biographer Ed Rice, on July 3, Sockalexis "was hitting .328 (81 hits in 247 at bats), with 40 runs scored, 39 runs batted in and 16 stolen bases."[9] Unfortunately, Sock quickly flamed out. He played only eight more games that season and only parts of the next two. A worsening problem with alcohol and a devastating foot injury that never properly healed led to his release the next year. He played parts of two seasons in the minors and was out of baseball after 1899.

Sock caught a break in 1902 because the man running the Lowell Tigers, Fred Lake, needed talent and a billboard attraction to field a competitive team and fill his newly constructed ballpark. He had competed against Sock in the major leagues as a catcher with Boston and remembered his impressive skills and popularity. He probably also knew that Sock had played reasonably well in his last stint for a minor league team in Connecticut before falling off the wagon. He had to be confident that if Sock remained sober, he could recapture his old magic.

A little over a week into the Tigers season, early signs on the baseball diamond were good. Sock was off to a strong start and on his way to becoming a star. The team was performing well, and fans were coming out to Spalding Park to see them play.

Sock made an immediate impact in his first game. A headline in the *Boston Globe* declared "Sockalexis Once More. Great Batting and Circus Catches Features of Dover-Lowell Game." Despite a narrow 5–4 loss, the reporter raved about Sock's diving grabs and domination at the plate: "The work of Sockalexis, the noted Indian player, was of the phenomenal order. Three of his catches were made after long runs and were followed by [somersaults]. His batting was a spectacular feature of the game. In five times at the bat he placed the ball safely four times. Coming from the field to the players' bench he was repeatedly cheered."[10] His play was near perfect, and the fans showed him their appreciation.

By the night of Lew's YMCA banquet, Sock had become one of the

Harry "Bucky" Lew

Louis Sockalexis with his 1902 Lowell Tigers teammates. Sockalexis (#11) is seated in the front row with a glove in his hands, and manager Fred Lake (#4) is seated in the center of the back row (*Spalding's Official Base Ball Guide for 1903* from Internet Archive).

offensive stars of the team. He was batting third in the order and hitting .324 with five walks and six runs. (While his runs batted in and stolen bases numbers were likely impressive as well, these statistics were not reliably reported in the papers.)

Sock's apparent good cheer also made him a fan favorite. He had withstood the predictable tomahawk chops and war whoops with a smile from his earliest days in the pros and he continued it with the Tigers.

Sockalexis played a prominent role in the press coverage of a recent two-game series with Nashua. In the first game, a 5–4 Lowell win over Nashua, Sock had two hits, three runs, and four putouts.[11] Further, in a series of sketches of the game that covered most of the top half of the page, Sock is featured twice. The likenesses are cartoonish but not caricatured, and Sock appears in exaggerated poses but without overly racial features. In one sketch, "Sock smiles," he wears a broad grin, and in another, "Sock gets dramatic on the coach line," he adopts a conspicuous stance as he coaches one of the bases.[12]

On his way out of the YMCA banquet, Lew likely heard the newsboys

Chapter 1. A Career on the Precipice

hawking the late edition with results from the second game on the series, maybe as he pulled his coat tighter while waiting to board the electric streetcar for home. If he picked up the paper, he would have seen that Sock drew attention once again for more than his play.

The *Sun* described a circus-like atmosphere as Lowell completed the sweep of the home team: "Sockalexis was the cynosure of all eyes and all the small boys in the town have gone hoarse from ripping out war-whoops every time he went to the bat," the account went. The "rubber-necking public, large and small, crowded about him and took as much satisfaction looking at him as though they were at a Wild West show."

How did Sock react? He went with it. According to the reporter, he remarked, "'It's great sport being an Indian.'" And he played along with more than just words. During a pause in the game, another player and "Sockalexis went through a war dance that made a great hit with the crowd."[13]

"Sign and symbol of a lost race"

Sock's success had come with a dark side going way back to his rookie year. After his first game in Cincinnati, a reporter from that city's *Commercial Tribune* commented favorably on the visitor's play: "The game was the initial appearance of Louis Sockalexis, the Penobscot full-blood Indian, and it was a most successful one. It seems the Cleveland Club has secured a star player in this recruit. He led his side at the bat, while his fielding was one of the features of the game."[14]

After a post-game interview, the reporter called him a "gentlemanly player" and could "hardly believe that Socks was the offspring of half-civilized parents." The racial swipe was bad enough, and Lew may have found Sock's take even more disturbing: "'It amuses me when I hear the crowd's warwhoops and yells when I go to the plate. Not that it reminds me of my early days, for I never heard them, but because they expect to see feathers sprouting out of my hair and a tomahawk in my pocket. I left my home when I was quite young.... After I received an education I found no more pleasure at my home, and I have been with the white people ever since.'"[15] As reported, Sock seemed to suggest he now belonged to white America exclusively.

It wasn't the only time an account appeared in the press noting Sock's apparent rejection of his people. A Hartford reporter claimed he had recently witnessed Sock abusing a tobacco advertisement featuring a Native American:

> Apparently he has lost all the love he ever had for his race. The other day he came upon a wooden Indian displayed as a cigar store sign. The Indian was a Narragansett, the same tribe to which Sock belongs. "Oh, you brute," he ejaculated in his purest English, "you sign and symbol of a lost race, take that, and that." And he gave the Indian two punches that would have sent him to the happy hunting grounds had he not been fastened too securely to this earth.[16]

This account is somewhat dubious. Sock, in fact, was a member of the Penobscot tribe of Maine, not the Narragansetts of Rhode Island. Also, whether Sock was sober or even serious at the time isn't clear. Regardless, the reporting was consistent with the popular perception of the man.

Pride and Prejudice

Someone with as proud a family history as Lew would have to be troubled by all of that. His great-great-grandfather Barzillai fought in the Revolutionary War and his great-uncle Zimri fought in the Civil War. His grandparents James and Elizabeth ran a station on the Underground Railroad, a network of homes, churches, and businesses maintained by people who provided safety and shelter to those escaping slavery. And his father William represented his city at an early Equal Rights convention in Boston. The Lews always seemed to challenge the status quo rather than play along with it.

To be fair, Lew had to acknowledge Sock was in a weaker position than he was. The U.S. government didn't recognize Native Americans as American citizens and wouldn't grant them that status until the Indian Citizenship Act of 1924.

African Americans were U.S. citizens, as the Fourteenth Amendment to the Constitution had established once and for all in 1868. That said, anyone reading the papers of the day had to have their doubts. The press was full of stories of violence against Black people who dared to exercise their Constitutional rights. They were also filled with accounts of African Americans accused of crimes who never received fair treatment or a just trial. Lynch mobs enforced their own brand of injustice, and the legal system didn't do much to discourage it—before or after the fact.

Chapter 1. A Career on the Precipice

When Lew finally made it back to the family home on 89 Mount Hope Street, the site of that old stop on the Underground Railroad, he had a lot to consider. If he did get a chance to go pro, was there anything he could learn from Sock's experience?

It was complicated, to say the least. While Sock had demonstrated that a person of color could succeed as a professional, he was almost always viewed through a racial lens and often regarded as a curiosity. Perhaps worse, he played along, acting according to stereotype for some audiences and distancing himself from his ancestors for others.

Lew could read *How to Play Basketball* for guidance on the court but there was no instruction manual for how to handle what might happen off the court. Based on his experience with the YMCA, it was obvious he had the support of the home fans. On the road, things might be very different. He'd be playing before hundreds to thousands of fans several nights a week. And while his YMCA games had seen some local press coverage, the pro game would bring another level of scrutiny. Every city in the league had one or more newspapers that carried daily stories about the games, and they needed something to write about.

It was a lot to take in for a young man who just wanted to ball out!

Chapter 2

Gateway City

When it came to race, Lew's hometown had a complicated history from the start. And the Lews were there every step of the way. In fact, the Lews were in Lowell before Lowell was Lowell.

Lowell's Ties to Slavery

Lew's great-great-grandfather, Barzillai, a Revolutionary War veteran, used his military pay to buy a farm in northeastern Massachusetts. His purchase was located on the north side of the Merrimack River, near Pawtucketville and its namesake Pawtucket Falls.

Not long after, a group of investors from Boston began buying land on the south side of the river. Looking to capitalize on a growing market for processed cotton goods, they built a series of textile factories and a network of canals to power them. Driven by a drop of more than 30 feet at the falls, the canals provided a reported 10,000 horsepower.[1] The mills were a success, the population increased, and the factory town of Lowell became a city. As it grew, it absorbed rural Pawtucketville for its undeveloped land and clean water.[2]

The original source of the investors' funds was the slave trade. When Massachusetts made importing slaves illegal in the early 1800s, those who had profited from the practice looked to diversify. According to author David Vermette, "By investing in textile manufacturing, the Perkinses, Cabots, Lowells, and allied family firms created a way out of their dependence on risky overseas trades. Merchant capital, gained, directly or indirectly, in the Atlantic slave economy ... provided the funds to establish the factories and to buy the raw cotton."[3]

The source of the cotton provided another link to slave-owning South. As the National Park Service says, "Lowell's textile-based economy was wholly dependent on the institution of slavery. To meet the demand for Lowell's cotton mills, enslaved people collectively worked

Chapter 2. Gateway City

around 33 million hours per year."[4] And in yet another tie, slaveowners could be customers as well as suppliers. One company produced a coarse cloth specifically for slaves, which was known as "Lowell cloth" in the South and "Negro cloth" in the North. No one who had a choice would wear it, as the "cheap fabric ... was uncomfortable and tore easily.... The Lowell Company made great profits selling this inexpensive fabric to enslavers."[5] So mill owners and slaveowners had a mutually beneficial relationship on multiple levels.

Perhaps inspired by their Southern partners, mill owners looked for a source of cheap labor to staff their factories. They started by recruiting young women from farms across New England. Women had few options to earn an income in those days, so they could be paid less than men and seemed less likely to agitate for better pay and better hours.

When the "mill girls" began to demand better working conditions, the mill owners turned to another source of labor—immigrants. Many Irish laborers were already in the city from building the canals, so mill owners employed them when they could, and they augmented their numbers by recruiting additional waves of immigrants from French-speaking Quebec and countries in southern Europe. The immigrants' lack of skills and limited English meant they too had limited options and their differences from each other would complicate any efforts to organize.

Allies and Adversity

Pro-slavery advocates had an obvious presence in the city. Mill owners, many workers, and the small businesses that catered to their needs were motivated to preserve the institution that provided their income.

Abolition groups were also active. Many religious leaders and some of the lowest levels of workers, marginalized themselves because of their lack of options, long hours, and low pay, had sympathy for those even worse off than them. The mill girls formed the Lowell Female Anti-Slavery Society and attracted hundreds of participants to their petition drives. Their efforts supported the abolition of slavery in Washington, D.C., opposed admitting Texas as a slave state, and donated money to support the Underground Railroad.[6]

Of course, the city's few Black residents, like the Lews, were opposed to slavery. Barzillai and his wife, Dinah, were members of the Pawtucket

Harry "Bucky" Lew

Society Church, which held the first anti-slavery meeting in the Lowell area in 1832.[7] That first meeting was organized within a decade of the opening of the first factories.

The activities of the opposing groups often led to conflict. When abolitionists invited a speaker from the London Anti-Slavery Society, George Thompson, to deliver a series of lectures in the city, the number of opponents grew with each talk. Before the third and final one, notices appeared downtown encouraging residents to disrupt it. One such notice was reprinted in *Cotton Was King: A History of Lowell, Massachusetts*:

> Citizens of Lowell, arise! Look well to your interests! Will you suffer a question to be discussed in Lowell which will endanger the safety of the Union?—a question which we have not, by our constitution, any right to meddle with…. If you are freeborn sons of America, meet, one and all, at the Town Hall, THIS EVENING, at half-past seven o'clock, and convince your Southern brethren that we will not interfere with their rights.[8]

A large crowd turned out as requested and in the expected mood. When members of the mob started to throw stones at the windows of the lecture hall, city leaders feared the violence would grow even worse and postponed the talk. Thompson agreed to the delay but refused to be silenced. Instead, he delivered his talk early the next afternoon when the protestors would be at work.

The Underground Railroad helped transport those escaping slavery through the city. One of the stops was the Lew family home at 89 Mount Hope Street. Lew's grandparents, Adrastus and Elizabeth, purchased and cleared a piece of woodland not far from Barzillai's original spread and built the house that remained in the family for generations.

Elizabeth told the *Sun* in 1912, "During slavery times, runaway slaves came to the house for protection. We would give them food and clothing and sometimes money to help them on their way to Canada."[9] Lew's sister Marion provided more detail when she spoke to the *Boston Traveler* in 1951: "A man would bring them to my grandfather. There was a large old closet upstairs that went from one end of the house to the other. They used to stay there during the day. My grandfather would take them to the New Hampshire line at midnight."[10]

When the Fugitive Slave Act of 1850 made sheltering slaves illegal and required citizens to return them to slavery, the Lews and many others refused to comply. That same year, when slave catchers were rumored to be in the city, abolitionists ran a defiant ad in a local paper:

Chapter 2. Gateway City

Manstealers in Lowell! We understand that one or more persons were in the city yesterday for the purposes of catching Mr. Booth ... formerly a slave in Virginia. He is now in Montreal, and his friend yesterday telegraphed to him that he had better remain there for the present. We hope, however, he will return to the city, for we think there are men enough in Lowell who believe in the "higher law" to protect him against all the efforts of the manstealers.[11]

Despite the new law and the presence of slave catchers in the city, according to University of Massachusetts Lowell professor Robert Forrant, no one who sought freedom in the city was ever returned to slavery.

Civil War Connections

When the Civil War came, its first combat casualties were from Lowell. Luther Ladd, Addison Whitney, and Charles Taylor were killed by a mob in Baltimore as they were on their way to Washington, D.C., to protect the capital.

Zimri Lew, Jr., Bucky's great-uncle, volunteered to fight. According to military records, he enlisted in the famous 54th regiment, the all-Black squad organized in Boston. As the regiment grew, he later transferred to the 55th, another all-Black unit.[12]

Both the 54th and 55th saw action in South Carolina, "the heart and soul of proslavery secession," according to author Douglas Egerton. The war had started in South Carolina when Confederates fired on Union troops at Fort Sumter shortly after Abraham Lincoln's election. And Sullivan's Island in Charleston Harbor was the place where 40 percent of slaves entered the U.S.

So it was a dramatic scene when Black troops captured Charleston in February 1865, and residents poured into the streets to salute them. "'The glory and triumph of this hour may be imagined, but can never be described,'" Egerton cites one soldier as writing. "'It was one of those occasions which happen but once in a lifetime, to be lived over in memory for years.'"[13]

The Civil War finally ended in April 1865, but Zimri remained in South Carolina with his unit. Its post-war mission was to clean up any remaining guerrilla fighters, notify former slaves of their freedom, and otherwise maintain the peace. Tragically, he never made it home. He became sick with dysentery and died in a military hospital in June. He lies buried in Orangeburg, South Carolina, the site of his grave identified by a veteran's marker.

Harry "Bucky" Lew

While his father's family was in Lowell from its earliest days, Lew's mother Isabelle came up from the South after the war. She accompanied one of Lowell's most prominent citizens, Benjamin Butler, a lawyer, politician, and Civil War general. The *Boston Traveler* reported that Isabelle was raised by her sister after her parents passed, then stayed with an uncle in the capital, and finally "came to Lowell with the family of Gen. Benjamin Butler."[14]

Butler achieved fame because of a key decision he made early in the war. His first assignment was to take charge of Fort Monroe in Virginia, and soon after his arrival, three Black men arrived seeking refuge from their enslaver. When the slaveowner, a rebel commander, sought their return, Butler refused.

According to Butler biographer Elizabeth Leonard, he had made a historic decision. "Butler had met with each of the runaways separately to hear their stories, his sharp legal mind slowly reasoning its way to the position that Virginia's recent claim of independence from the United States meant that escapees from bondage there ... were no longer subject to the US Fugitive Slave Law."[15] Some historians credit the choice with inspiring President Abraham Lincoln to issue the Emancipation Proclamation that ultimately freed all of the former slaves.

Unfortunately, Butler had previously supported the series of compromises before the war that sought to preserve but contain slavery, largely by balancing the number of free and slave states. His views only became hardened after South Carolina attacked Fort Sumter and the mob in Baltimore killed the three Lowell soldiers.

After the war, Butler led an unsuccessful impeachment effort against President Andrew Johnson. Johnson opposed efforts to help former slaves and refused to enforce laws protecting them against the rising Ku Klux Klan. While the impeachment failed, Butler and others successfully fought for a series of Constitutional amendments intended to guarantee the former slaves their rights as citizens.

Butler maintained his support for the oppressed for the rest of his political career. He said his interest in siding with marginalized groups had its origins in his childhood in Lowell. His mother was a widow who ran boarding houses for mill girls, and he grew up listening to stories of the challenges they faced.

Chapter 2. Gateway City

Jim Crow Spreads Its Wings

Isabelle married William Lew, and the couple moved to the Lew family home on Mount Hope Street. Two years before Bucky's birth, they opened a dye works and dry-cleaning business in downtown Lowell. Their work consisted of dying fabric for the mills and cleaning and otherwise restoring clothing for consumers.

In addition to running a small business with his wife, William was also active in the early civil rights effort. He "was a delegate to the 1891 Equal Rights Convention held in Boston," according to the UMass Lowell Library, which was a "predecessor to the National Association for the Advancement of Colored People (NAACP)."[16]

Such a civil rights movement was needed even after the Civil War because early hopes of equality for Blacks were soon dashed. Despite the work of Butler and others, Southern leaders passed a variety of laws that made it nearly impossible for former slaves to improve their lives. The laws blocked their access to property ownership, the vote, and education.

Then came Jim Crow. The system of separating whites and Blacks started in the South and spread to a large part of the country after the Supreme Court's infamous ruling in the *Plessy v. Ferguson* case of 1896. The court said that forcing people to use facilities segregated by race didn't violate their Constitutional rights.

While formal segregation did not exist in Lowell, racism still took place. Leonard describes how Butler represented a Black man who was abused and removed from the audience of a musical performance in the city. Despite the unfortunate incident, Butler won the case, and a jury awarded the man $200 in damages, roughly $8000 today.[17]

Lowell's schools were open to all. When the state of Massachusetts examined the state of its schools in 1846, the mayor responded that:

> the public schools of Lowell, of every grade—primary, grammar, and high—are open to colored children, on the same conditions as to white children.... The colored child, as the white, attends the school that happens to be located in his neighborhood, and no fault is found or questions asked. He has the same right to present himself for admission to the high school. And if, upon examination, he is found to have the requisite literary qualifications, he is admitted there, on an equal footing with his white brother.[18]

Caroline Van Vronker was Lowell High School's first Black student. Yet when she graduated and applied for a teaching position there, she faced pushback. According to the UMass Lowell Library, she encountered "objections on account of her color."[19]

Harry "Bucky" Lew

As a lifelong Lowellian, Lew was undoubtedly aware of his city's complicated racial history. And while 50 years had passed since Van Vronker had tried and failed to achieve professional status, given what was happening in most of the country, he might wonder, how much had really changed?

Chapter 3

Other Options

As an outstanding athlete, Lew excelled at more than basketball. Baseball, boxing, and bicycling were the most popular sports of the era, and Lew had an interest in all three. His exploits in baseball and cycling were noteworthy enough to make the newspapers, and while the depth of his interest in boxing is unknown, his granddaughter Wendy remembers watching "Friday Night Fights" with him. Whether he was good enough to go pro in any of these other sports—and whether he would be allowed to try—was, like his basketball dreams, to be determined.

Boxing

Boxing often featured integrated competition in Lew's day. Several matches between Black and white fighters took place in his hometown as he was growing up and they received significant attention in the press.

John Butler, a Black fighter from nearby Lynn, came to Lowell to face George Gardner at the Nutone Club in 1899. The *Sun* reporter described the "meeting" as "the most interesting of its kind ever seen in Lowell." After several preliminary matches, which included John Dion, "the boxer, wrestler, and basket ball player" who would later die in the ring, "the stars of the evening came in," namely Butler and Gardner.[1]

The story was mixed in terms of its consideration of race. The reporter noted that the Black fighter was a skilled one, saying, "Butler is a man of reputation in the ring,"[2] and he didn't identify him as "colored" until late in the story. However, the large illustration that depicted the match clearly shows a white man against a Black one, and since it shows Gardner facing the illustrator, with Butler's back to the reader, it's clear the white fighter is intended to be the focus of the fans' admiration.

The story took a turn for the worse near the end. The fight ended in the seventh round when the referee stopped it. Gardner took control of

Harry "Bucky" Lew

George Gardner fighting John Butler from the 1899 *Lowell Sun*. Note Gardner is facing the viewer while Butler has his back turned (NewspaperArchive).

the match in the third round and by the seventh he had Butler trapped in the corner and unable to defend himself. Butler fell twice and the match was called. The story describes all of this by saying that while Butler dominated the first few rounds, Gardner took control after adjusting his technique and starting to attack his opponent's body, "doing the proper thing against colored game."[3] It's a chilling description. Not only is Butler stereotyped as part of a group, but the group is also compared to an animal hunted for sport.

Another account of a fight published a few years later managed to insult both the Black fighter and Native Americans as a whole. The *Sun* story from 1901 describes the appearance of a boxer called Young Starlight, whom the promoter brought to the city to take on challengers from the audience. When a local man volunteered and showed himself to be an even match for the fighter, "the darkey realized that he was up against it, and he began to butt the Lowell man with his head."[4] Apparently Young Starlight had to resort to dirty tricks to win.

Chapter 3. Other Options

The reporter further said the challenger objected but the promoter refused to tell the fighter to change his approach. A police officer, who was monitoring a group of Native Americans in the cheap seats, had to come down and intervene: "Officer Moffatt saw Starlight's act from the gallery where he was watching the Indians in the ten cent seats and noticing that the darkey intended to keep it up he went down stairs" to stop it.[5]

In the account, Starlight is often referred to by his appearance, described either as "colored" or "the darkey." And, of course, he is also portrayed as a cheater. The Native Americans are poor, only able to afford the cheapest seats, and beyond their impoverished state, they have to be monitored by the authorities to keep them in line.

Cycling

While we don't know if Lew tried his hand at boxing, we do know he tried another popular sport of the era, bike racing. It also included integrated competition. And it was dominated by Black racer Major Taylor, who was based in nearby Worcester, Massachusetts.

Lew was compared to the famous racer when he began appearing in local competitions in 1901. In a preview of the coming racing season, the *Sun* said, "Harry Lew, the Major Taylor of this city, is a little wonder and the race going people of this community will have a chance to see a star in the different events of the season."[6] Lew was undoubtedly compared to Taylor because he was both Black and talented.

Taylor achieved fame when he set a series of new records in Philadelphia in 1898. His fame increased in late 1899 when he became the first Black world champion sprinter by winning an international race in Montreal. He appeared in Lowell twice that year, once before his championship, and once after it, and he was well received both times.

The cyclist first appeared in Lowell in March. A *Sun* reporter described him: "Major Taylor is a most pleasing man to meet, an excellent conversationalist, very intelligent and well versed in all matters pertaining to bikes."[7] While the story did call out Taylor's race, describing him as colored, it contained no stereotypes or other negative references. Also, an illustration of Taylor posing on his bike accompanied the story, and it was a realistic depiction of Taylor without any exaggerated racial features.

Taylor's second visit to Lowell came a month after his world

Harry "Bucky" Lew

Marshall "Major" Taylor from the 1899 *Lowell Sun*. The world champion cyclist was undoubtedly a role model for Lew. Note the artist's realistic depiction of Taylor (NewspaperArchive).

championship and he was met by far more than a single reporter. In an appearance at the local fairgrounds, he attempted to set a new city record in the mile. The lead for the story went like this: "'Major' Taylor ... was the drawing card of the day and an attendance of about 2000 people were present, despite the very cold weather."[8] The attempt at a record was a success and Taylor became the first man in the city to finish a mile in under two minutes.

As he finished, he was cheered by the standing-room–only crowd: "As he came down the home stretch he was given a great reception by the people in the grandstand and also the spectators on either side of the track."[9] Not once in the story was Taylor's race mentioned, nor was any racial reference made to his appearance or his ability. He was simply treated as an individual.

Chapter 3. Other Options

Cycling's Color Wall

Despite his success, Taylor did face racial difficulties. According to the Fitchburg Historical Society, "In the spring of 1900, the American Racing Cyclists Union drew the color line, excluding Taylor because he was Black. But public opinion favored Taylor's reinstatement, and in May, the ARCU's executive board voted him back in."[10] With the support of the public, he was able to break through the union's attempts to build a wall.

Taylor biographer Andrew Ritchie provides more detail on the support he received:

> Taylor's popularity as a person and a star performer was of critical importance in determining the outcome of the struggle ... his popularity with the general public was his biggest asset. They loved his style of winning and the excitement he generated on the track, and they were eager to see him race again. The track owners and promoters, too, understood in terms of dollars and cents how good he was for the sport.[11]

Taylor made enough of an impact that President Teddy Roosevelt wanted to meet with him. In his autobiography, Taylor says the pair shook hands as the president told him:

> Major Taylor, I am always delighted to shake the hand of any man who has accomplished something worth while in life, and particularly a champion. I know you have done big things for your profession because I have followed your racing through the press for many years ... whenever I run across an individual who stands out as peer over all others in any profession or vocation it is indeed a wonderful distinction, an honor and pleasure enough for me.[12]

President Roosevelt was considered progressive for his times. And while he was known to honor individual Black men for their achievements, he shared the common opinion of the day, captured by the phrase "the white man's burden." It meant the white race represented the best of civilization and thus had a responsibility to govern those who otherwise would not be able to do so themselves.

This attitude was perhaps most clearly illustrated by Roosevelt's actions in the early 1900s. The U.S., fresh off victory in the Spanish-American War, took control of Spain's former possessions in Cuba, Puerto Rico, Guam, and the Philippines. The effort to exert American control over the locals, even when they sought their own independence, had racial undertones. When Filipinos objected, the "white man's burden" became a bloody conflict.

Harry "Bucky" Lew

"The local Major Taylor"

Lew's name first appeared in a *Sun* sports story in a summary of the races at the city's Fairgrounds in October 1900. He participated in the one-mile race and finished third in his qualifying heat. He did not, however, place in the finals.

While his race was clean, the headline event was not. Newspaper coverage suggested it was fixed. One of the top racers, Pat Keegan, "was given a barefaced 'cold deal' by his pacemakers ... and was not given an opportunity to win." It was obvious that "Keegan wasn't getting a square deal and the crowd raised an angry protest." Both the racer and fans with money on the line demanded that his pace setters go faster but they did not. As a result, "many criticized the judges for not declaring the bets off in view of the fact that they believed the race was unfair and that much money had been wagered on the result."[13] While the controversy and open gambling didn't affect Lew, it was an unfortunate stain on his first race.

Lew's name appeared in the papers again at the beginning of the next racing season: "Harry ... has shown wonderful speed and acquitted himself very creditably Patriots' Day when he won sixth place in the Medfield road race."[14] While there was no cash for the winners, there were prizes, and Lew was awarded a couch valued at $25, worth roughly $1000 today. Unfortunately, the finish and prize were later taken from him, with a bare-bones story appearing a few weeks afterward announcing that some of the racers were disqualified. Lew was not one of the four cheaters, who "stayed out a lap in the woods, remounting when honest riders came in sight and then finishing ahead of them." But instead of moving up in the rankings, Lew moved down instead. "Al Haynes who was mistaken for Harry Lew because of a change of numbers, gets second prize."[15] Lew's new place was left unsaid.

He qualified for a two-mile race in mid-summer but fell ill and could not finish. He then took some time off. The *Sun* reported that "Harry Lew, the 'Major Taylor' of this city, is on the fence, having given up riding for a week or two owing to ill health. It is expected that he will be able to mount the silent steed in a week or two and then start in training."[16]

Lew returned and finished third in his heat to qualify for the finals of a one-mile race. Overall, 3000 fans attended the match at the fairgrounds, "a grand success" in which "the grandstand was taxed to its utmost capacity." Lew was in the mix as the race neared its conclusion.

Chapter 3. Other Options

"Diette set a merry pace, but Harry Lew, the local Major Taylor, crawled up" close to him as the racers came down the stretch before other racers passed both of them. Lew finished fourth and he just missed out on one of the diamond rings awarded to the top three finishers.[17]

Baseball

While Lew was waiting on his basketball future, he was playing baseball for the YMCA. As Sockalexis appeared with the Lowell Tigers at Spalding Park, Lew was playing for the Y team on the city's South Common.

In late April, only a few weeks before the basketball banquet, the YMCA posted a blurb in the *Sun* announcing its roster and asking for opponents:

> The Young Men's Christian Association have organized a base ball team for the season of 1902. The team is made up as follows: Holmes c, Field and Patrick p, Devlin 1b, Lindsay 2b, Simpson ss, Lynch 2b.... Lew and Spencer, fielders. Send all challenges to the Y.M.C.A., Hurd Street.[18]

The two players who left the Y basketball team to go pro, Skip Field and Dan Lynch, appeared on the roster of the baseball team. Field was a pitcher, an obvious skill position, and Lynch was a second baseman, another important position in the deadball era when most balls stayed in the infield. Their places suggest they were two of the better players on the team. Lew was apparently an outfielder, and it's not clear if he was featured in centerfield, hidden in right field, or something else entirely.

The *Sun* also reported on the results of two of their games that May, however they were high-level summaries with no references to individual names or box scores. Both games were played Saturdays at the city's South Common. They were high-scoring affairs, with the YMCA winning 18 to 14 on May 5 and losing 18 to 17 on May 19. How Lew figured into either game is unknown.

Early Baseball and Integration

Lowell had a long history with baseball, fielding an early professional team in the New England Association as far back as 1877, a year in which Lowell won the championship. While the local team was all white, they did play exhibition games against independent Black teams. In *The New England League: A Baseball History 1885–1949*, Charlie Bevis writes:

> These games between Caucasian and black teams helped to establish a black-friendly attitude in the New England League, which extended into the late 1880s, several years after the color line was established in the major leagues.... On August 10, Lowell played the Mutuals, a team of blacks from Washington, D.C. Before about 600 spectators at the fairgrounds, Lowell defeated the Mutuals 7–0.[19]

Lowell moved to the International Association in 1878, where they may have faced an early integrated team, the Lynn Live Oaks, who featured Hall of Famer Bud Fowler. Fowler made several starts as a pitcher that May, but when the team merged with a Worcester squad in June, he did not continue with the new team.

Like the Harlem Globetrotters in basketball generations later, some Black baseball teams emphasized entertainment as much as their expertise. In *The Birth of the Modern NBA*, Josh Elias writes that they tried to please crowds, following the tradition of minstrel shows, whose history he provides:

> Actor Thomas D. Rice popularized the character of Jim Crow in the 1820s, portraying an enslaved black man through blackface performance, exaggerated language, and stereotypical traits. Rice's act gained immense popularity, leading to the emergence of minstrel shows featuring white actors in blackface and perpetuating racist stereotypes.[20]

This type of comedy created an opportunity for African Americans too, and Elias says the Cuban Giants incorporated it into their style of play:

> Managed by Cos Govern, a Danish West Indies native with a background in hospitality and acting, the Cuban Giants incorporated elements of minstrel show–inspired comedy into their games, establishing the first instance of clowning in professional sports. This style of performance was emulated by other early black baseball teams and enjoyed popularity among diverse audiences.[21]

Whether the Mutuals, the team Lowell played as far back as 1877, followed these techniques is unknown, however, the city would later host the Cuban Giants too.

Baseball's Color Wall

In July of 1887, pitcher George Stovey was set to take the mound for Newark against the National League's Chicago team in an exhibition

Chapter 3. Other Options

game along with catcher Moses Fleetwood Walker. That is, until their star and leader, Cap Anson, refused to face the Black players.

In *Only the Ball Was White*, Robert Peterson describes what happened: "The White Stockings ... were led by Adrian Constantine (Cap) Anson, one of the greatest players in baseball's history" when "Anson refused to field his team if [they] played. It was another first in organized baseball. This triumph of race prejudice determining a manager's judgement."[22] Unfortunately, it was the start of a trend.

Later that year, the St. Louis Browns boycotted a game against the Cuban Giants set for New York. The *Boston Globe* reported that "for the first time in the history of base ball the color line has been drawn and the World's Champions, the St. Louis Browns, are the men who have established the precedent that white men are not to play with colored men." Apparently referencing the Stovey affair, it did acknowledge, "There have been little dissensions before, but only about a player here or there."[23]

According to club president Chris Von Der Ahe, the race card was only an excuse. He said his players wanted to nix the game because they had other plans. The *Globe* quoted him as saying, "'Two or three of them had made arrangements to stay in Philadelphia on Sunday, and this scheme was devised so they would not be disappointed.'"[24] Whether the Browns were racists or only used racism as an excuse is almost irrelevant. The damage was done and the movement against integration was gathering momentum.

Lowell hosted the Cuban Giants a few weeks later in September. According to Bevis, the *Lowell Courier* reported that "attendance was sparse at the two games." He speculates that "publicity about the 'color line' being established in professional baseball likely kept the attendance down."[25] While the turnout was disappointing, the fact that Lowell had scheduled two games with the Cuban Giants suggests they had expected more fan interest.

The next year, in 1888, the Worcester team in the New England League signed Stovey, the man Cap Anson had refused to face the previous summer. Stovey's stay with Worcester was brief and he was released in mid–July. Bevis reports that Stovey received some support in the Lowell press:

> The *Lowell Daily News* ... wrote "We blush to be compelled to say it, but it may as well be said: Stovey is an A No. 1 pitcher, but his color, over which he has no control, barred him from receiving the support of his so called 'white associates.' And this is civilization."[26]

A Worcester paper disagreed with this assessment. The *Worcester Spy* said the team found Stovey impossible to manage. The paper challenged Lowell's club to sign him if they wanted to keep him in the league. Stovey remained unsigned.

In what may have been an example of hardening attitudes, the *Lowell Daily News* seemed to change course a few years later. When Frank Leonard, the owner of the Portland, Maine, franchise, proposed that the Cuban Giants represent his city in the New England League in 1891, the paper objected. Bevis says it wrote, "The idea of putting the Cuban Giants in Portland as members of the New England League is preposterous. It would simply mean the breaking up of the league."[27] The Portland owner faced opposition from his fellow owners too and soon withdrew his plan.

The Cuban Giants next joined the Connecticut League and represented the city of Ansonia. Unfortunately, that league dissolved at the end of June, and it was the last chance Black baseballers would have to play in an integrated game for generations to come.

Sockalexis Goes Pro

Despite all that history, Sockalexis first received an invitation to join a New England League team way back in 1895. Walter Burnham signed him to play for the Kennebecs, a regional team based in Augusta, Maine, which took its name from the Kennebec River Valley.

Sock didn't join the NEL until he finished his season with a Warren team in a Knox County town league. He appeared with the Kennebecs in the last game of the season on September 7 in Bangor, Maine, batting fifth and playing centerfield before 600 fans. According to biographer Ed Rice, Sock had "one hit, a double, in four at bats, scored a run, and made three put-outs."[28] After the game, with the Kennebecs season concluded, Sockalexis joined Bangor. The former opponent was apparently impressed enough by his performance and fan interest that they wanted him to play with them in a benefit game.

Lowell too was willing to wait for Sock in 1902. Lowell manager Fred Lake visited him at home in Indian Town, Maine, in 1901 as Charles Scoggins describes in *Bricks and Bats*:

> He coaxed one of the game's most popular and colorful players, the famed Indian Louis Sockalexis, out of retirement while on a road trip to Maine in late June. He signed Sockalexis to a contract, but the alcoholic native

Chapter 3. Other Options

American star ... was in no condition to play and would not report to Lowell until the following spring.[29]

When Sock did report to the team, he dominated, so Lake found he was worth the wait.

What Did It All Mean for Lew?

When it came to integrated sports, the scene was a bleak one. Racism was rampant, and chances were few, but opportunities, in rare circumstances, did exist.

Louis Sockalexis from the May 1902 *Lowell Daily Courier*. **Note the dignified pose and realistic depiction (NewspaperArchive).**

Despite his interest in boxing later in life, we have no record of Lew ever appearing in the ring, and the press coverage of the sport may reveal why. Boxing was open to Black athletes, but due on the questionable legality of the sport and negative portrayal of minorities by those who followed it, it seems unlikely that Lew would want to pursue it as a career.

As far as cycling went, Major Taylor had cleared a path, but plenty of obstacles remained. And Lew certainly had his share of ups and downs in two seasons. He witnessed a race overshadowed by a gambling controversy, lost an impressive finish and the resulting prize in a cheating scandal and alleged number mix up, and suffered a serious injury. While none of the newspaper reports referred to his race, they didn't have to, because the consistent comparison of him to Taylor made his color clear. Cycling looked more promising than boxing, but it was still complicated.

Baseball looked to be the least promising sport of all. Jim Crow was firmly in place and had been for years. There was no sign of change on the horizon. Sockalexis had broken through, but he was a Native American, not an African American.

Harry "Bucky" Lew

If Taylor and Sockalexis had something in common, it was that they received strong public support, and owners recognized that support meant more ticket sales and bigger profits. Maybe Lew just had to be good enough that fans demand he play!

Chapter 4

A New Hope

While pro basketball hadn't included integrated competition by early 1902, both the game itself and the professional version of it were still relatively new. The first pro contest took place in 1896, and the first two pro leagues started in 1898. Since it all happened within a few years of Lew turning 18, he might wonder if anyone had even attempted to integrate the pro game.

Good News, Bad News

As the well-known story goes, Dr. James Naismith invented basketball in 1891 at the International YMCA Training School in Springfield, Massachusetts. His goal was to give his bored baseball and football players something to do over the cold winter months.

Claude Johnson describes the bigger picture in *The Black Fives: The Epic Story of Basketball's Forgotten Era*. The YMCA was a driver of the "muscular Christianity" movement that sought to counteract the negative effects of growing industrialization in the country and the relocation of people from farms to sedentary lives in cities. Naismith's boss, Luther Gulick, feared physical boredom would lead to mental and spiritual decline as well.

So Gulick charged Naismith with developing "a challenging activity requiring so much skill, sportsmanship, and physical exertion that it would lead not only to student engagement but also spiritual growth. This would apply in Springfield and in YMCAs everywhere."[1] Gulick's mindset was illustrated by the Y's triangle logo, which he designed. The three-sided symbol represented its commitment to body, mind, and spirit. And he wanted Naismith, a former athlete and divinity student, to address all three with his new game.

Naismith quickly concluded "the problem was not the students but the outdated indoor fitness routines" available to them and took on the challenge "to make indoor fitness exciting again."[2] Basketball was his last try. He described it as "a team game demanding a high degree of accuracy, judgment, individual skill, initiative, self-control and the spirit of co-operation."[3] He thought he hit the mark, and his students agreed—they loved the game.

Basketball attracted both players and spectators. In *Cages to Jumpshots*, Robert Peterson writes, "Within a couple of weeks, 200 people were lining the gallery for the daily noon-hour games."[4] Word spread beyond Springfield when Naismith wrote an article for the Y's newsletter, *The Triangle*, and his students left for home at winter break and taught their friends the game. Peterson adds, "With the impetus furnished by article and the missionary work of Springfield's students, basketball quickly became the rage in YMCA gymnasiums."[5]

Lew was a lot like the youth Gulick and Naismith had in mind. He was growing up in a planned industrial city and had recently left school to learn his parents' business. He eagerly played baseball and cycled in the warmer weather, and he needed a similarly engaging activity for the winter. And when he was old enough to play, he took to the game as quickly as Naismith's first students.

Unfortunately, while basketball was spreading rapidly, not all athletes, even those who had access to local YMCAs, had access to the game—not all Ys had the gym space. According to Johnson, "most of its branches had their own gymnasiums, though it must be pointed out that that did not yet apply to the organization's numerous 'Colored' branches."[6]

Settlement houses, established in big cities to provide services and shelter to the poorest residents, picked up the game too. However, many of these also lacked proper facilities for basketball. As Johnson writes:

> Though there was also a growing number of "Colored" settlement houses in the North and South, often funded and run by White philanthropists, they did not yet have the same opportunity for basketball immersion. No settlements had yet been established in Chicago, Maryland, Washington, D.C., Missouri, New Jersey, Buffalo, Brooklyn, or Milwaukee. Those that existed did not have a gym.[7]

When basketball grew too big for the YMCA to handle, it transferred control of the game to the Amateur Athletic Union in 1897, and the situation worsened for Black athletes. Johnson says the AAU continued to aggressively promote the game: "The AAU believed basketball to be a great vehicle for social progress, specifically for Americanization,

Chapter 4. A New Hope

especially for European newcomers. So the amateur sports organization pushed the game for that purpose, signing up participants and setting up leagues." Yet it left Black athletes out in the cold. "The AAU, despite its stated ideals, would prohibit African American membership until 1914." No team that wanted to comply with AAU rules could include or compete against Black athletes.[8]

Fortunately for Lew, his city did not observe the Jim Crow system of segregating whites and Blacks into separate YMCAs. Further, the game was well established in Lowell before the AAU took control.

"A Game New to Lowell"

The first exhibition of basketball in Lew's hometown took place in December of 1892, within a year of the game's invention. At that time, F.L. Marion of the Springfield YMCA traveled to Lowell and organized a game between two teams comprised of members of the local Y.

While penmanship and bookkeeping classes were featured on the calendar the previous night, this evening would be all about basketball. Even the *Lowell Daily Courier* covered it under the headline "Basketball: A Game New to Lowell Played at the YMCA Gym."[9]

> The game of basket ball was introduced in the city last evening, at the Y.M.C.A. gymnasium, and the athletes there went wild over it. There is no doubt the sport will become a popular one, for it combines the elements of exercise and chance, with an opportunity for skill without roughness.[10]

In what at times sounded like a game of human foosball, each team featured nine players, with rows of guards, centers, and wings. "It takes nine men to a side ... placed in three lines with intervals.... The science is in passing the ball down the line and in blocking it when it is thrown."[11]

The reporter goes on to describe a chaotic scene in which most players hadn't yet taken to the science of the sport:

> The ball was tossed up in the air and both captains jumped for it. Snyder got it and passed it along to one of his men, who tried to throw it into the basket on the wall. Instead of that it hit the wall and bounded into the arms of the goalkeeper who threw it over to his side. It didn't get into the basket there, but went sailing into the air toward the ceiling, where it hit the gas pipe, nearly turning the gas off, and came down, causing two of the men to run into each other and upset. The fun was fairly on.[12]

Harry "Bucky" Lew

Not surprisingly for a game where the players had so much to learn, it was scoreless for much of the contest. Play improved as the game continued and two late scores by the team that almost shut off the heat prevented it from ending in a scoreless tie.

Despite the challenges, the game was a success and plans were made to continue the momentum. "The young men took hold of it wonderfully well.... The game will be played often at the gymnasium now and a team to represent the association will be formed. It is a sport that affords great amusement to spectators and an attempt will be made to introduce it at the annual exhibition."[13] Much like the players in that first game in Springfield a year earlier, the players in Lowell became immediate evangelists of the new game.

The Lowell YMCA soon formed a team, and it began to compete with other organizations, such as the team sponsored by the Burke Temperance Institute. Named after an Irish priest, Father Thomas Burke, an anti-alcohol crusader, the Institute sponsored sports teams to promote healthy lifestyles for youth.

The Burkes were into basketball in a big way. On January 11, 1896, a *Lowell Sun* story mentioned that a "hot game of basket ball was played in the Burkes gymnasium last evening, the players showing great superiority. A tournament will probably be arranged."[14] The Burkes too seemed eager to evangelize the game.

Before long, the YMCA and the Burkes began to play each other. In April 1896, the YMCA won by a score of 2 to 1 in a game that received only passing attention in the papers. The game was preceded by a concert, which received more press attention. Coverage of the game was limited to a single sentence reporting the result.

The Burkes got revenge the next month when they defeated the YMCA by a score of 5 to 4. In a sign that interest in the sport was growing, the *Sun* gave this game more detailed coverage. While there was a concert beforehand, the game dominated most of the story, with three of five paragraphs devoted to it. It also includes a box score.

The additional details revealed that the game had not changed much since the earliest one in Springfield. The teams played nine-on-nine. Each basket, whether a field goal or free throw, was worth one point. The story was also complimentary of both teams, describing it as a "very exciting" game, with the Burkes being "superior in all-around work," while the Y "did well to score as often as they did." That said, it also pointed out that the "Burkes admirers were very jubilant over the result."[15] Players and fans were taking the new sport very seriously.

Chapter 4. A New Hope

Lew's Amateur Career

Lew started playing organized basketball in 1898. According to the UMass Lowell Library, that was the year he "joined the Lowell YMCA 'young employed boys' basketball team."[16] He was eligible to play because he completed his education after the eighth grade and never went to high school. Instead, he worked at his parents' dye house in downtown Lowell, where he would learn to dye fabric, dry clean clothing, and run the business he would one day manage.

He caught a break when Victor Meister became Lowell's YMCA's physical director and basketball coach in 1900. Meister's standing with the players was shown at the YMCA banquet: "Before the gathering adjourned, speeches were made by some of the fellows and three cheers were given for Mr. Meister, the most popular instructor who has ever been in this city."[17]

Born in Worcester, Meister was originally a cabinet maker but moved to a role at the YMCA because of his love of sports. Previous to joining the Lowell YMCA, he also taught at Ys in Hyde Park, Brockton, Newburyport, and Salem. He was in Salem four years and was well thought of there too: "He was a very popular man at Salem and was responsible to a large degree for the success of the association in that place." And he was an early advocate for basketball: "He very successfully conducted the basket ball games and the Salem team had an enviable record for the last two years."[18]

He apparently engineered the YMCA's triangle league, of which Lowell was the pivot point. Lowell competed as one of three teams in a northern division (against YMCAs in Manchester and Nashua in New Hampshire) and one of three teams in a southern division (with Lawrence and Haverhill in Massachusetts). They also played against local high schools, such as Lowell High School, and college teams like Lowell Textile School and the Massachusetts Institute of Technology.

Meister's success as a basketball instructor was evidenced not only by his team's winning ways but also by the high regard in which he was held by the city's professionals. He had already sent two players to the next level, and when the two pro teams in Lowell were considering which referees to use for a city series, an item appeared in the *Sun* noting that Meister's name was advanced by one of the owners as a solid candidate.

He may also have been a mentor of sorts for Lew. In a YMCA game that Meister refereed on November 28, 1900, when the Lowell Y played the Haverhill Y, the box score lists Lew as the official scorer. It's not clear why Lew didn't play, it may have been due to injury, or perhaps the founder of the triangle league was looking to develop Lew in other ways. What is more important is that Lew worked as an official in an era when most Black youth didn't even have the opportunity to play the game.

A Scrapbook for the Ages

Of course, Lew's immediate future in the game was as a player and not an authority. And if Lew needed to build fan support, like Major Taylor and Louis Sockalexis had, he could look to the papers to help his cause. And their coverage suggested he was well on his way.

A scrapbook of his play at the YMCA might include these highlights:

- Impressing fans in leading his team to a 28–14 win: "The playing of Lew … was as usual up to the standard and delighted their admirers."[19]
- Scoring 12 of his teams 36 points in another win: "Lew did the best work of the association team."[20]
- Being heralded as a star in a rare loss at Manchester—and by the Manchester paper too: "The star of the Lowell team was Captain Lew, who succeeding in running the ball the length of the hall several times, staying with it to the finish."[21]
- Outscoring the opposing team in a 39–8 win: "Lew again clinched the victory with his sensational shooting, scoring 9 points for his team."[22]
- Securing a win with an end-of-game shot: "It was a close and hotly fought battle from the time the referee blew his preliminary whistle until 'Bucky' Lew threw his phenomenal basket a second before the close of the last half."[23]

And a reporter's reflection on him ending with a championship:

> I can remember one game especially, when he was pitted against a big strong man about twice his size and weight. Bucky was in his element that night and scored nine goals to his opponent's none. He was captain of the Y.M.C.A. team all last season and his quintet won the championship of the Merrimack Valley League with ease.[24]

Lew could only hope the men running the city's two pro franchises were reading the papers too!

Chapter 5

Relapse

ONE BRIGHT SPOT THAT SUMMER was the emerging friendship between Fred Lake, Sock's manager, and James Gray, the manager of one of the local entries in the New England Basketball League. While there was good news off the field, there was also bad news. As Sockalexis' season progressed, he suffered a relapse and was suspended. Although the local press ignored his return to drinking, the truth was revealed by out-of-town papers. It was an unfortunate event, and the racial overtones involved in a Native American's struggle with alcohol made it worse. Sock went from a curiosity to a caricature, and that did not bode well for Lew's pro prospects.

A Potentially Helpful Connection

Fred Lake, manager of the Lowell Tigers, and James Gray, manager of one of Lowell's pro basketball teams, the Pawtucketville Athletic Club, developed a friendship that summer. And since Lake had challenged the status quo in signing Sock, it might help Lew's chances with Gray.

Gray was also baseball man—the PAC had a baseball team too, and he was its player-coach. The team played other amateur outfits and often placed side bets on the games to make things more interesting. One story had them competing for a $50 purse,[1] roughly $1800 today. Later, when Lake left Lowell to manage in the major leagues, Gray ran the Tigers for several years. (He played such a prominent role with the team that they became known as the Lowell Grays.)

In what is likely the first instance of granting corporate naming rights to a stadium, Lake named his new baseball field "Spalding Park," and Gray seems to have played a role. Scoggins writes that the park's namesake was "Albert G. Spalding, the former star pitcher who had become a club owner, a wealthy sporting goods manufacturer, and the most powerful man in baseball."[2] Gray was a sporting good salesman,[3] so he undoubtedly knew the men running Spalding's local stores, and he could make sure word got back to Albert himself.

When he heard the news, Spalding rewarded Lake. Scoggins says that "Spalding sent two dozen of his firm's expensive baseballs as a gift when he learned of the honor."[4] While it might not sound like much, the approximate value of the baseballs was $30 at the time, roughly $1100 today. Also, since balls were so expensive, a single ball would stay in a game a while; in the dead ball era of baseball, "balls were used until they unraveled."[5] And, of course, besides helping Lake equip his team, the gift from Spalding attracted press attention as well.

The promotional move sounded like something Gray might do. He demonstrated an eye for getting headlines while running the PAC basketball team, and it's reasonable to think he suggested Lake name the park in such as a way as to attract corporate favor and press attention. Playing in a new, out-of-the-way park, Lake could use all the help he could get.

Gray and Lake's friendship continued past the season. When Lake moved on to the majors a few years later, Gray took control of Tigers. Later, when Lake was manager of the National League's Boston Doves, he sold the contract of pitcher "Red" Wolfgang to Gray. It was quite a gift. Wolfgang had three, 20-win seasons for Lowell before moving on to a five-year career with the Chicago White Sox. In making that deal, Scoggins wrote that "Lake wanted Gray to succeed."[6] The feeling appeared to be mutual and likely began that summer of 1902.

Sock Cools Off

Sock's good start continued through mid–June, but there were some bad signs as well. While the coverage in the Lowell papers was almost exclusively positive, the *Sun* did run some stories from out-of-town papers that presented a more balanced view.

One story, which initially appeared in the *Manchester Union*, suggested Sock had stopped playing along with fans who expected him to put on a Wild West show:

> One of the principal attractions of the game was the appearance of the melanocomous Sockalexis, whose ancestors assisted in parting the early pioneers from their toproots. It was advertised that Socky would bound into the arena in full war paint rent the air with war whoops and pluck the

Chapter 5. Relapse

eagle feathers from his head to distribute as souvenirs. But Socky refused to whoop, being overmuch afflicted with pococurantism, and being college bred and a gentleman, he doesn't wear fathers in his head.[7]

According to the reporter, fans were led to believe Sock would act like the character they expected, but he "refused" to play along. If the series of silly racist references in the article were reflective of the treatment Sock was still receiving over a month into the season, it may have finally been growing old. However, the shift in mood might be indicative of other changes that were taking place.

The reporter also suggested Sock wasn't the only player on the team with a history of drinking. "Lowell may have a team of gone-bys, an aggregation that do not observe the hours that produce good athletes, and all of those other things that have been said about Lake's men may be true, but they can play ball at any stage of the game."[8] It sounded like a backhanded compliment, an apparently positive comment with a negative undertone. While the team's wild ways hadn't caught up to them yet, including "all of those other things that have been said" that the reporter didn't mention, it was still early in the season.

Lake may have thought he could keep the men in line by adopting a disciplined approach. He set such a tone early in the season, levying a warning and then a fine on Bennie Cassidy, the "bright and particular star of the team thus far,"[9] for not hustling to first base. According to the *Sun*, Cassidy was batting around .300, leading the team in steals, and fielding well. He typically hit third in the order to Sock's fourth.

The *Sun* ran a report from a different Manchester newspaper, the *Manchester Mirror*, in June that seemed to provide more detail on Lake's approach to player drinking: "The manager of one of the down country teams, which had the reputation for 'fishing' at times, is credited with a novel way of meeting the weakness of his men for the cooling beverages of summer."[10] It went on to say that the manager does not allow his men to wear their uniforms into a bar after a game, but once they take a moment to clean up and change, he'll buy a round or two before telling them it's enough.

The reporter went on: "The players know that a man who sneaks out for a drink after the manager has said 'enough' is bound to have trouble ahead and they stick to the rules. The work which this particular team has done shows that the system may have good results."[11] While the story does not mention the specific team it references, it sounded a lot like Lowell. The Tigers were in first place at the time, and the city is "down country" from Manchester, roughly 30 miles to its south. And, if the story wasn't about the home team, why would the *Sun* run it?

Before Lake signed Sock, he must have known the disciplinarian approach had worked in his most recent successful season, when he played for a demanding manager in the Connecticut League in 1899. Sock's boss at that time was Roger Connor. In a lengthy major league career, Connor was one of the game's first home run hitters and is a member of the baseball Hall of Fame. When he left the majors, he returned home to Waterbury, Connecticut, purchased his hometown team, and ran it as a family business.

As biographer Ed Rice writes, "Perhaps the answer simply lay in management. All the others who attempted to manage Sockalexis, could not seem to manage his drinking problem.... Described as a deeply religious and moral man, Connor may well have been able to reroute the path of the rapidly sinking star."[12] Sock did seem to respond to the stricter approach.

The proof was the success he had in Waterbury after several years of struggles. Rice adds, "Sock ended his 1899 season to the sound of cheers and adulation. Sockalexis had played in a total of sixty-one games for the team. He had 85 hits and batted .320 (with a slugging average of .421), scored 35 runs, and had four stolen bases."[13] The team found success too, rising from a slow start to second in the standings.

Unfortunately, Sock started drinking again that winter in Connecticut, and he was in no condition to play when the start of the next season rolled around. In March of 1900, he was living on the streets of Hartford, Connecticut, and in August he was arrested for vagrancy in Holyoke, Massachusetts, where he spent 30 days in jail.

Lake gave him another shot, and it was paying off. Lowell's hot start in May continued through mid–June. The team remained near the top of the standings throughout that stretch. Despite the new stadium's distance from the city center, attendance was good, and a capacity crowd of 3500 people showed up for a Memorial Day game.

Sock was a big contributor to the team's success both on the field and at the box office. According to the *Sun*'s "Diamond Notes" of June 9, Sock was batting .331, good for second on the team.[14] The *Daily Courier* said, "he seems to be the Sockalexis of old."[15] The reporter's words may have been closer to the truth than he intended. Before long, Sock returned to his "old" habits.

Chapter 5. Relapse

Off the Wagon

Given his history of alcoholism and the presence of other drinkers on the team, it's probably not surprising that Sock relapsed. When he missed a week in mid–June, the Lowell papers ignored it, and it was left to a Lawrence newspaper to reveal what happened: "'Sock' has fallen off the water wagon and has been suspended by Manager Lake. 'Sock' will have to keep the best care of himself to keep up with the procession."[16]

The Lowell papers covered for Sock, with neither mentioning his suspension. As Sock's return drew closer, the *Daily Courier* claimed he missed the games due to arthritis. "Sock, who has been laid up with rheumatism, will probably resume his position in right field."[17] The *Sun* took the same angle, suggesting his return would wait for agreeable weather. "Sockalexis is due to go back to right field today, though if the weather is bad he will remain on the bench."[18]

Sock rejoined the team without returning to his earlier form. As the season wore on, and as the fortunes of the team took a downward turn, coverage in the local papers turned negative. One *Daily Courier* reporter described him a symbol of physical and moral decline:

> Sock, out in center, offers a striking example of baseball degeneracy. His splendid work of the first part of the season has been succeeded by ability that is only known to amateur baseball. He hits the ball quite frequently, but in the field he is all to the bad, and on the base lines he is also a loser. Failure to keep in condition is the only explanation.[19]

Louis Sockalexis from the August 1902 *Lowell Daily Courier*. After he struggled on and off the field, he became a caricature (NewspaperArchive).

Before long, Sock had become a caricature, as evidenced by a sketch of him in the *Daily Courier.* Titled "Sock in His Glory," it shows him dropping a fly ball as he leans on a crutch. Worse, he is depicted with exaggerated racial features and wearing face paint and feathers.[20]

The full truth about Sock's drinking would come out after the season ended. While the papers largely ignored his troubles during the season, after it was over, they piled on:

- "Poor old Sock was a great player in his day, but the alcohol put him out in a round once it got started. Sock would still be fast enough for this league if he could be induced to behave."[21]
- "Sock ... proved an attraction all along the circuit, and for a time played excellent ball, but Old Barley Corn got at him once more and put him out of the game for all time. He finished the season with Lowell and was not reserved."[22]
- The *Daily Courier* ran a dig from another paper describing how a team in Fall River was interested in his services, but it suggested that once he was paid, he would spend his money on liquor and fail to show. "Wonder where Sox is? Has he obtained advance wampum? If so, the jig is up."[23]
- A story about an inebriated Native American who resisted arrest that winter used Sock to reinforce the racial stereotype of the drunken Indian. It said the woman "was full up to the neck with 'fire water' and her Indian Spirit made her as dangerous as a regular Sockalexis."[24]

The stories confirmed the worst. While the Lawrence paper was the only one to mention Sock's suspension during the season, once it ended, the Lowell reporters acknowledged his drinking had become problem.

Second Half Collapse

When Sock first returned to the field after his suspension, the fans were happy to see him: "Sockalexis received an ovation as he stepped to the bat after a week's lay off."[25] He struggled at the plate in his first two games then hit a home run in the third. Rice writes, "On June 18 Sockalexis snapped [his] hitless streak with a home run and gave Lowell its 4–3 margin of victory over Dover." Even then, Rice says Lowell was "just percentage points out of first place."[26]

Unfortunately, it wouldn't last. Charles Scoggins says, "The Tigers

Chapter 5. Relapse

stayed in the thick of the pennant race until the middle of June.... Then Lowell started losing regularly, and by the end of the month, the Tigers were six games behind first-place Manchester."[27] They were still in second place, but the margin between first and second had grown significantly.

It wasn't all Sock's fault. Two of the team's players left the team in mid–July, including one of its best offensive players in Cassidy. When Lake suspended Cassidy for "poor playing,"[28] after previously fining him for not hustling, he had had enough. The *Sun* concluded that "Cassidy will be greatly missed"[29] and he was. Cassidy missed a month and when he returned to the team in mid–August, they had fallen to fifth place.

It only got worse. "The Tigers could never get going during the second half of the 1902 season," says Scoggins, "losing 16 of their final 22 games, and ended up in sixth place."[30] The team collapsed and finished well under .500. Once in first place, they finished in sixth.

Sock turned it on at the end, perhaps hoping to leave on a positive note and receive an invitation to return to the team the next year. Rice says he hit .391 in his last five games (nine hits in 23 at bats). Overall, Sock:

- played 105 of 113 games, had 117 hits, scored 50 runs, and batted .288;
- finished 10th in average in the league for players who appeared in more than 100 games[31]; and
- led the team in hits and was third overall in batting average.[32]

While Sockalexis' statistics were more than respectable, Lake did not reserve him for the next season. The *Daily Courier* cited his alcoholism and bad foot as the reasons: "Sockalexis, whose fondness for firewater made him a burden to the Lowell team at times last season, will pitch his wigwam elsewhere ... 'Hobbles Sock' was a good hitter, but in the field and on the bases, he was a 'heap bad Injun.'"[33] Sock had his shot, and he had his moments, but his inconsistency paired with the team's collapse was too much to overcome.

Perhaps worse, Sock had become a caricature of the stereotypical drunken Indian. If Lew struggled, would he have to face false stereotypes about his own race?

Chapter 6

Problematic Professionalism

Reporters turned their attention to winter sports once the baseball season ended. As they did, some promising news appeared in the papers—both of the city's two professional basketball teams had open roster spots as the rivals looked to bolster their squads for the upcoming season.

Lowell Leads the League

As the birthplace of basketball, Massachusetts was naturally at the forefront of its move to professionalism. And as a city that hosted an exhibition game within a year of its invention, it also made sense that Lew's hometown was right in the middle of the action.

"Lowell [was] a hotbed of enthusiastic and knowledgeable basketball fans," according to William Himmelman, basketball historian and founder of the *Pro Basketball Encyclopedia*. "The two Lowell clubs led the league in attendance ... drawing over 2,000 fans for some games, big numbers for turn of the century sports."[1]

While that figure may not seem impressive today, in the NBA's inaugural season in 1946, "only three of the teams—Philadelphia, New York, and St. Louis—averaged paid attendance of more than 3,000 per game."[2] And it's worth noting that Boston, roughly 30 miles from Lowell, was not one of them.

Lowell's two pro teams were the Pawtucketville Athletic Club and the old Burkes of the Burkes Temperance Institute. And in some good news for Lew, the *Lowell Sun* said that "both managers have their eyes on the YMCA stars. The latter are in the amateur class which they will have to forsake if they become members of either of these league teams."[3]

Chapter 6. Problematic Professionalism

The reporter offered more detail on the state of the Pawtucketville Athletic Club:

> The teams will line up about the same as last year except that the P.A.C.'s will be without the services of [Michael] McManmon. In his place Manager Gray will pick up some likely youngster and get him in shape for the big games.... This will be Manager Gray's first full season with the P.A.C.'s. The team has always been weak at the opening of the season and those who have followed the game will be interested to see if they show any change this year.[4]

It was encouraging that the PAC had an opening, because Gray had already shown a willingness to dip into the YMCA's talent pool. He was the one who signed Lew's former teammates Dan Lynch and Skip Field last season. Both played only parts of the year, with Lynch appearing in 15 games and Field seven.

Of the two, Field had a more significant impact. In his short stint, he had the highest scoring average on the team at 6.3 points a game. While a modest number today, it was more than respectable then, with the team averaging only 24 points a game. Like baseball, it was basketball's dead ball era too. If Field had played enough games to qualify, his average would have placed him in the top 10 scorers in the league.

Lynch was a role player. A defensive specialist and utility man, he played all positions that season—guard, forward, and center. Definitely not a scorer, Lynch averaged only a point per game. While it's not fair to judge his scoring by today's standards, it wasn't an impressive average then either. He had the second-least number of field goals on the team.

Gray held the rights to the two men for the upcoming season, per the league's reserve clause, which allowed managers to retain players from the previous season. Still, the *Sun* reported a week or so later that he decided to let Lynch go: "Lynch is not among those named [to the team]. Manager Gray says that Dan is a good man alright and should be in the game but he could not afford to carry seven men and a business representative."[5] The business representative was undoubtedly Gray, so the quote made it clear he would draw a salary and run with a roster of six players. As substitutes were only used in emergency situations, a team of six players was common for the times.

Included in the six was Bill Halloran of South Framingham, whom Gray had made an offer. Halloran had not yet accepted it, and why Gray assumed he would sign was not clear. The league had a salary cap, and Gray could offer him no more than the team Halloran had just

Harry "Bucky" Lew

captained to a championship. Perhaps it was just a cover story intended to let Lynch off easy because of his local connections.

That said, it didn't appear Lynch would be a free agent for long. The *Sun* also suggested the Burkes would sign him to complete their own roster: "It is whispered that Manager Redmond may take a chance with the former P.A.C. man."[6] The team was mostly Irish, and since Lynch was born in the old country, he seemed like a good fit.

If Gray was still looking for a "likely youngster," Lew's best chance seemed to be with the PAC.

Evolution of the Game

The development of pro ball in Lew's hometown matched the larger evolution of the game. After a few years of amateur play, some teams moved to professional status. When they began to struggle as independents without the protection of a larger organization, teams formed leagues. The Burkes followed that model to a tee. And while the team from the Lowell YMCA did not jump from the amateurs to the pros, the PAC did, giving the Burkes a cross-town rival.

The evolution was fueled by basketball's rapid growth, which become a problem for many YMCAs. The way the game dominated the gym bothered non-playing members and its violent nature troubled many leaders. Himmelman noted that "members complained that basketball monopolized gym time to the detriment of regular gymnasium work and that it attracted a rowdy, decidedly un–Christian element into the organization."[7] So some YMCAs took action: "The Philadelphia YMCA League, one of the strongest in the country, was disbanded."[8] With nowhere else to play, players began renting halls and hiring officials to stage their own games.

Frank Basloe said the first such pro basketball game took place in Herkimer, New York, in 1893. In *I Grew Up with Basketball*, he says players took matters into their own hands after the YMCA directors ended the Herkimer Y team because the players were caught drinking wine on the train ride home from Syracuse after a victory. They invited the Utica Y team down for a game, rented the local opera house, set up 150 folding seats, and charged 20 cents admission. He says, "the Herkimer Boys each took home some change after paying their own and Utica's expenses."[9] Every seat was sold, and players seemed surprised that they made an unintended profit.

Chapter 6. Problematic Professionalism

Robert Peterson maintains that the first professional game took place in Trenton, New Jersey, in 1896. In *Cages to Jumpshots*, he acknowledges Basloe's account "could be true" but says "there is no documentation."[10] The game in Trenton, in contrast, was well recorded. The players ran an ad promoting it in the city's *Daily True American* beforehand and a story on the game appeared afterward. It was both a popular and profitable enterprise. The paper said 700 people attended and Peterson estimates that each player made $5,[11] roughly $200 today.

Either way, pro basketball was a hit and word traveled quickly. Peterson writes, "the Trenton Basketball Team's success in making basketball a paying proposition was soon emulated by other teams."[12] More games were organized, and players were paid to play. Sometimes players were paid a guaranteed amount, sometimes they played for a percentage of the gate, and other times they played for a winner-take-all bet.

These first pro games did not always go well. While playing professionally could be rewarding, the independent nature of the games presented a number of risks. Basloe writes:

> Unscrupulous managers took up the sport as a money-making scheme.... Games were cancelled at the last moment.... Good teams were robbed of their just victories by incompetent and biased officials. The established playing rules were disregarded to such an extent that many of the contests degenerated into pure rough and tumble fights.... Somehow, this unruly bearcub had to be tamed before it ran completely wild.[13]

Himmelman agrees: "Star players could do quite well financially, but they were often the victims of unscrupulous promoters or of their own inability to properly finance exhibition games. The players were anxious for the stability and protection of an organized association."[14] The solution was for teams to organize into leagues.

Teams found that leagues provided additional benefits. Set schedules and familiar opponents attracted interest from newspapers and fans. And improvements in mass transportation helped too. According to Murry Nelson in *The Originals: The New York Celtics Invent Modern Basketball*, this "golden age of passenger rail"[15] and the availability of "intercity trolleys"[16] made travel convenient for players and fans. These transportation systems were only convenient to a point, of course, and since early players still had day jobs, the early leagues remained regional.

Harry "Bucky" Lew

The First Pro Leagues

Basketball's first two pro leagues formed in 1898. The so-called National League included teams from Philadelphia and nearby New Jersey, while the Massachusetts State League featured teams from the eastern part of the state. While Lowell did not yet have a franchise, the city was well represented from the start by some of the league's best players. The city's Jack O'Neil was a top 10 scorer that first season, and Lowell's Albie Allard led the league in scoring the next one.

In 1900, the third year of pro ball, the city was represented in the league, by not one, but two, teams. Himmelman says "The two new clubs brought energy and some fine young players into the Massachusetts League."[17] O'Neil and Allard came home, with O'Neil joining the Burkes and Allard playing for the PAC.

The Burkes were managed by businessman James Redmond, a former player who was on the Burke's first squad in 1895, when they defeated the YMCA two out of three games.[18] Perhaps it wasn't surprising that he led the team in its move to professional status, because he appeared to be more devoted to basketball and business than the Temperance movement. City records show he applied for a liquor license in 1898.[19]

The PAC started as a sporting club, and it had a similar history to those Himmelman sketches here:

> By the final decade of the 19th century, the men's sporting club was a well-established part of the American scene.... By the turn of the century many of these clubs had added basketball to their agendas. These organizations soon discovered what the Y.M.C.A. had realized almost a decade earlier. It was virtually impossible to maintain a truly amateur rivalry for very long. A fierce competitiveness and creeping professionalism quickly corrupted the basic concept of members representing their club. It soon became apparent that the favorable newspaper publicity that accompanied sporting successes could be translated into financial gain for the club, either as a means of attracting new members or simply by charging admission to the event. A club seeking to enhance its prestige was quick to pad its membership with professional players.[20]

After their first season in the league, the two Lowell clubs did so well that they left the original Massachusetts State League and formed their own. Himmelman also writes:

> During the summer of 1901, the two Lowell-based teams broke away from the three-year-old Massachusetts League to organize a new league, which

Chapter 6. Problematic Professionalism

they brazenly called the Massachusetts League, forcing the established league to change its name to the Massachusetts Central League. In addition, the new league ... added a team in Maynard and two Boston teams, Somerville and Cambridge.[21]

The next year the league expanded even further by adding teams in two New Hampshire cities (Nashua and Manchester). With its larger footprint, it rebranded itself the New England Basketball League.

Naturally, the two Lowell clubs developed a significant rivalry. In addition to the league games they played against each other, they also played non-league games during the season. While technically exhibitions, they were every bit as fierce as the regular games, if not more so. The *Sun* described the rivalry this way: "In the days of the P.A.C.-Burkes combats many a fan forgot all about supper, so anxious was he to get to the hall and land a seat. By game time the hall was generally packed to its capacity. And the games were among the most bitterly contested ever seen in this city."[22]

Gambling only added to the drama. Technically, gambling was illegal, but teams promoted it to add interest to games and bring in additional fans. Himmelman says, "The better quality of play in turn stimulated attendance because the more easily recognizable performers made gauging the strengths of teams an easier task, an important factor in an era when betting on contests was a major part of the sport's popularity."[23]

People came to games looking to place bets and it was easy to find someone to accommodate, especially when the regional nature of the circuit meant fans of the road team attended games too. Generally speaking, odds were even, but fans would sometimes adjust them in favor of a point spread, where one team had to win by a certain margin. Newspapers often covered the gambling as if it was an event in itself. One report went, "On all sides the long green was put up and the excitement was almost as intense as at any time during the contest itself."[24]

On at least one occasion, a referee was responsible for both ensuring the fairness of the game and the gambling. When the winners of the new and old Massachusetts leagues faced each other in a post-game series a month before the YMCA banquet, the fourth game of the series ended in controversy. South Framingham had a late one-point lead over Webster—but exactly how late was up for debate. Each team had their own timer, and they disagreed on how much time remained. When the South Framingham timer said time had expired and tried to stop the game, the Webster timer disagreed—violently.

Harry "Bucky" Lew

The *Sun* reported:

> Timer Green claimed that time was up and attempted to blow his whistle. Timer Prout disputed him, saying there was still ten seconds to play, and as Green persisted in attempting to announce the end of the game Prout knocked the whistle from his mouth. Green, it is alleged, then punched the Webster tax collector. The blow was returned and in a minute a general mixup occurred.[25]

The fans got into it too, and when they rushed the floor, the referee suspended everything: "The game was declared off by the referee, who also declared that all bets were off."[26] The referee stopped all of the action, both on the court and in the stands.

James Gray Gambles and Wins

As the *Sun* said, Gray had taken over the PAC basketball team partway through the 1901–1902 season. After a poor start, the PAC finished strong, rising to fourth in league standings, one game behind the Burkes. They even won their last two matchups with the Burkes.

Confident in his chances, Gray challenged the Burkes to a city championship series. He told the *Sun*, "I realize that my supporters would rather see our team defeat the Burkes than win the league championship." And in an effort to increase the pressure on Redmond, he expressed a willingness to back his team with more than words. "I have a little wad of money that I would like to wager with him that I can defeat his team. Of course it would not be the proper thing to have the men in the game bet, so I have offered to make a side issue with the manager."[27] A few days later, Gray further upped the ante, by repeating the challenge in an open letter to Redmond published in the *Sun*. The letter made the front page of the evening edition under the headline "$200 Challenge,"[28] roughly $7500 today. The money was to be split between the players alone with the winners taking 60 percent and the losers 40 percent.

The *Daily Courier* also jumped on the gambling angle. It reported, "Manager Gray has good courage to wager $200 on his P.AC. team in a series of games with the Burkes."[29] Redmond agreed to play a best-of-three series and apparently matched Gray's figure, because the pot grew to $400, or close to $15000 in today's money.

PAC won the first game of the series, 14–7. The *Sun* said about 1500 fans watched the first game and many got in on the action: "There

Chapter 6. Problematic Professionalism

was plenty of money around and it was taken up quickly before the game started. No odds were offered as it was felt the teams were about equal."[30] Lew's old YMCA teammate, Skip Field, featured prominently, scoring half the team's points.

The second and final game attracted even more fans. Roughly 1800 fans turned out to watch the PAC win the series. The PAC defeated the Burkes 18–12 and while Field was held in check, he still contributed more than his share of the offense with four points.

Even more gambling took place that night as a supremely confident Gray engaged in a series of individual bets with Burkes fans too. The *Sun* reported, "The betting men came into evidence and there was something doing. Jimmie Gray had his bundle out and he was not afraid to risk it. The Burkes had good supporters who were willing to put their good coin to back their opinions."[31]

With the win, the PAC swept the series to become city champions. Gray marked the achievement with a party at his home a few days later. Of course, he invited the *Sun*, and the paper described the event as follows:

> The members of the Pawtucketville A.C. basket ball team celebrated their victory over the Burke team in the series for the championship of the city at the home of Manager James Gray.... A large party of admirers of the team were present and a delightful time was enjoyed. The punch bowl which was won by the P.A.C ... was a conspicuous feature of the event.[32]

The *Daily Courier* also described Gray's success: "With a huge punch bowl and a large bunch of money won from the Burkes, James Gray must feel tickled with his first season of basket ball."[33] While the Burkes had historically been the top team in the city, it looked like the PAC were poised to overtake them.

Both Gray's boldness and the Burkes' decline seemed like good news for Lew. The Burkes had to feel threatened, so they might be willing to go outside of their comfort zone and sign a player like him to re-establish their dominance. Of course, the PAC was a more likely fit, with Lew's neighborhood ties to Pawtucketville and his relationship with old YMCA friend Skip Field.

Despite winning the city championship, Gray didn't seem like someone who would stand pat. Like Lake signing Sockalexis, Gray signing Lew would seem be a headline-making move, and Gray had shown he wasn't afraid to make news—he actually sought it out!

Chapter 7

Opening Night

As the opening night of the New England Basketball League's 1902 season approached, Lowell's two pro teams announced their rosters—and Lew's name didn't appear on either of them. Then, injuries created an opening with the PAC, and apparently prodded by the press and the fans, Gray asked Lew to join them. It wasn't a contract offer—Gray made it clear he would be an emergency substitute for one game only and shouldn't expect to play. Fortunately for Lew, it wasn't entirely up to Gray.

An Open Spot or Not?

Two weeks before the official start of the season, the *Lowell Daily Courier* listed the players on the city's teams. The story only identified five men for each squad, and it didn't include one of the men Gray said he'd signed for the PAC, Oscar McFarland. Instead, it reported, "McFarland has not decided where to play."[1] The Burkes roster appeared in print for the first time, and it too included only five players, with Dan Lynch's name not being among them. Either Gray or Redmond might have an open spot. If so, neither manager approached Lew about it.

Lew continued to play as an amateur and his YMCA team traveled to Lawrence the same night as the PAC played their first exhibition game. Under the shared headline "Basket Ball On," *Lowell Sun* readers learned that "Lowell Defeats Lawrence" while the "PACs lost to Maynard."[2]

The *Sun* said the YMCA tilt featured "sensational throws by Lew." The "game was fast and furious at times and it was only a garrison finish at the end that saved the local boys from defeat."[3] Lew had a team-high six points in the 22–14 victory.

The PAC played in Maynard the same night, losing 14 to 12. In contrast to the "sensational throws by Lew," the *Sun* reporter said, "both

Chapter 7. Opening Night

teams showed a lack of practice, especially in shooting baskets."[4] Gray couldn't have liked the comparison—it sure sounded like the PAC could use a player like Lew.

McFarland played for the PAC that night just as Gray had said he would. Skip Field did not. A Halloran also appeared on the roster, but it wasn't the Bill Halloran that Gray had hoped to sign away from South Framingham. Instead, it was John "Bucky" Halloran, who had played with the PAC for parts of the last two seasons. Whether that meant anything for Lew wasn't clear. They played the same position and shared the same nickname. He might wonder how many guards called Bucky you could have on a roster!

The PAC dropped their next exhibition game too. Worse, it was against the rival Burkes. It wasn't the official season opener because it wasn't a league game, but it felt like one. The *Sun* reported that a band paraded through the streets beforehand, players were brought to the hall in horse-drawn carriages, and the mayor attended and threw out the opening ball. The *Sun* reported that the game drew 1500 fans and that "basket ball is the same old game, full of life and overflowing with excitement."[5]

Despite all the festivities, the PAC lineup shuffle continued. Field played, but Harry Tighe, who had been on the roster the whole time, did not. While the PAC never led, it was a tight game throughout and went right down to the wire. The Burkes won by a single basket at 18–16. The day after the initial game report, the *Sun* appeared to place the blame for the loss on the other Bucky, who hadn't scored. Apparently, he failed to cash in on some opportunities to change that in crunch time: "Halloran lost some dandy chances to place his team in the lead."[6]

Gray wouldn't appreciate that analysis either. His team's lack of preparation—and resulting lack of offense—was cited as the reason for the first loss, and the blame for the second, against his cross-town rivals no less, was placed squarely on the shoulders of his most recent addition. Given the contrast the *Sun* drew between the PAC's performance and that of the YMCA, and the struggles of the Bucky on one team with the leadership of the Bucky on the other, at least one paper seemed to be pulling for Lew.

Lew Travels with the PAC

When the PAC traveled to Marlboro for their first game of the season a few days later, Lew joined them. His excitement likely matched

Harry "Bucky" Lew

that of the press and fans. The *Sun* reported that "no season was ever opened under more favorable circumstances.... And judging from the make-up of each team, the fastest kind of basketball will be witnessed."[7]

Marlboro had already played—and won—their first game. The team was returning for their home opener, and the *Marlboro Daily Enterprise* tried to hype up the crowd. "The P.A.C. team of Lowell, the opponents, are expected to prove one of the strongest in the league, and the Marlboro team has already shown itself to be strong." The reporter seemed to begrudgingly accept the fact that Lowell fans would make the trip down for the game, while suggesting rising local interest would soon make such a thing unlikely: "as time goes on there won't be room on our streets for a 'fan' of any of the other basketball towns."[8]

Fans attending road games was commonplace in those days. Teams planned for such interest, providing transportation in the form of special trains or trolleys. Murry Nelson writes that "intercity trolleys ... allowed fans and players to move from one city in a region to another on a more timely basis. In some cases, extra trolleys were provided for special occasions."[9] Interest in this game was high because it was the season opener. It's also possible that Lew's presence brought some fans out too.

How many fans actually knew Lew might play is unclear. When the PAC roster for the game appeared in the local paper in the run-up to the game, he wasn't on it. Tighe, who had missed the game against the Burkes, was listed as an expected starter.[10] While no announcement was made in advance, Tighe's injury had created a potential opening, and Gray brought Lew along as a substitute.

When Lew reflected on the event decades later, in an interview with Gerry Finn of the *Springfield Union* in 1958, he said Gray only asked him to come to that one game and told him he would only play as an emergency substitute: "A series of injuries forced the manager to take me on for the game. I made the sixth player that night and he said all I had to do was sit on the bench for my five bucks pay."[11] (That $5, roughly $200 today, was the standard rate.)

In those days, running subs was far less common than it is today. Teams could only substitute for players during the course of a game in a case of an injury or someone fouling out. If they wanted to replace a player who was playing poorly, they had to wait for the break between periods to do so. And once a player left a game, they could not return.

All that said, the unexpected emergency occurred. When a teammate, apparently Tighe, was injured or re-injured during warmups or

Chapter 7. Opening Night

early in the game and couldn't play, Gray balked at using his sub. Lew said, "It just so happens that one of the Lowell players gets himself injured and had to leave the game. At first this manager refused to put me in. He let them play us five on four."[12]

This is where the Lowell fans came in. The fans who travelled with the team made their objections to Lew staying on the bench loud and clear: "The fans got real mad and almost started a riot, screaming to let me play,"[13] he said.

It's not surprising that the fans were so fired up. They were undoubtedly invested in the outcome, both emotionally and financially. Some may have traveled just for the chance to see Lew play and many others likely had money on the line. Only sending four players out to play the other team's five wasn't likely to give them a good return on their investment.

Lew Plays—and Plays Well

Gray finally relented and put Lew in the game, and he credited the fan reaction with the assist. "That did it. I went in there."[14] While none of his opponents objected to him taking the court, they seemed surprised to see it. "I can almost see the faces of those Marlboro players when I got into that game."[15]

As you might expect, it wasn't easy for Lew. Whether he was referring to this game or another (or more likely several others) is not clear when he recalled:

> All those things you read about Jackie Robinson, the abuse, the name-calling, extra effort to put him down ... they're all true. I got the same treatment and even worse.... I took the bumps, the elbows in the gut, knees here [and there] and everything else that went with it. But I gave it right back. It was rough but worth it.

He said he quickly earned his opponents' respect: "Once they knew I could take it, I had it made. Some of the boys that gave me the hardest licks turned out to be among my best friends in the years that followed."[16]

Lew appeared to have help from more than just the fans. His old teammate Skip Field finished one foul shy of the limit, and the four fouls he had made up half of the team's eight. In the coverage of the game in the *Lowell Daily Courier*, the reporter added a note about Field's play:

Harry "Bucky" Lew

> "Skip" Field of the P.A.C. team is one of the hardest men playing basket ball ... to be put up against. While he does not resort to out and out rough work, still he gets in a tap, which is not of the love variety, now and then, to let his opponent know that he is there with the goods if the latter wishes them delivered.[17]

It sounded like Field used his fouls strategically. And he may have done so protecting Lew.

Lew also seemed to get a fair shake from the referee. According to the *Marlboro Daily Enterprise*, the game featured "fast work but [was] not altogether clean ... the Marlboro team being penalized heavier than the PAC."[18] The referee's strictness with the home team came despite his local connection. The paper said the referee was "Charlie Connors, son of Patrolman Connors of this city."[19] Marlboro had 14 team fouls to the PAC's eight. While Lew had only one foul, the man matched up with him, Jack Punch, had four, and another Marlboro player, Joe Lynch, fouled out with five.

The game was a close one, with the score tied going into the final period. The *Daily Courier* reported that a "large crowd turned out" and "interest in the game was intense throughout." It said the game was tight until the end when a Marlboro player, Jimmie Healey, went on a scoring binge. The man, who was not known as a scorer, apparently slipped through the defense and "made four baskets in rapid succession, clinching the game."[20] Marlboro won 28–19.

Healey was guarded by Lew's teammate and team captain Albie Allard. Lew basically played his man, Jack Punch, to a draw. While Lew did not score, he only had the one foul. Punch had two points and four fouls. Since teams were penalized a point for every three fouls, Punch effectively gave the PAC a point.

The account of the game in the *Daily Enterprise* was largely positive. It mostly focused on the hometown team and described the game as having "the kind of playing that brought the fans to their feet with whoops of joy."[21] Lew's name appears in the box score but not the game story.

The *Sun* also covered the game, with a big headline, an even bigger picture of Gray, and a slim game account. It was another positive take on the event, saying it "was well contested and abounded in brilliant playing."[22] The only PAC player mentioned in the game story was Allard's. Lew's name did appear in the box score.

The *Boston Globe* also featured a small recap of the game. Unfortunately, Lew's name is misspelled as "Low" in the box score.[23] However,

Chapter 7. Opening Night

Bucky Lew with the 1902-03 Pawtucketville Athletic Club from the 1903 *Lowell Daily Courier.* **Back row, from left: manager James Gray, timer J. Murphy, and Skip Field. Albie Allard, Bucky Halloran, Jimmy Harrington, Bucky Lew, and Harry Tighe are sitting (NewspaperArchive).**

given the coverage from the other papers, it's obvious that "Low" was actually Bucky Lew.

The *Daily Courier* gave the game its most visible hometown coverage. Under the primary headline "P.A.C. Lost," a subhead read, "McFarland and Lew Play Well." And the last line of the story reported that "the features were the playing of Healey and W. Sheridan for the Marlboro team and of McFarland and Lew for the PAC."[24]

McFarland led the PAC with eight points, so his contribution is obvious. Lew did not score, so his impact is hard to assess based on the limited statistics of the day, when only points and fouls were tracked. Given the type of game he demonstrated at the YMCA, he likely contributed with defense, passing, and ball control.

Why Didn't Gray Want to Play Lew?

Gray's reasons for initially refusing to send Lew into the game are unknown. He died in 1914 and never commented on that first integrated game in pro basketball. (Lew himself didn't comment on it until he spoke to Finn in 1958.)

So, while it's hard to know where Gray was coming from, there are several obvious possibilities. One is that he felt pressured to sign Lew but never actually intended to play him. Lew said the reporters pushed Gray: "Some of the local papers put the pressure on by demanding that they give this little Negro from around the corner a chance to play."[25] He may have signed him just to quiet those critics.

Gray certainly kept his eyes on the headlines, so he probably realized signing the hometown hero would generate some favorable publicity. Then, once his roster returned to full health, he might release him and cite business reasons for it, similar to what he had done with Dan Lynch.

It's also possible he didn't want to play Lew because he didn't want to make history. As mentioned earlier, Black athletes were active participants in individual sports at that time, like boxing and bicycling, but team sports, not so much. While a Native American like Sockalexis was allowed to play pro baseball, African American players had been excluded for close to 15 years. Maybe Gray didn't want to challenge baseball's precedent.

Gray may also have been reluctant to play Lew out of fear for his safety. Basketball was a violent game, and with only one referee on the floor, players knew they could get

Coverage of the PAC's loss on opening night in Marlboro from the 1902 *Lowell Sun*. Note the large illustration of James Gray that accompanies the game story (NewspaperArchive).

Chapter 7. Opening Night

away with a lot. It was a road game and Gray may have thought it risky to play him then. He may have preferred to wait for a home game to play him, so that he would be surrounded by a more protective environment.

While we'll never know what Gray was thinking, we do know the facts. He signed Lew, and while he may have been reluctant to play him, he did put him in the game. The rest is history.

Just Getting Started

After interviewing Lew in 1958, Finn speculated that Lew's historic achievement would have made headlines in the papers the next day. He wrote, "That day the headlines went something like … 'Lew Breaks into Lowell Lineup, Makes Pro Basketball History.'"[26] It didn't happen. None of the papers mentioned the fact that his playing that night made it pro basketball's first integrated game.

Although the papers didn't trumpet his achievement, they did document it, and the Naismith Hall of Fame acknowledged it in a 1978 letter to the Lew family. The letter, appearing on the official letterhead of the Naismith Memorial Basketball Hall of Fame, is direct from Lee Williams, its executive director at the time. He wrote, "It will be our position that … we will consider Mr. Lew as the first Negro to play professional basketball."[27] Lew did indeed make history that day—and he was just getting started!

Chapter 8

Basketball's Dead Ball Era

LEW'S TEAM LOST THAT FIRST GAME 28–19, an incredibly low score by today's standards, but not according to those of the day. Like baseball, the early 1900s was basketball's dead ball era. Scoring was low to an extreme. For example, the PAC averaged only 23.3 points per game the previous season.[1] There were a number of reasons for it, including crude equipment, primitive skills, challenging court conditions, and the philosophy of the league itself—whose managers thought fans preferred a defensive game and tried to skew the rules to favor it.

The Equipment

The dead ball era started, naturally, with the basketball. Robert Peterson described it as "a leather-encased pumpkin somewhat larger than today's molded ball, with laces along one side creating a bulge that made shooting and dribbling an adventure."[2] The ball was made by hand and the results varied. Its size might range from 30 to 32 inches[3] in circumference while today's limit is 29.5 to 30 inches[4] around.

An early player, Joe Schwarzer, described the construction of the ball in detail: "The ball was four pieces of leather sewn together, with a slit in the center where they put the bladder and the laces over that. When you shot the ball, you could see it going up leaps and bounds depending on how the air would hit the laces."[5]

The laces could be a problem. While they provided convenient access to the inflatable rubber bladder inside the ball, they also resulted in an awkward lump once the bladder was filled with air and the laces were re-tied. Irregularities like that might provide advantages to a pitcher in baseball, but a player shooting a basketball didn't want to see it knuckleballing through the air on its way to the basket.

The ball wasn't perfect to begin with, and its condition worsened with use. Peterson added that "after a few minutes of fast action [the

Chapter 8. Basketball's Dead Ball Era

ball] was rarely a true sphere."[6] Basloe agreed: "Balls did not hold their shape long. That's one big reason for low scores in early games. You just couldn't dribble and shoot with a lopsided ball."[7]

The design of the rim also presented a number of challenges. The flexibility of today's collapsible rim helps shooters as well as dunkers, but in the dead ball era, the hoop was a rigid steel ring—there were no friendly bounces. If you didn't manage to score cleanly, you might not score at all. Schwarzer said of shooting the ball, "If it hits the rim on the laces, God knows what would happen."[8]

The rim was smaller too. When Lew joined the New England Basketball League, the hoop was 15 inches in diameter, roughly 47 inches circumference, while today's hoop is 18 inches wide, roughly 56 inches around. So, he and his teammates were shooting a larger, lopsided ball through a smaller hoop. As a reporter from the *Lowell Daily Courier* said at the time, "With the rim only two inches larger than the leather, a man will have to be pretty accurate to get a basket."[9]

Backboards—or the lack thereof—could be another issue. While some leagues used them, others didn't. YMCAs started using them to prevent fans standing and watching on elevated running tracks from interfering with shots. The NEBL played mostly in open halls, without suspended tracks, so managers thought backboards unnecessary. Players in other leagues could use backboards as a shooting aid, either as a visual break to help them distinguish the rim from the background or as a bumper to redirect the ball into the hoop, but it wasn't an option in the NEBL.

Skills and Drills

Players had a long way to go before they came close to perfecting techniques and training routines. With the game a little over 10 years old, it's not surprising that the best way to shoot, pass, or dribble may not have been discovered yet.

The most common method of shooting the ball was the set shot. Players planted both feet on the floor and released the ball from about the waist level. Given the low angle of the shot, getting off a clean one required plenty of room to do it, so teams had to be patient in moving the ball and moving their feet to get an open look at the basket.

While some players also used a one-handed overhead shot when close to the hoop, few players appear to have mastered this technique.

Shooting like that may have given players more distance from the defender's attempt at a block, but given the large ball, and its lopsided nature, it was more difficult to do so in a controlled way.

Since so few statistics were tracked at that time, the shooting accuracy of early players is difficult to assess. The few references to makes-and-misses that are available suggest players shot a very low percentage, with 30 percent considered acceptable.

In *The National Basketball League*, Murry Nelson writes about a game between the Oshkosh All Stars and the Whiting Ciesars in 1938 where shooting percentages were tracked:

> In a rare (but very much appreciated) instance, the *Daily Northwestern* carried shooting percentages for each player for the game and it was not pretty. The All Stars went seven for 78 from the floor, for 9 percent while the Ciesars burned the nets at a rate of 18.5 percent with 10 for 54. What was even more amazing was that not a word was mentioned in the article about the horrific shooting, leading one to speculate that it was not that unusual.[10]

Nelson found coverage of another NBL game from 1941 which included shooting percentages. In this one, he writes, "Chicago outshot the Oshkosh team, 29 percent to 28 percent from the floor, figures the *Oshkosh Daily Northwestern* saw as 'fine percentages.'"[11]

Another author found a story from the era that confirmed Nelson's research. In *Pioneers of the Hardwood*, Todd Gould writes that when Indianapolis re-joined the NBL in 1945, the team hired one of the Original Celtics, a dominant early team, to lead their squad. According to the *Indianapolis News*, coach Nat Hickey was "counting on a shooting average of .300 ... to keep the team in the thick of the ... race this season."[12] Considering Hickey played for one of the top teams of his era, it is clear experts found shooting 30 percent a reasonable performance.

No Layups

Since field goals were hard to come by, players might compensate by taking advantage of free throws—if their league allowed it. The NEBL, for one, did not. By the time Lew joined the league, they had stopped shooting free throws. Instead, a single point was awarded every third time a team was fouled.

Since the other games of the day, notably baseball and hockey, were low scoring, owners feared fans thought high scores meant teams weren't defending. Some reporters seemed to agree, with one reporter

Chapter 8. Basketball's Dead Ball Era

from the *Lowell Daily Courier* saying of a 52–17 win by Lew's team, "the game was rather exciting despite the high score."[13] It may sound surprising, but it's not unlike fans who don't find today's All-Star games interesting because players don't play defense. As early player Charley Martens said of the modern game in an interview he gave the *Springfield Union* in 1953: "The ball goes into the basket too much."[14]

In a game without free throws, players were incentivized to foul. Taking someone going in for a layup out of the play only cost your team, on average, one-third of a point. Mathematically, it made sense. Of course, it resulted in fewer points and a rougher game. "We'd just as soon grab a fellow by the back of the neck as let him shoot,"[15] Martens also said.

That mindset was further illustrated by a revealing conversation between PAC manager James Gray and Manchester manager John Smith overheard by a *Lowell Sun* reporter.

Smith ran teams in both the NEBL and the National League. (The National League name is misleading as the league was not truly national in scope. Its teams were exclusively from Pennsylvania, New York, and New Jersey.) In describing the difference between the two leagues, Smith told Gray:

> Basketball is played differently in the National league than it is played here in the New England league. Here the men play each other, but in the National league they must play the ball all the time. That is to say it is an open game and in this vicinity it is a close game. I believe that if the National league game was played here ... the fans would go crazy over it. There is no more scientific game played and you never saw such a chance for excitement.

Gray disagreed: "I'll bet that if you brought the Bristol and the Trenton [teams], the two greatest rivals in your league here, and played in Associate Hall at that style of game the fans would think you were playing ping-pong."[16]

For perspective, Smith's NL team, Bristol, averaged roughly 30 points a game the previous season. While still very low by today's figures, it was roughly 10 points, or 30 percent higher, than the PAC. The difference in mentality—and the fact that the NL shot free throws—had an obvious impact on the scores.

The rules also favored more physicality. A reporter reviewing the NEBL rules said that "every possible method of blocking the player with the ball is allowed, except tackling, and holding with both arms."[17] Even the NL rules allowed roughness as long as defenders made a play on the

Harry "Bucky" Lew

ball, as Smith had mentioned. Peterson quotes one early referee, Marvin Riley, as saying:

> In those days you must know that when a guard met forward, or any other player, head-on ... it was not called a foul. All that was necessary was to make a play on the ball, just as you make you make the play in football on the man who is carrying the ball.... If the player who was dribbling happened to be right in the back of the ball—that was his fault.[18]

Players were limited to five fouls, however they were often allowed to play even after exceeding that number if no substitute was available. Also, for some big games where managers didn't want to take a chance at displeasing fans by having star players removed, the limit was lifted. In those games, players didn't have to worry about any personal penalty for fouling whatsoever.

Of course, even when there was a foul, it had to be seen to be called. Leagues only used one referee, and he could only see so much. Naturally, the referee's focus was on the ball, and a lot of off-the-ball contact was missed. Flip Dowling told Peterson, "We only had one official.... The official couldn't cover everything, and when he had his back to you there were a lot of pick-offs—that kind of roughness."[19]

Referees might not call all they saw. Potential fouls aren't always black and white and subjective judgement can be a factor. And even today, referees can be intimidated by managers, players, and fans. As one of Lew's peers, Dan O'Connor, observed later in life, "There was very little whistle in those days."[20]

Steel Cage Matches and Other Court Conditions

Another factor in the low scores was the small size of the playing surface. NEBL games were held in halls and fans needed space to stand or sit and watch too. Peterson writes that courts were "likely to be only 65 feet long and 35 feet wide."[21] Most playing surfaces were limited to about half the size of today's court, which made it difficult for players to find space to safely dribble, pass, or shoot.

The court was also surrounded by a metal fence, usually made of chicken wire. Peterson says courts were "enclosed in a cage with wire rope or netting walls from 10 to 35 feet high."[22] The fence was designed to protect fans from the players. In Naismith's original rules, the first player to touch a ball after it left the court was awarded possession, so

Chapter 8. Basketball's Dead Ball Era

a ball traveling off the court often had a pack of players going after it. With fans hugging the court, it could get ugly.

Players often took advantage of the fence on defense and used it as hockey players use the boards that surround their rinks. Joel Gotthoffer told Peterson, "You could play tic-tac-toe on everybody after the game because the cage marked you up; sometimes you were bleeding and sometimes you were not. You were like a gladiator, and if you didn't get rid of the ball, you could get killed."[23] Lew himself once needed stitches after being caught in the fence.

The cage was part of the court, so the ball was live the whole time. With no free throws and no out of bounds, games were largely continuous. As Lew said later, "The ball was always in play and you were guarded from the moment you touched it. Hardly had time to breathe, let alone think about what you were going to do with the ball."[24]

After each score, players lined up for a center tap, and that infrequent event was about the only respite they got. There were no timeouts. The NEBL played three 15-minute periods with five-minute breaks in between. Most teams carried a minimal number of players, five or six, so players had to be prepared to play the whole way. Substitutes were only allowed for emergencies or between periods. And once someone left a game, they couldn't return. A player had to be injured or extremely ineffective to be removed.

Playing surfaces were also a challenge. Given the multi-purpose nature of the floors, which could be used for dancing, roller skating, military drills, lectures, and so on, they were uneven and sometimes slick. If players were fortunate enough to have them, they wore sneakers with suction-cup soles to help them maintain their footing. The Spalding catalog advertised Spalding BBs which, according to the catalog, were helpful because "the wearer cannot slip because of the unique construction of the sole, which is made of rubber with holes in it so as to form a sufficient suction when in contact with the floor."[25]

Courts could be obstacle courses. Some had poles to support the roof in the middle of the playing surface. Others had furnaces, boilers, coal stoves, or steam pipes located on the court or just off of it. Lighting could also be challenge. Ideally halls were lit via electricity, however some relied on gaslit lamps. Obstacles and uneven lighting made scoring even more difficult.

Harry "Bucky" Lew

A Game Skewed Toward Defense

Even in a game skewed toward defense, some positions were more defensive than others. Lew played guard and, as the name suggests, his role was to protect his team's basket by staying at the back of the offensive formation. He wasn't a goalkeeper, but he played behind his teammates like a safety might in football.

Himmelman writes,

> The game began with a tip off at the center of the court, with the controlling team moving slowly into offensive position. The center and the two forwards moved toward the basket with one guard positioned about twenty feet from the basket and the other "standing guard" well back in the other half of the court.[26]

Nelson also talked about this "one guard, the standing guard ... [who] did not go much into the forecourt, but instead laid back on defense and directed the ball in and out on offense."[27] This was the position Lew typically played, so instead of scoring himself, he more often looked to stop the other team from scoring, gain possession of the ball, and move it ahead to his teammates.

Himmelman describes an early expert's take on the primary focus of the role:

> The first and most frequent thought in the mind of a back should be to stick to his opponent like glue and he should follow these tactics without varying. In fact, if a back should prevent his opponent from throwing a goal, and yet during the whole game has not once touched the ball himself, he has a right to think he played a good game.[28]

It was often a thankless job. In his early instructional manual, George Hepbron wrote, "The position of guard is the most unsatisfactory on the team. He does the hardest work and gets the smallest amount of praise.... If he lets his man score a goal he is severely reprimanded. No matter how often he has 'blocked' the man before. Few or none notice the 'blocks,' but all see the goal."[29]

The low scoring game persisted for decades. Himmelman writes that as late as the 1940–41 season, of the two major pro leagues in existence at the time, "[National League] teams averaged 30 points per game.... In the American League, teams averaged 36 points per game."[30] Equipment needed to improve, skills needed to evolve, and rule changes that sped up the game, such as the 24-second shot clock, would help too. It would be a long time before scores would reach the triple-digit figures we expect to see today.

Chapter 9

Star Turn

Another PAC player missed the team's second game and Gray gave Lew an extended look. He continued to impress and when the player left the team, Lew took his spot on the roster, quickly making a name for himself all over the league for his athleticism and defense. And the team? After a seesaw start, the PAC went on a winning streak, dominated their cross-town rivals, and looked to test themselves against the best player of the day.

Not One and Done

The man Lew replaced in the lineup, Harry Tighe, was back on the roster when the PAC traveled to Worcester for the second game of the season. Another player, Oscar McFarland, missed the game, so Gray was still a player short.

McFarland soon became the focal point of a league-wide controversy. The early reporting of the *Lowell Daily Courier* that he hadn't decided where he wanted to play turned out to be accurate. The paper said he signed with both the PAC and the Maynard franchise.[1]

Lew took McFarland's spot in the lineup, and the PAC defeated Worcester for their first win of the season. Team captain Albie Allard had 24 points, an incredibly high amount in those days. The game coverage didn't include a box score, so it's not clear who else contributed to the team's 38 points. What is clear is that Lew played well again.

Besides the obvious mention of Allard, the game story in the *Lowell Sun* singled out Lew for praise: "Lew, a young Y.M.C.A. player, gave a good account of himself."[2] The reporter also suggested the team was starting to gel and building momentum. "They outplayed their rivals at every point in the game. Their team work was admirable and the passing they did will win four out of every five games for them.... Manager Gray was well pleased with the victory and says now that his boys are started there will be no stopping them."³

Praise for the team's performance appeared in the *Daily Courier* too: "They played their opponents to a standstill with good, clean, fast, basket ball." Still, the report included an ominous note: "The visiting players were much lighter than their opponents but the weight of the Worcester aggregation was inferior to the science of the visitors."⁴ The small size of the PAC would become a recurring theme that season.

At the next league meeting, Burkes manager James Redmond suggested the league ban McFarland and the motion carried.⁵ Now there finally was an open spot on the PAC roster and the *Sun* carried the news that Gray signed Lew to fill it: "Manager Gray announces that he will hold young Lew ... for a regular player."⁶ Lew had a contract for the season. "All the Lowell players are under salary now and no matter how large or small the crowd they get their coin."⁷

"An attraction in every city"

While the PAC experienced mixed results the rest of that November, Lew received praise whether the team won or lost.

He scored his first official pro points in the third game of the season, contributing six points in a 28 to 8 win over Maynard. The *Daily Courier* said his play demonstrated he belonged on the club: "Lew is a new comer in professional basket ball, and his work of last night gives him clear title to membership in the P.A.C."⁸ The *Sun* offered even more praise: "'Bucky' Lew is an attraction in every city and town where the P.A.C. plays. He is a little chap but lively on his feet and has a pretty good eye for the basket."⁹ After only three games, Lew had established himself as a player of note.

The PAC won game four in a "close and exciting"¹⁰ but extremely low-scoring game as they defeated South Framingham 11 to 7. Lew, like most of the players, was scoreless. Of the 18 points scored by both of the teams combined, roughly half were awarded on fouls. With the win, Lew's team improved to 3–1 and moved up to second place in the standings.

A rematch with undefeated Marlboro followed and the press buildup was fitting for a game between the league's two top teams. When Marlboro's manager sent Gray a note with a challenge, Gray had the *Sun* reprint it. Appearing under the headline "Visiting Team Will

Chapter 9. Star Turn

be Accompanied by Crowd of Rooters with Plenty of Money," the letter from Hugh Healey goes "We will be accompanied by about 50 rooters with a whole lot of money, so if you think your chances are good have the long green with you."[11]

A thousand fans showed up, and if they arranged bets with the visitors, they lost as badly as the PAC. Marlboro doubled the score of the home team in a 29 to 14 win.

Lew didn't score, but neither Lowell paper blamed him for the result. The *Sun* reported that "Little Lew used all his basketball knowledge and gave a very fine exhibition" and also noted that "the visiting men were all larger built than the locals and in this respect had an advantage that helped them wonderfully."[12] The *Daily Courier* also noted, "Allard, Tighe, and Lew played well against their sturdy opponents."[13] Marlboro was the "sturdiest" team in the league and the PAC's lack of size was most pronounced when they faced them.

According to the *Pro Basketball Encyclopedia*, Marlboro had three men in their starting lineup that were six feet or taller, while Lowell's team had none. The PAC roster featured

- Skip Field at 5'10";
- Albie Allard at 5'8";
- Bucky Lew and Harry Tighe at 5'7"; and
- Jimmy Harrington and Bucky Halloran at 5'3".

Marlboro may not sound huge by today's standards, but people in general and players in particular were smaller in those days. Peterson writes, "In the game's early years, most professional players were not much taller than the average male—at that time 5 feet 8 inches."[14] He also said, "Until about 1930 a six-footer was considered a big man."[15] This was certainly true a generation prior. In an interview with the author, Gerry O'Connor said his father Dan, a teammate of Lew's, talked about "six footers" with the same awe people talk about "seven footers" today.

The PAC closed out the month with a loss to their cross-town rivals, the Burkes, in another low-scoring affair. The *Sun* said a capacity crowd of 2000 watched "one of the fiercest games these teams have ever played" with a final score of 12 to 9. The reporter wrote, "From the time the referee called play and the whistle blew at the close of the [game] it was a case of yelling and shouting on the part of the spectators and roughing on the part of the players." Only a combined four field goals were scored with most points awarded on fouls.[16]

Harry "Bucky" Lew

The loss to the Burkes dropped PAC to 3–3 and fourth place in the standings. Despite the two-game losing streak, Lew's play continued to draw rave reviews. According to the *Daily Courier*, "Lew is a fast man. He covers his man in grand style and is quick to uncover himself when the opportunity presents itself."[17]

He received even more praise from the *Sun* a few days later:

> Harry Lew is known to be a fixture with the P.A.C.'s now and they have obtained a fast and coming player. Lew was known when he played on the amateur circuit when he played on the Y.M.C.A. team as "Bucky" and he was a general favorite all along the line. His playing has been of the phenomenal kind and his success is caging the elusive sphere has been remarkable.... Lew is a coming man all right and is one of the fastest men on his feet in the league.[18]

A December to Remember

The PAC started December with a big win, scoring 45 points while holding Nashua to 11. In a game in which "the entire team played well together,"[19] Lew added a field goal. He also played the whole way, while Tighe sat for a spell, with Halloran replacing him for the final period.

The seesaw season continued when they dropped their next game 36–16 to Maynard then followed that with a 28–25 win over Hudson. Lew had six points in helping right the ship. Of the victory, the *Sun* said, "It was a case of hustle from beginning to end and that the P.A.C.'s won is a matter of pride for the little men from across the river."[20]

Buzz was starting to build around the league about the best player in the game joining the Manchester franchise. The *Sun* said the "leader and ex-champion of the national league," Harry Hough, was "the best man playing the game in America today." His manager, John Smith, who also held his National League rights, wanted to play him in the New England league "to show the people ... what basketball really is when played by an expert."[21] Smith continued to say, "'When he gets the ball.... He will go down the court like a streak of lightning and not one of the players will be able to take it from him. He is a crackerjack and will surprise the local admirers of the game.'"[22]

A full scouting report on Hough is available in the *Pro Basketball Encyclopedia*:

> Harry Hough was the most influential player, on and off the court, during the first dozen years of professional basketball.... Hough was undisputedly professional basketball's brightest and most highly paid star. He possessed

Chapter 9. Star Turn

incredible agility and speed. He was unequaled in his ability to break free for a clear shot. If a defender played him tight, he would drive around him for an easy layup. If the defender backed off to defend against the drive, Hough could show off the fact that he was among the best set-shooters of the era. On the court, Hough was an extremely intense, high-strung figure who raged at referees, opponents and even teammates at times.[23]

Hough had already played one game with Manchester. Playing under another name to avoid violating NL rules for playing for another team ("Hough ... was billed [as] Simpson"[24]), he fulfilled his manager's wishes by scoring 26 points.[25]

Working to fulfill their own manager's wishes, the PAC finally won consecutive games by defeating South Framingham 18–16. The *Sun* said Harrington won it for them by scoring "just as time was called."[26] Lew added a field goal.

The *Daily Courier* continued to praise the team and the man: "The work of the Lowell team was fast and great team work was showed at all times. Lew was as usual one of the stars and he had his man going early in the first period. He is considered ... one of the slipperiest players on the P.A.C. quintette." The paper also noted that Lew continued to work on his game despite his early success. "Some of the P.A.C. players who are members of the local Y.M.C.A. are seen on the floor nearly every day, throwing goals. Lew is a crack shot now, although he always was pretty good at caging the ball."[27]

Another sign things were heading in the right direction came when the PAC increased their winning streak to three games by defeating the Burkes. They won 21 to 14 in another well-attended game watched by 1500 fans.

It was also another rough one. "Forty-eight fouls were called," according to the *Sun*, and the high number was perhaps not surprising since "the five foul rule was suspended." According to the paper, the Burkes cut into the smaller team's lead late in the game as "the P.A.C. team seemed to weaken but the time limit was too close." It sounded like the PAC was saved by the bell.

Despite the extreme physicality, Lew and his opponent were credited for their clean play. "[Michael Qualey] and Bucky Lew, the colored lad, put up the cleanest game of the night. It was a treat to watch these two youngsters who by the way, know as much about good, clean basketball and its fine points as any player in the league ... what they did was in strict accordance with the rules and was all the more appreciated because it required cleverness to carry it along."[28]

Harry "Bucky" Lew

The roughness of a typical PAC-Burkes tilt was later described in the *Daily Courier*. "According to the rules there are about 300 fouls committed in every P.A.C.-Burke contest," the reporter said, and he went on to describe the rules violated. "Holding, tripping, shouldering ... slugging, dirty playing, profanity, abusive or insulting remarks addressed to referee, spectators, or anyone else in the hall."[29]

The PAC took their three-game winning streak into Marlboro to face the still-undefeated league leaders. Marlboro remained perfect with a resounding 30–12 win. Despite the disappointing loss, Lew was still singled out for praise: "Lew guarded Punch so closely that the Marlboro man was unable to find the basket for a score." The *Sun* story included the note "The feature of the game was the playing of Henry Sheridan for Marlboro and Lew and Harrington for the visitors."[30] Harrington had eight points as the high scorer on offense, so Lew's contribution likely came on defense.

Looking for a Christmas Miracle?

Heading into Christmas, Marlboro was first in the league at 11–0 and the PAC second at 7–5. Gray intended to make the most of the holiday, scheduling three games in two days, one on Christmas eve, another on Christmas afternoon, and another on Christmas night.

On the other side of the holiday, the best player in the game lay in wait. The *Sun* touted the matchup in a home-and-home series and predicted a one-on-one battle between Hough and Allard:

> Manchester will come to town Wednesday. Harry Hough, the famous player of the National League, will be in the Manchester lineup, and will be played by Allard. Manager Smith says that Hough is the greatest player in the game today. Lowell fans think that Allard cannot be beaten ... the pair will give the greatest exhibition of playing the local rooters have ever seen.[31]

First, the PAC would have to survive the three holiday games.

In the first game, the PAC beat Maynard 36–15 in Lowell on Christmas Eve. The game recap did not include the box score, so individual totals are unknown. Mike McManmon, a former player who was home from college for the holiday break, started the game before being subbed out for Harrington. Lew played the whole way.

Next, in the Christmas afternoon game, the PAC defeated the Burkes 28–12 before 1800 fans. It was the PAC's second consecutive win

Chapter 9. Star Turn

over their rivals. Lew contributed four points. McManmon subbed for Harrington this time while Lew again played the whole way.

Gray and Redmond had again agreed to lift the foul limit, and 50 fouls were the result. Lew, who seemed to be adjusting to the physical game, had eight fouls himself. The *Daily Courier* said that "Lew, the P.A.C. man, naturally a clean player, committed enough fouls to be ruled off the floor. Bucky did the wrong thing eight times while the watchful eye of [Referee] Davis was upon him."[32]

Lew was far from the worst offender. The Burkes' Frank Devlin left the game with 10 fouls before the end of the second period. Perhaps he thought he could foul with impunity. According to the paper, it wasn't the number of fouls, but their intentional nature, that forced the referee's hand.

The PAC victory seemed to mark a turning point in city basketball. "Never before," the reporter wrote, "since the Burkes and PAC have been battling for honors in the basketball arena for four or more years past, had the latter aggregation shown such superiority in the rudiments of the game."[33]

It appeared to be a historic performance on both sides of the ball:

> The Pawtucketville aggregation has presented the fans of Lowell with exhibitions of team work in the past that were thought, at the time, could not be improved upon, but yesterday's work in this line excelled anything in this line in the past.... On the other hand, they prevented any semblance of team work that the Burke players tried, and time and time again the P.A.C. players brought their admirers to their feet by the manner in which they broke up the playing of their opponents.[34]

On Christmas night, the team traveled to Nashua for the final game of the holiday. With two huge wins behind them, and Hough in front of them, it was a classic letdown game, but the PAC kept their focus and won 32–13. McManmon started and Harrington subbed for Allard. Lew played the full game as he did for the entire three-games-in-two-days stretch.

Gray was going all out and so were the players. The *Sun* recognized their incredible effort. "Three games in two days are quite a task on the players. There is no game where greater exertion is required than basket ball."[35] Only time would tell if the aggressive schedule and trend toward rough play would catch up with what was the smallest team in the league.

Harry "Bucky" Lew

And a Happy New Year!

Manchester came to Lowell for a New Year's Eve game and the first part of a home-and-home series, but "the unequaled" Hough was not with the team. Gray even offered the 1400 disappointed fans their money back if they wanted it. Lew settled the refund question by putting on an offensive display of the kind Hough was famous for in a 51–9 win.

Hough, the no-show, averaged 14.4 that year in the National League, and Lew put up a season-high 14 points of his own. And it sounded like Lew could have added to his team-leading total if he were so inclined. "The colored boy, Bucky Lew, had his basket eye with him and sent the ball flying into the cage seven times. If pushed hard the little fellow would have scored several more."[36]

The PAC then traveled to Manchester and the league finally got the matchup it wanted—almost. Hough was there, but the PAC's captain, Allard, didn't defend him.

Defending Hough was left to Lew. "It was hoped that Allard, the star P.A.C. player, would be pitted against the little 'Wizard' but that was not the case," the *Sun* said. "Manager Gray, however had plenty of confidence in Bucky Lew, the star little colored player of the visitors and he covered Hough to perfection."[37]

It didn't look good early as Hough scored right off the opening tap. But Lew matched him basket-for-basket the rest of the way. Hough finished with six points and Lew four in a 32–20 PAC win. "At the start of the game Lew was a bit nervous," the *Daily Courier* wrote. "But as the game progressed he had the heralded champion player of the world on the weary list."[38] Never mind the team, the reporter said. "It was a great victory for the Lowell player."[39]

Lew may have learned something from his battles with the Burkes. The referee announced before the game that the managers had agreed to lift the five-foul limit and Lew finished with seven fouls. He may have deserved even more, as the *Sun* said, "his methods were very rough and time and time again he got away with tactics that were not seen by the referee."[40]

Gray told the *Sun* he considered it "the best victory of the season,"[41] and the Manchester paper was impressed too: "The P.A.C.s presented the strongest aggregation of players that has been seen in this city and their combined team work was the winning factor in the game.... It is doubtful if another such game will be seen here again, as far as excitement and all around playing goes."[42]

Chapter 9. Star Turn

The *Sun* offered their take a few days later:

> Bucky Lew covered himself with glory at Manchester Thursday night. Even one of the Manchester papers comes out and admits that the Lowell paper had the trifle better of the argument. When a home paper comes out in such a fashion you may conclude that the visiting player did even more of what they claim of him.[43]

The PAC had wrapped up the holiday stretch and prepared for some much-needed rest. They were riding a seven-game winning streak and had a solid hold on second place. Lew played a key role in the team's dominance over the Burkes and sweep of Manchester. And while Hough returned to Pennsylvania to complete the National League season, he'd be back for more basketball in New England the next year.

Chapter 10

Face of the Franchise

IN THE SECOND HALF OF THE SEASON, the PAC took control of the city. They extended their winning streak over the Burkes and their rivals relocated to New Hampshire after their sponsor dropped them. Next, it was the PAC's turn to fall off the map. Their aggressive schedule and the excessive roughness of the games caught up with what was the smallest team in the league. Injuries mounted and the squad started to lose. Despite all the adversity, Lew continued to shine, and by the end of the season he had become the face of franchise. When a local school asked him to coach and level up their program, he integrated college basketball too.

Burkes Dropped

As the PAC and Burkes prepared for a mid–January matchup, the *Lowell Daily Courier* revealed it would be "the last game the Burkes are to play under the Temperance banner."[1] The team had been dropped by their sponsor, the Burke Temperance Institute, who had supported them since they started playing in 1895.

The Temperance Institute sponsored sports teams to promote a healthy lifestyle, and they couldn't have been pleased with the headlines the team generated, which often involved violence and gambling. The *Daily Courier* said their style of play received "censure all down the line." The reporter expressed concern it "may do permanent harm to the sport" and "cannot be tolerated much longer."[2] Apparently the Temperance Institute agreed and they dropped the team.

The Burkes kept their nickname but relocated 30 miles north to Manchester, New Hampshire. John Smith held the NEBL's franchise rights there and after Harry Hough returned to the National League, Smith released the remaining players. The roster had included several other men from Pennsylvania, whose salaries and living expenses Smith

Chapter 10. Face of the Franchise

had to cover while they were in the city. Since the team had won only three of nine games, he may have decided the imports weren't worth the extra cost.

The Burkes had played against Smith's original Manchester team, and like many others, the local paper wasn't impressed with the way they played. The *Manchester Mirror* called into question the tactics of one player in particular:

> Pete Regan [resorted to] suddenly squatting in front of a running opponent in an effort to throw him to the floor. He was frequently seen holding and once he ducked between [another player's] feet, and catching an arm around either leg, threw him. He was then cautioned by the referee and this together with the hisses and other remarks of disapproval from the audience made him somewhat more cautious.[3]

The *Mirror* also criticized some of Regan's unnamed teammates: "Another disgusting trick was played by some of the big fellows on the team. Encountering a Manchester player in a rush they would throw an arm around his neck in a strangle hold and twist his neck violently."[4] Either the reporter was exaggerating the move, or the Burkes gave the traditional "clothesline" a little extra.

The PAC's concerns seemed to focus on one specific player. "Every man on the P.A.C. roster accuses Devlin," reported the *Sun*, "of being a rough player. In fact they are afraid of him and say he does not play the game as he should but gives his attention to the players with a view to making them incapable of putting up their regular game."[5] The report may have been diplomatically worded, but the message was clear—they thought Devlin played dirty.

Lew, for one, wasn't intimidated by any of the Burkes and he was willing to give as good as he got. Matched up against Regan in that mid–January game, he showed he could play physical too. According to the *Daily Courier*:

> Lew and Regan faced each other. Both men played a covering game throughout and it would have been necessary to hire one man on the side to catch the many fouls these two committed. Referee Connors caught Lew 10 times doing that which the rules do not allow, while the little Burke man was only four behind his opponent.[6]

Since both players exceeded the five-foul limit, the managers had obviously agreed to lift it for the game. While many had concerns about the way the Burkes played, apparently Gray wasn't one of them. The *Sun* would later report that "the Burkes and P.A.C. have been used to a game from which the ordinary rules of blocking and tackling have been omitted."[7]

Gray's eagerness to lift the personal foul limit, and the PAC's willingness to play as physical as their opponent, seemed to be a case of choosing valor over discretion. The smallest team in the league would have been better off if they focused on finesse rather than force. Gray was giving the fans what he thought they wanted, but it would come at a cost.

That last game the teams played as representatives from Lowell was as violent as any of the previous ones. In the ugliest incident of the season, a scrum between Devlin and Tighe degenerated into a fistfight, as described earlier, and Tighe had two teeth knocked out and was left unconscious.[8]

The PAC won 20–14 regardless and the victory extended their winning streak to eight games. While they only made seven field goals—Allard had three, Field made two, and Lew added another two—the Burkes only made three. The rest of the points were awarded as a result of fouls.

Perhaps adding insult to injury, the *Daily Courier* once again suggested the PAC had established they were the better team: "The Pawtucketville team was much superior of their opponents in every department of the game. They played their usual excellent passing game and their individual work was always in evidence. The Burkes ... were up against a superior set of players."[9] By defeating their rivals three games in a row and chasing them from town, the PAC may have felt like they won the war. Winning the battle and losing the war might be closer to the truth.

A PAC Collapse

The PAC were 13–5 and their next opponent was the bruising Marlboro team. The *Daily Courier* called the game "very rough." One man was expelled for five fouls but "two other Marlboro men should have been ruled off the floor if [Referee] Sawyer had seen fit to call fouls on them."[10] Marlboro ended another PAC winning streak by a score of 12 to 8.

In the aftermath, accolades were few, except for Lew. He had scored the only field goal for his team until Allard added one at the very end of the game. The *Daily Courier* said, "Lew was the only man who

Chapter 10. Face of the Franchise

performed with superior skill to that of his opponent."[11] The *Sun* agreed that "Bucky Lew ... played the best game for his side"[12] and suggested more efforts like his would have resulted in a win: "Had the PAC braced in the second period after Lew threw his goal the chance of a victory would have been excellent for Marlboro was just about ready to quit. The home team failed to take advantage of the opportunity and then the visitors pulled themselves together and regained their feet."[13]

The PAC had plenty of reasons to struggle. Allard, their top scorer, was "off play" (he would soon miss several games with an injury), and several others were in worse condition. The *Sun* said, "Jimmy Harrington was in no condition to give a good account of himself as he was suffering with that bad eye and besides his arm is in bad shape. And so with Harry Tighe."[14] It's a wonder the pair played at all, never mind that they played the whole way.

Players finally began to miss action, and the PAC dropped their next four games. They lost 20–5 and 31–24 to South Framingham, 37–17 to Hudson, and 36–9 to the Burkes in Manchester. The first half of the season ended, and the team was in a free fall, with their record dropping to 13–10. With the games Gray added around the holidays, the team had played three more games than anyone else in the league.

Despite all that, it looked like the PAC would finish the first half in first place when Marlboro left the league. Every one of its players left the team to represent Chicopee in the rival Massachusetts Central League. (That was the league from which the New England league had split two years prior.) The *Daily Courier* reported that Chicopee offered the players a sweetheart deal. While the NEBL capped salaries at $5 per game, the paper said with their new team "each man is to receive $25 weekly, his board and lodging free, and traveling expenses."[15]

The move to the top of the standings would have guaranteed the PAC a spot in the championship. Like many early leagues, the NEBL championship featured the team that finished in first place over the first half of the season with the team that finished in first place over the second half of the season. With a spot in the finals assured, the PAC could have eased up and made sure they were healthy and ready for the playoffs.

It was not to be. Marlboro's manager soon put together a new roster, and the franchise remained in the league—and in first place. PAC dropped back to second place. It wasn't clear whether or not Gray fought the decision, but the press didn't report any complaints.

Besides the Burkes switching cities, and Marlboro changing

players, there was drama in the PAC clubhouse as well. In the loss to the Burkes that ended the first half of the season, Skip Field refused to stay on the court after his fifth foul. It's not clear why. He may have been taking a principled stand against yet another lifting of the foul limit or he may simply have been tired of the abuse. The *Mirror* said, "Field ... was ruled out under the five-foul rule, and ... refused to get into the game after Manager Smith consented [to him staying]."[16] Reports also surfaced that the unhappy Field planned to leave for the rival league.[17]

Field wasn't the only one to have issues with the lack of enforcement of the five-foul limit. A *Manchester Mirror* reporter wrote at length about the impact it had on the game:

> The practice ... in suspending the five-foul rule may be carried too far. While most fouls are accidental rather than intentional, some are committed deliberately to prevent an opponent from scoring. As six fouls count as no more than a basket, it is easily apparent that a judiciously placed foul now and then may win a game.... Another bad result of the suspension of the rule is the tendency to roughness that results from it. The press reports show that rough playing has characterized a number of recent games in which the limit has been suspended and it can reasonably be blamed to that cause.[18]

Representatives from the rival league may have tried to capitalize on the locker room issues by recruiting Lowell too. The *Sun* reported that entire team had received an offer similar to that of Marlboro. "The P.A.C. players admit they were asked to jump Lowell but they say they have refused all offers and are here to stay.... There was some little misunderstanding between the players but this has all been explained satisfactorily and it has been learned that an outsider was responsible for any trouble that may have been brewing." In the same article, the reporter defended Gray, which suggests that unhappiness with his decisions may have been the cause of the trouble: "There is not in the league today a squarer manager or one who uses his players better than the man at the head of the P.A.C. team."[19]

Regardless, the entire roster, including Field, returned for the second half of the season.

Limping to the Finish

The injury issues persisted throughout the second half of the season. Various newspaper reports called the PAC "patched up,"[20] "crippled," and "weak."[21] Their roster was described as "remnants" of their

Chapter 10. Face of the Franchise

former selves and Gray as "handicapped for players."[22] Not surprisingly, they lost more games than they won.

Harrington and Tighe continued to sit games out. Allard missed several himself. Lew didn't dress for a game due to injured hands, and it sounded like he should have skipped another: "Lew ... was at a disadvantage, however, as both his hands are injured."[23] Adding insult to injury, a rival newspaper referred to Lew as his manager's servant about this time. In previewing a battle for second place with Hudson, the local paper called him "Jimmie Gray's colored valet, Mr. Lew."[24]

McManmon, the team's holiday substitute, was apparently healthy, but he had to return to school. The only player who appeared in that brutal Burkes game that didn't end up missing time was Field.

In one matchup against the Burkes, Gray tried to incentivize his players by offering the winning team a $50 bag of gold coins and a new pair of sneakers. The PAC lost anyway 31–25. Allard might have appreciated the offer a few games earlier, because it was disclosed that he was out with an injured foot.

Tighe returned for the sneaker game but probably regretted it. In one of the more eyebrow-raising pieces of commentary that season, the *Sun* said that "the five foul limit had to be omitted or the cage would have been empty of players before the game was half over."[25] Describing the decision of the managers to lift the limit as a *result* of the high number of fouls rather than its *cause* was an interesting take.

Gray's decision to give sneakers to the opposing team was also surprising. As a sporting goods salesman, he would be up on the latest tech, but it didn't appear that the PAC were outfitted with the best shoes for their home court. As the *Mirror* said in reporting on that very game, "The one handicap to the success of the game was the frightful condition of the floor. It was worse than glass, it was as slippery as a greased pig.... The players would often slide halfway across the cage and a runner was likely to fall at least half the time if he attempted a sudden change of direction."[26]

Quality footwear did seem to make a difference. When the PAC later played South Framingham, the *Sun* reported that "South Framingham was greatly assisted in its victorious march by the fact that they have solved the secret of the suction sole slipper, so while they galloped over the floor and had no difficulty in keeping their feet, the less fortunate Pawtucketvillians navigated with difficulty and fell frequently on the slippery surface."[27] Instead of giving away sneakers as a promotion, why didn't Gray just equip his players with the best?

That loss to South Framingham, 58–11, was the PAC's "worst defeat of its career." Yet Lew continued to shine. The *Sun* said, "Lew was the man picked as the PAC star," a "great player," and "redeeming feature," who "covered two men and he did it well too." Apparently, there was no quit in him either. Despite his team's large deficit, "he never tired and kept at the grueling as if his team was having the better of the argument."[28]

The season ended on a positive note, with the PAC winning two of their last three games, both over the Burkes, by scores of 21 to 14 and 19 to 16. Gray had finally added some new, healthy players, importing Jimmy Kane and Jack Tighe from Pennsylvania. (Jack Tighe was unrelated to Devlin's punching bag, Harry Tighe.) At 6'2", 220, Kane was the biggest man to wear a PAC uniform, and he could play too.

The response on the floor and in the papers was promising. The *Sun* said, "The pair played a corking game and showed what they are capable of doing."[29] And while Kane and Tighe put up a disappointing performance in the South Framingham loss, Lew didn't. The *Daily Courier* reported, "The only man who was not outclassed by his opponent was Bucky Lew."[30]

Of course, the final game of the season against the Burkes wouldn't have been a true PAC-Burkes battle without someone being knocked out of the lineup. This time, it was Lew's turn. "While jumping for the ball Qualey accidentally struck Lew in the left eye and it closed soon so he had to retire."[31] The PAC won anyway, and despite their woeful second half, they closed things out with two consecutive wins over their rival.

City Championship

The Burkes fared better in New Hampshire than they had in Lowell. Apparently rejuvenated by the move and new management, they finished the second half at 10–5, just behind first-place South Framingham. Like the PAC in the first half, the second-place finish meant they missed a chance to move on to the finals.

So Gray invited the Burkes players to return to Lowell to play a best-of-three city championship series. In the battle between the NEBL's two second-place finishers, the winner would get bragging rights, the full gate receipts, and a $300 pot. Gray had to be feeling good about things considering the way his team had dominated the Burkes so far.

Chapter 10. Face of the Franchise

Game 1 was held on Saint Patrick's Day and 1200 fans attended. Both teams augmented their rosters, with the PAC featuring two new starters, and the Burkes adding one of the top scorers in the league in Joe Kynoch. Of course, Lew defended him, and the *Sun* highlighted the matchup: "Bucky played [Kynoch] as he was never played before and the great goal thrower never got a look in at the basket. Lew's work was cheered repeatedly by the audience."[32]

Other than the roster changes, it was a typical Burkes-PAC war. The game was played without a foul limit, and seven of the 11 players who appeared fouled more than five times. It was another rough one, and Lew had to leave the game after being kicked in the stomach.

Only one field goal was scored, with the rest of the points awarded on fouls, and the Burkes won 12–8. Despite the loss and the fact he had to leave early, Lew's picture accompanied the game story over the caption "'Bucky' Lew, a P.A.C. Star."[33]

For the second game, 1600 fans came out to watch as Lew returned. Tighe had to leave due to injury and Field didn't play at all. The *Sun* renewed its focus on Lew and Kynoch: "All eyes were on Lew and Kynoch," it said, and "Lew ... played Kynoch off his feet." The reporter concluded,

Coverage of the PAC's loss in the city championship from the 1903 *Lowell Sun*. Despite the defeat, Lew has become the face of the franchise. The caption, "'Bucky' Lew, a P.A.C. Star" has been cropped out (NewspaperArchive).

"Lew [was] the liveliest man on the floor and, by the way, the chap who did all the playing for the P.A.C.'s."[34]

Once again, the foul limit was lifted, and once again more points were given as a result of fouls than field goals. The Burkes won, 16–14, taking the game, the series, bragging rights, and all that money too.

No wonder Gray was so upset afterward. The *Sun* reported there was quite a commotion when the receipts changed hands. "After the game there was the greatest excitement in the vicinity of the box office when the money was handed to [the Burkes]," the *Sun* reported. "The latter and Manager Gray, who lost heavily on the series ... became involved in an argument that attracted quite a crowd. There was all kinds of talk about wagers and finally it was agreed to play a game next Tuesday night in which only local men can appear."[35]

So the teams played a meaningless third game anyway. For the first time in the series, the Burkes featured their full roster from their Lowell days, while, despite the apparent agreement cited above, Gray added yet another outside player, Bill Sheridan from the original Marlboro team.

Only 1000 fans attended the PAC's anticlimactic and irrelevant 18–16 victory.[36] Neither Tighe nor Field appeared, and Lew played the whole way. He scored the first PAC field goal to get the festivities started. It was one of only a few baskets, but with the series decided, the intensity was lessened, and for the first time in the series, points earned from field goals exceeded those awarded on fouls.

Historic Honors

After the season ended, Gray announced that he had re-signed most of his players for the next one. The lone holdout was Field, which was perhaps not surprising given the rumors that he might leave the team at mid-season. According to the *Sun*, he was unsure if he would return to the game. Lew agreed to come back.

Lew also made an all-star team. He was asked to appear on a team made up of the best players from the PAC and the Burkes to face the old Marlboro team. The first game was held in Chicopee in late March. The *Daily Courier* relayed to its readers that the "*Springfield Union* speaks in complimentary terms of Lew's work. After wearing down one opponent, the colored boy took on a fresh player and held his own with him."[37] A second game was held in Lowell in early April as a benefit for striking textile workers. While the papers didn't report on the game, perhaps

Chapter 10. Face of the Franchise

because they were busy covering the strike, the *Daily Courier* said that Allard, Fields, and Lew would be there.[38]

He made more history when he received another honor late in the season. In a short piece on the Lowell Textile School and the college's basketball team, the *Daily Courier* revealed that "the coach of the team is Harry H. Lew of the P.A.C."[39] It was a remarkable achievement for a Black man in those days to be asked to lead the sons of New England's elite.

Textile is now known as the University of Massachusetts Lowell, home of a successful Division 1 basketball team. Hoops seemed important then too. In 1903, the school had just moved into its newly constructed flagship building, Southwick Hall, whose high-ceilinged top floor was designed for basketball. (Now home to the robotics lab, parts of the markings for the circles at center court and the free throw lanes from Lew's day are still visible.)

How could Lew pull off playing pro and coaching college at the same time? Because coaching in those days wasn't as time-intensive at it is today. Lew wasn't running up and down the sidelines like he was playing on the college court too. In fact, coaches were not allowed to talk to players during games. While that seems strange today, bear in mind, the game's inventor, James Naismith, did not think basketball was suitable for coaching at all. According to author Kenneth Johnson, "Naismith didn't consider himself a coach.... Naismith thought of himself primarily as a doctor, secondarily as an educator, and never as the Jayhawks' basketball coach. He preferred the term 'teaching.'"[40]

Team managers and captains owned some of what we consider coaching responsibilities today. Textile's student manager, James Dewey, would have been responsible for operating the team on a day-to-day basis, and the captain, referenced as only Captain Clapp in the papers, would have been responsible for directing the team's performance on the court. Lew's role was to provide strategic direction and skills-based instruction before and after games.

Still, Lew was a busy man, playing pro ball, coaching college, working out at the YMCA, and working at the family dry cleaning shop. Somehow, he pulled it all off. It obviously helped that the school was located only blocks from both home and work, and that Lew presumably had a flexible work schedule at the family business.

Overall, Lew's rookie season was a smashing success. While the PAC finished out of the running for the league championship and lost the city championship, no one blamed him, and his play was praised from beginning to end.

Harry "Bucky" Lew

The limited statistics of the day make it hard to quantify his performance, but the qualitative reports from the newspapers show he had a dramatic impact. And further proof is provided by Gray renewing his contract for the next season, his peers inviting him to join an all-star team, and the local college asking him to coach its team as they tried to level up their program.

Of course, his season was a historic success too. As player and coach, he had single-handedly integrated both the professional game as well as college basketball. And it looked like more was to come. While Gray's picture appeared in the *Sun* next to its story on the PAC's first game, Lew's picture appeared alongside its penultimate one when he was heralded as its star. Lew had replaced his showy manager as the face of the franchise and the leading figure in local hoops.

Chapter 11

Over to Haverhill

Basketball's growth in New England continued and the NEBL expanded for Lew's second season. Gray left Lew exposed and a new franchise in Haverhill acquired him. The league further leveled up when both the National League and the other Massachusetts league folded after half a season and their best players came over. Among them was Harry Hough and his ongoing rivalry with Lew would make headlines across the basketball world.

Lew on Loan?

After Lew re-signed with the PAC at the end of his rookie season, he was caught up in the shuffle of a reorganized New England Basketball League the next year. New teams were added, including an upstart franchise in Haverhill, run by Nixie Coughlin, and another one in Chelsea, awarded to Gray's friend and current Lowell Tigers owner Fred Lake.

Gray's association with the Pawtucketville Athletic Club ended too. In the upcoming season, he would be owner as well as manager of the team now simply known as the Lowells. Gray also signed several new players. Apparently, he blamed the team's small size for their second half breakdown, rather than his aggressive schedule or willingness to engage in rough play, as three of the new men were over six feet tall.

One of the new men was Guy Abbot, who had been a former multi-sport star at Dartmouth College. Abbot played with South Framingham the previous season, but the franchise did not return for the new one. Gray also named Abbot captain, which was a curious move given he was new to the team and that he had demonstrated an inability to guard the most visible star in the game, Harry Hough. When Hough faced him last season, the *Lowell Sun* said, "He threw 13 baskets against Abbot."[1] (Lew guarded Hough in his next game and he scored only six points.)

Harry "Bucky" Lew

Rumors of a split between Lew and Gray started in the off-season. In early September, the *Sun* reported, "It is whispered that Bucky Lew and Field may be among the missing in the lineup of the Lowell team and there are others, too, that will get the go-by."[2] The news likely surprised fans. While Field seemed unhappy about the lifting of the foul limit, he was a fixture with the team and the only player to appear in every game the previous season. And Lew had become a star.

That said, Lew wasn't free to sign with any team—or even league—of his choosing. The very next day, the *Boston Globe* reported Lew had been reserved for the NEBL over the Western Massachusetts league after the leagues came to an understanding. "The presidents [of the leagues] have signed an agreement regarding the reservation of players. No transfers of players will be permitted without the consent of the officers of both leagues."[3] (The Western league called itself the Massachusetts Central League the previous season.)

If Lew wanted to play major league ball in New England, he would have to wait and see where he was assigned. Playing for Fred Lake in Chelsea may have seemed enticing, since Lake had managed Sockalexis the summer before Lew went pro, but it wasn't Lew's choice to make. (When a similar situation happened a year later, after John Smith dropped the Burkes and sold them to New Bedford, the players objected, but officials ruled they had to go if they wanted to stay in the league.[4])

Before long, Lew found out where he was headed. He and teammate Jimmy Harrington were moved to the new team in Haverhill. Jack O'Neil, another new man signed by Gray, was also moved. It sounded like it might be a temporary measure to help Haverhill build a roster. The *Sun* reported that at least O'Neil would stay in Haverhill only "until a new centre is signed."[5] (Gray would later claim that Lew too was just a loan, but the league decided his attempt to re-acquire him came too late.)

The change was likely a difficult one for Lew. While Haverhill was only a little over 20 miles from Lowell, he would no longer play for his hometown team. It also appeared to cost him his college coaching role, as his name was no longer associated with the Textile school. The distance from work was inconvenient too.

It's not clear why Gray made the change. If Lew had joined Field in questioning Gray's lifting on the five-foul limit the previous season, there was no evidence of it. While he was never accused of playing dirty, he was not shy about accumulating fouls, and he played as physical as anyone in those games. Given the fact that Gray had moved to take full

Chapter 11. Over to Haverhill

control of the team as both owner and manager, and the high profile he maintained in the press, it's possible the publicity-loving manager resented the perception that Lew may have replaced him as the face of the franchise.

"Here it is all Lew"

Since Haverhill was a new team, it wasn't surprising that they struggled out of the gate. Without much of a supporting cast, Lew looked to score more, and the *Sun* noticed: "Bucky Lew has his eye on the basket judging from the scores he has been making."[6] In one of the team's early wins, he had 12 of his team's 23 points, which equaled the opposing team's total of a dozen.[7]

Attendance was good in Lew's new city. The team drew 1000 in an early home win over Lowell, 18–16, with the *Lowell Daily Courier* reporting, "Haverhill is developing into a red hot basketball town." The number of fans was apparently more than the hall could support. During the game

Bucky Lew individual photograph from the 1904 *Boston Journal* (NewspaperArchive).

Harry "Bucky" Lew

"part of the bleachers collapsed, hurling 200 spectators to the floor."[8] Fortunately, while some fans were "slightly injured," no one was seriously hurt.

The team was also making money. The *Daily Courier* said a league meeting revealed that "Manchester and Lowell were chock full of basketball life, while the figures from Concord and Haverhill also showed a generous margin on the profit side."[9] It wasn't the case everywhere, as Fred Lake disbanded his Chelsea team after three games and Nashua soon dropped out too. Instead of that fate, Haverhill became a core city in the league. "Haverhill is one of the leading cities in the state for basketball. It is fast approaching Lowell in the matter of attendance,"[10] according to the *Sun*.

Despite the success in the ticket office, reporters suggested Lew needed help with his new team. The *Sun* agreed: "Here it is all Lew and the colored boy is making good in grand style."[11] And the *Daily Courier* opined after an early loss, "Bucky Lew was the star for Haverhill. Had there been another man of his caliber playing for Haverhill a different story would doubtless have been in order."[12]

The paper even made specific recommendations for improving the roster. Another story advised they needed "a strong player at centre" and recommended Field. "With a player of Field's ability in Tuesday evening's contest I dare say that the down-river aggregation would not have taken the small end of the tallies."[13] Despite the earlier rumors, Gray kept hold of Field and there was no reunion of the old friends in Haverhill.

Interest in Lew remained high in his hometown. The *Sun* speculated that Haverhill would soon replace the Burkes as Lowell's main rival: "Haverhill is fast displacing Manchester as the great Lowell rival, and when the 'colored wonder' and his white friends come to Lowell again they will be greeted by a house that will surprise them."[14]

Despite the change in uniform, the *Sun* reported that Lew was still a popular figure:

> Bucky Lew ... was the big fellow for Haverhill and what he did was worthy of [the] applause that greeted his performance.... He found little difficulty in avoiding the interference of the local men and at times he held the ball by dribbling and dodging while two Lowell men tried to get it away from him. Lew seems to get faster every day and never tires of his work. That he is a favorite in this city was demonstrated by the applause accorded him every time he appeared on the floor.[15]

Chapter 11. Over to Haverhill

Even the money continued to follow him. The *Sun* said some gamblers were putting their money on the visiting star. "There has been some betting that Bucky Lew will score more baskets from the floor tonight than any other man in the game."[16]

Haverhill Levels Up

Things began to change on the court for Haverhill when Connie Driscoll bought out Coughlin. The *Sun* said he fully intended to make over the roster and build a winner: "Connie Driscoll ... wants the best and so do the people of Haverhill. They deserve it for the support they have given their team."[17]

The *Daily Courier* painted a word picture of the man that showed he took his basketball very seriously: "Connie Driscoll is the hardest loser that basketball has ever seen. Tears, copious tears, flow down Connie's cheeks very time his team loses a game, and words that defy Webster's dictionary pour from his voluble lips. Connie stands alone."[18]

Driscoll's power move was well-timed. When the league's Nashua team folded, Driscoll signed Pat Doyle, one of their top players. Doyle's scouting report from the *Pro Basketball Encyclopedia* says, "Doyle was a talented athlete who was adept at both baseball and basketball and also was a fine wrestler.... Doyle was a capable scorer and a feared defender who intimidated opponents with a combination of athleticism and his hair trigger temper."[19]

Then, when the Western Massachusetts League failed, Driscoll bought the contract of future Naismith Hall of Famer Ed Wachter. According to the *Total Basketball: The Ultimate Basketball Encyclopedia*, his successful offer of $100 for Wachter was "apparently the first sale of a basketball player's contract."[20]

Wachter was almost as young as Lew, having been born a year earlier in 1883. He was a pioneer of sorts too. In *Cages to Jump Shots*, Peterson says he was "sometimes credited with inventing the bounce pass and fast break" and also "took pride in team play and crisp passing."[21]

Wachter too had a scouting report:

> Wachter possessed a combination of size, speed and agility that few centers of the era could come close to matching. He excelled as a rebounder and defender and was equally adept at scoring on tap-ins or set shots. In addition, Wachter was a fine [shooter]. Wachter was an intelligent and innovative performer.[22]

Harry "Bucky" Lew

It took until February, but Lew finally had the help he needed. The team was taking shape.

Of course, Wachter was far from the only addition to the league. Two full teams came over. The old Marlboro squad returned, and Hough's team joined the league too. The NEBL closed out the first half of the season and started the second half with the new teams.

Hough and his teammates were the ultimate free agents. In the past two years, they had played for several cities in multiple leagues. In the National League, they had represented Bristol, Pennsylvania, and Burlington, New Jersey. In the Western Massachusetts League, they would represent Pittsfield, Chicopee, and Springfield. And the musical chairs would continue in the NEBL, as the team played in Lynn for only a few games before relocating to South Framingham. Regardless of where they played, Hough was one of the top scorers, and his teams were one of the league leaders, but they struggled to draw enough paying fans to cover costs.

"Lew Equal to Hough"

Haverhill and South Framingham clashed soon after the second half of the season began. After Haverhill defeated Manchester and Lowell in their first two games, they lost a close one to Hough's team, 31–30.

Hough himself didn't do much in the game. Not starting, he came off the bench. Lew guarded his predecessor, Joe Fogarty, while he was in the game, then played Hough when he replaced him. Lew scored two, held Fogarty to four points, and kept Hough scoreless.[23]

In the next matchup of the two teams, Hough did not play at all. Wachter left early and South Framingham won again. Lew guarded Bobby Mayham this time out and matched his two points. According to the *Sun* coverage, "Lew excelled for Haverhill."[24]

At this point, a report suggested South Framingham had an issue playing Lew, and it's possible this is why Hough avoided him. The *Daily Courier* said, "There is a story going the rounds that Bucky Lew is given the right of way by So. Framingham on account of his color. Most of the So. Framingham players come from the South and they dislike the idea of playing against a colored man."[25] They were from south of New England, anyway, mainly hailing from New Jersey and Pennsylvania.

Regardless, Hough finally played a full game against Lew when the two teams next faced each other at the end of February. Perhaps

Chapter 11. Over to Haverhill

trolling the rumored racist with a headline that read "Bucky Lew Equal to Hough," the *Sun* reported, "Bucky Lew held his own with the world beater, Harry Hough. Each man tossed four baskets."[26] Haverhill won 34–21 before a home crowd of 1000 fans.

If fans were hoping for more where that came from, they might be disappointed. Lew suffered what looked to be a season-ending injury in his next game, in what the *Sun* called "one of the roughest games ever played in [Haverhill],"[27] when the Burkes came to town. A "record-breaker" crowd of 1300 turned out and it would have been bigger if Driscoll could find a place for them. Fans were "refused admission to the hall, there being no room."[28]

The game was rough from the very start. Haverhill's Doyle "floored" the Burkes' Qualey with "a straight blow" and both men were tossed in the first period. The roughness continued when Lew "was thrown by Devlin and his right shoulder knocked out."[29] The injury was a serious one, and with only a few weeks left in the season, it seemed unlikely Lew would return.

While the initial report clearly blamed Devlin, his Burkes teammate Dan Lynch later said it wasn't his fault. The *Sun* reported that "Dan ... states that Bucky Lew collided with the goal post and was not the victim of rough work by Devlin as stated in telegraphic dispatches in newspapers."[30] Lynch might be expected to back his teammate, but he was also a friend of Lew's, with the pair still known to train

Bucky Lew in his Haverhill uniform from the 1904 *Boston Globe*. Note the wrap or brace on his left shoulder (Newspapers.com).

Harry "Bucky" Lew

at the YMCA together. So it's possible Devlin's reputation led reporters to blame him for what was not his fault. Then again, Devlin had a reputation for a reason. He was known for his questionable tactics and had many mix-ups with opposing players, most notably the PAC's Harry Tighe.

Haverhill won the game 35–23 but Lew's injury looked to be a significant loss. The implications for Haverhill's chances against the team with the league's leading scorer became an immediate point of discussion. The *Sun* said, "Lew's loss with be a severe one … as the colored lad was putting up a wonderful exhibition and was considered the only player in the league … that could cover Harry Hough properly."[31]

So it was a shocking event when Lew returned to play a little over a week later in a 33–28 win. Playing his former team may have been a motivating factor. The *Sun* described his return: "'Bucky' Lew went in for two periods and displayed his usual cleverness despite the fact that he is badly injured. 'Bucky' managed to locate the basket twice."[32] Based on the box score, it appears Lew played the first two periods and sat the final one, which wouldn't be a surprise as he was obviously still hurt.

Next up was the PAC. Skip Field and a few others had left Gray's new team and re-formed their old one late in the season and Lew may have been unable to resist playing against his friends. Haverhill won going away, 41–17. The *Sun* said Lew again played well, scoring six points and moving the ball to open teammates: "Wachter and Doyle threw baskets from fine passing by Lew."[33] It was rare that game coverage included a description of a player earning assists. Lew clearly had several that night and along with other anecdotal reports it suggests passing was part of his game.

Post-Season Matchup

When Haverhill met South Framingham in the last scheduled game of the regular season, Lew's team destroyed Hough's 72 to 23. The *Daily Courier* reported that Lew dominated Hough yet again: "One of the most interesting features was the plucky work of little Lew, who played the doughty Hough to a standstill."[34] Lew even outscored Hough, finishing with four points while Hough only had two.[35]

Haverhill finished at 32–34 and fourth in the standings. The team improved under Driscoll's leadership but fell short of qualifying for the finals. Hough's South Framingham team finished first, but they were

Chapter 11. Over to Haverhill

ruled ineligible for the championship since they joined the league so late.

Naturally, with neither team advancing to the post-season, Driscoll challenged them to a matchup: "So confident is Driscoll that Haverhill is the better team in the league today," the *Daily Courier* reported, "that ... he wagered $100 that in a series of games with South Framingham, the games to be played on neutral ground, his team could defeat [them]."[36] It may have been a case of irrational exuberance, especially with Lew still only a few weeks out from his injury.

The two teams did play one more time, and it didn't go well for Haverhill. South Framingham turned the tables and crushed Haverhill 55–15. The benefit game was held in Lowell with half the receipts going to a re-building fund for Saint Patrick's church after the historic church was destroyed in a fire. For once, Hough played against Lew like he did against everybody else, and he went off for 18 points in front of the crowd of 1500. Lew himself did not score in the game. Perhaps worse for local fans, many bettors, including Lew's old manager James Gray, gambled that Lew would hold Hough under five baskets. They were sorely disappointed.[37]

Haverhill played one more exhibition game, this time against Lowell. Lew did not start, suggesting he still wasn't 100 percent. The *Sun* described the game as "very rough and was stopped several times owing to injuries."[38] Lew entered the game as a substitute, presumably for one of his freshly injured teammates, and scored four points. Haverhill won 31–25.

All in all, it was a successful season for Lew. While it took some time for the team to come together, he bookended the year with wins over Gray's rebuilt team. And Lew's new team seemed to be on its way. As the *Sun* said of Haverhill in an end-of-season wrap-up, "the playing of this team as of late has showed marked improvement." And despite missing time to injury, then playing hurt when he came back too soon, he still finished 16th in the league in goals scored.[39]

At the league meeting that closed out the season, the Haverhill and South Framingham clubs reserved all of their players for next year.[40] So Lew's rivalry against Hough would have a full regular season to play out—and maybe more.

Chapter 12

Injuries and Indignities

Talent levels in the New England Basketball League remained high for Lew's third year. Rival leagues remained dormant and according to basketball historian William Himmelman, "Massachusetts remained in the spotlight by signing the best available professional talent."[1] The franchise shuffle continued as Marlboro left for Newburyport and Hough and his teammates moved to Natick. Haverhill stayed in place, anchored by fan support that would lead the league. Lew and Hough's teams separated themselves from the pack immediately and it would be a two-team race all year. When they played each other, fans could look forward to a matchup of the league's best teams as well as its best offensive and defensive players. Given Hough's issues with Lew, however, only time would tell whether their matchups would prove to be showdowns or letdowns.

An Ominous Start

Hough's new team, Natick, was the favorite to win it all despite Driscoll's continued efforts to strengthen his roster. The *Globe* reported that at an off-season meeting, James Gray and some of the other owners speculated that "the only way to make the games interesting was to weaken the Natick team, as it was far too strong for the others." Driscoll countered, "Never mind [that]. I intend to wallop you on your own floor and also Natick."[2]

Driscoll signed two new players to bolster his returning squad. The first was New Yorker Jimmy Williamson, who William Himmelman calls "one of greatest guards in the early history of professional basketball."[3] The second was Flo Haggerty, another early star, who hailed from Springfield. The first of many in the family to play ball, he was the older brother of future Naismith Hall of Famer "Horse" Haggerty.

Haverhill started well and the fans responded. According to the

Chapter 12. Injuries and Indignities

Newburyport Daily News, "Haverhill seems the banner town for attendance so far this season. Lowell beat that town out on the opening game but ever since then Haverhill has led them all in the number of people going to the games."[4]

That was the good news. The bad news was Lew re-injured his shoulder in an early season road game in Newburyport. The *Daily News* reported, "During the game, 'Bucky' Lew, the colored favorite of the Haverhill team, dislocated his shoulder."[5] The *Globe* said he "will probably be unable to play for the balance of the season."[6] It was a curious statement, given Lew's quick return the previous season. The *Globe*'s reaction may simply have been an acknowledgment that the shoulder had never properly healed.

It would become a recurring issue all year, and when the season was over, a *Daily News* reporter would say, "Bucky Lew will have to lay off as much as he can during the summer to get his arm and shoulder back in shape again. He will have the arm treated, as the tendons and muscles are all stretched and will not hold the bone in the socket."[7]

Regardless, Lew was back before long, returning once again in a little over a week, this time sporting a brace to keep his shoulder in place. "Bucky Lew of the Haverhills is playing with a dislocated shoulder," the *Fall River Daily Globe* reported, "having a pair of shoulder braces that cost $14 to keep his dislocation in place."[8] The expense, roughly $500 in today's money, demonstrated how motivated Lew was to return despite the apparently unhealed injury.

The dislocated shoulder was another in a long list of injuries suffered a little over two years in the league. He had to leave one game because he was kicked in the stomach and another because he was hit in the face so hard his eye closed. Another time he needed "surgery" (presumably stitches) on a hand after being run into the fence around the court and on a separate occasion he missed a game due to undisclosed injures to both hands.

Lew's race was likely a factor in his rough treatment. It was a physical game anyway, as his former teammate Harry Tighe's concussion and lost teeth attest. But as mentioned earlier, when Lew spoke to *Springfield Union* reporter Gerry Finn on the eve of the opening of the Naismith Hall of Fame, he experienced verbal and physical abuse similar to that of Jackie Robinson. And the abuse was about to take a new turn.

Harry "Bucky" Lew

The Boycott

Haverhill fans were expecting a showdown and possible championship preview when their team met Natick early in the season. Instead, they experienced a letdown. "Hough drew the color line and would not mix up with Lew," the *Lowell Daily Courier* said, "Baby Hough refused to play against Lew, and in this stand, was supported by the entire Natick team."[9] Natick took the court but refused to participate in the game. Apparently, they only moved to dodge the balls thrown at their heads by Lew's teammates.

The referee, Charles Connors, asked Natick's manager if they were forfeiting and he said no. They said they were ready to play—once Lew left. Connors warned them they would be fined but they still refused to engage.

Haverhill scored at will and built a big lead, but it wasn't good enough for the fans. They wanted to see Hough matched up against Lew and they let Natick know about it: "The spectators at the game did not take kindly to Hough's actions and hissed him for the stand he took."[10]

Perhaps fearing the game would descend into a riot, Lew asked to sit. Driscoll objected but Lew insisted. So he went to the bench, and the game was played without him. Natick never recovered from their early deficit and Haverhill won 62–19. Why Lew elected to sit out is unknown. He declined to discuss the affair after the game other than saying he trusted that "his friends in the league should take care of his interests."[11]

For his part, Hough was willing to talk to the press. He said he "liked Lew personally and would treat him in a gentlemanly manner anywhere but in a basketball rink."[12] The problem was that "it was against his principles to play against a colored man."[13]

The press suggested Hough was motivated by something else—Lew's exceptional defense:

- The *Waterbury Evening Democrat* of Connecticut said, "Hough quit because he was afraid to measure his abilities with the colored boy.... Bucky Lew is one of the best backfield players in the country."[14]
- The *Daily Courier* added, "Hough has found that the goals from the floor don't come with the usual frequency when he is pitted against [Lew] ... this reason is set forth by many as the real reason"[15]
- The *Boston Globe* commented, Lew is "credited with being the only able opponent for Harry Hough."[16]

Chapter 12. Injuries and Indignities

- Perhaps the *Sun* said it most directly: "Harry Hough seems to fear Bucky Lew."[17]
- The *Haverhill Evening Gazette* suggested it went beyond the individual players and that Natick knew the team's chances were greater without Lew playing: "Haverhill seems to be about the only team that can beat Natick."[18]

The Decision

As the best player in the game, and leader of the reputed best team in the league, Hough may have thought he had leverage. Lew's response, in contrast, is an interesting one. He may have handled his business so quietly because he had inside knowledge.

Apparently, it wasn't the first time Hough had tried to bar him. The issue had been brewing a while, and the *Boston Journal* provided the full history on the matter:

> The trouble started last August when some mention of the "color line" was made at the league meeting and at that time President Fred A. Cummings took the matter in hand and prevented an attempt to oust the player. Lew heard of the matter, and not wishing to cause any trouble among the basketball managers, wrote to the president and asked if there was to be any trouble over his membership in the league and asking the head official "how he stood." The president's reply was typical of him—"I am behind you"—and Lew remained in the league.... Lew was a popular favorite and rated one of the best players in the league.[19]

Recognizing the importance of the moment, Cummings called an emergency meeting. "At midnight Saturday night a special meeting was arranged," the *Daily News* reported, "and at 2 o'clock Sunday afternoon there was a conference of the directors, at which the case of the Natick club was thoroughly discussed."[20]

It may not have been a quick resolution, but the league came to a firm decision. The *Daily Courier* said, "After much discussion it was decided to fine the management of the team."[21] Natick was fined $50, $1500 in today's money, for their actions. And it would only get worse if "the Natick aggregation refused to abide by the ruling in regards to the color line."[22] Every team voted against Natick.

The same paper also reported that Natick was threatening to leave the league. Their manager, William O'Neil, claimed the team would be re-locating because "he could no longer make expenses here and for that reason would no longer keep his men in pay."[23] The timing was suspect to say the least and the *Daily Courier* wasn't afraid to state the obvious: "It is assumed from Natick's recent action with reference to Bucky Lew of Haverhill, the colored player, might have had something to do with the withdrawal from the league."[24]

Regardless, Lew's faith in the league was rewarded. "When it came to the show down between Bucky Lew and the Natick team, the New England League stood back of Lew."[25] It was a historic decision. The league would not become a segregated one—there would be no color line.

More Adversity

If Lew thought he was in the clear after the league's decision, he was mistaken. A few days later, fans targeted him with abuse, with fans in Fall River calling him a "coon."

"One of the Haverhill players was 'Bucky' Lew, a colored man, one of the fastest basket ball players in the league, and when he began to make things lively for the home team, some of the more excitable sports called the attention of the locals to him," the *Daily News* said. "Some of the spectators yelled out 'look out for the coon' and 'get after the coon.'"[26]

The referee wouldn't have it. "Referee Packard stopped the basket ball game," the paper reported. He "refused to let it go on until he warned the audience to stop that kind of talk ... the talk was dispensed with for the rest of the game."[27]

It's interesting that this incident followed Hough's attempted boycott so closely. Was it really the first such incident, with the fans more emboldened by Hough's stance against Lew? Or did the referee just feel empowered to do something about it because of the league's decision? Or was the press just more willing to report on it? Looking back, it's hard to say, but it seems unlikely Lew hadn't experienced anything like it before.

Gray Makes a Play for Lew

Another interesting development in the boycott saga was the play James Gray made to re-acquire Lew. Only a few days after the boycott, the *Daily Courier* said Gray was chasing him:

Chapter 12. Injuries and Indignities

> Manager Gray is after the pennant and he knows he has to have a man who can keep Hough from scoring. For this reason, he is negotiating with Connie Driscoll of the Haverhill team for Buckey Lew. Driscoll thinks a great deal of Lew, and it is possible that Gray will not be able to secure the colored wonder.[28]

Gray said he had only loaned Lew to Haverhill when the franchise came into existence at the beginning of the previous season, so he now had a right to ask for him back. And he had evidence to prove it. "Gray claimed that he had an agreement and later produced it, to the effect that Lew was considered a loan to Haverhill and was returnable at the request of the Lowell manager. The agreement was signed by Nixie Coughlin, former owner of the team."[29]

One of the other players who left Lowell for Haverhill, Jack O'Neil, did return promptly, so there might be something to Gray's argument. That said, while O'Neil returned, Lew did not, and the *Globe* reported after the conclusion of the season that Haverhill, not Lowell, had reserved him for the next one.

The *Sun* even reported that Gray had his man. "Manager Gray made a deal with Manager Driscoll last night and there is little doubt that it will be ratified by the league directors."[30] Since Lew did not control his own rights, he would have to once again wait and see what the league decided.

The agreement reportedly involved Gray purchasing Lew's contract for $500. It seemed an astronomical offer, five times what Haverhill had paid for Wachter, and roughly $18,000 today. Seemingly confident he would get his man, Gray also announced he had a double header coming up against Natick and planned to use Lew against Hough.

As is often the case with Gray, going back to when he brought Lew along to his first game but was reluctant to play him, it's not entirely clear what he was thinking. His actions could have been a sign of support for Lew. He was also clearly hoping to capitalize on the controversy by making headlines and attracting fans to games.

Haverhill had overtaken Lowell as the league leader in attendance, and he may have hoped to reverse that. He may have been feeling nostalgic for the good old days when Lew played for him and he led the league in fan support.

In reporting that the league was on solid financial footing, the *Daily Courier* said, "Haverhill is conceded to be the best city in the circuit.... Lowell has braced up and is now giving Manager Gray a fair return for the money he has expended in the sport."[31] If Lowell had to

Harry "Bucky" Lew

"brace up," it meant they were off to a rough start. One reason for that might be that Huntington Hall had burned down, and Gray was playing in a smaller arena, the Westford Street Armory, which had a capacity of only 800 fans. Another was likely Lew's absence.

He even added music and dancing to the program when he found interest in his team was declining. Commenting on the state of the league in 1905, the *Daily Courier* said "Manager Gray makes no mistake when he gives fans a good music program along with the game. The fans should respond."[32]

For its part, the *Haverhill Evening Gazette* objected to any agreement that would send Lew back to Lowell. "If Bucky Lew is worth $500 to Manager Gray of Lowell, he is certainly worth that much to Manager Driscoll," a reporter wrote, "and the popular colored boy should not be allowed to leave Haverhill, especially as he prefers this city to any in the league."[33] Lew had established himself as a favorite in the city and the *Gazette* suggested the feeling was mutual.

The reporter also suggested Driscoll could make money by keeping Lew: "If Manager Driscoll wants to fill the hall all he has to do is put 'Bucky' Lew against Harry Hough and keep him in the game."[34]

For his part, Driscoll insisted he didn't make a deal. He also said he wasn't bound by the agreement Gray had with the team's previous owner because he wasn't a party to it.

The league sided with Driscoll and Lew one more time. According to the *Daily Courier*, "Connie Driscoll said when he bought the Haverhill team he bought all of its players and the league stood by him in this contention."[35]

Gray was disappointed with the league's decision and would be further disappointed with the light turnout for his team's doubleheader against Hough. "Two very small basketball audiences welcomed Natick to the city," the *Daily Courier* said. "It may have been because of the recent action by Natick against 'Bucky' Lew that the people stayed away."[36] Perhaps the fans decided to give Hough the same cold shoulder he had given Lew.

Haverhill fans were happy to have him stay with their team. Perhaps still battling injury, he made a token appearance in the next home game but didn't stay for long. "Bucky Lew appeared in the lineup for a short time and made a hit with the crowd," the *Daily Courier* reported: "Local people think a great deal of Lew, and are pleased that he is to remain here."[37] Where Lew wanted to end up is unknown, however there's no reason to think he wasn't happy to be back with the team with the most wins and best fan support in the league.

Chapter 13

Near Misses

Lew returned to play, Haverhill continued to win, and the team closed out the first half of the season in first place, punching their ticket to the league championship. The second half started similar to the first, with Haverhill jumping toward the front of the standings, and Lew re-injuring his shoulder. Natick, which didn't follow through on its threat to leave the league, started out strong too. They won their first 13 straight games and finished the second half of the season in first place. It meant the two rivals would face each other in the finals. Hough did his best to avoid Lew after the failed boycott, so it wasn't certain Lew would guard him, but with a championship on the line, it seemed inevitable.

Seasons End

Haverhill won the first half of the season with a record of 28–8 and Natick finished just behind them at 19–11. With a guaranteed spot in the championship, Haverhill could afford to make sure they were rested and ready for the finals. That wasn't Lew's style, however, and after he re-injured his shoulder in the second half of the season, he only missed a single game before returning to play.

Natick started the second half in dominant fashion with an extended winning streak. Haverhill finally stopped it, defeating them 29–21 in early February, but by then the streak had grown to 13 games. According to the box score, Lew guarded Natick's other guard, Joe Fogarty, not Harry Hough, that night.[1]

Hough tried to avoid Lew after his failed boycott. When the two teams played each other, he missed some of the games and switched positions in others. Sometimes, the switch involved moving to guard, and at others, he played the forward spot on the opposite side of the court from the one Lew was defending.

He could make this work because of some differences between

Harry "Bucky" Lew

Bucky Lew with his Haverhill teammates from the 1904 *Boston Globe*. Lew stands in the back row at right. Hall of Famer Ed Wachter, the tallest player in the photograph, stands second from left (Newspapers.com).

early basketball and today's game. Back then, most possessions started off a jump ball. When teams set up for the tap, guards positioned themselves in the back to protect their basket, while forwards set up at the front to be closer to their opponent's basket and in a better position to score. Guards defended forwards, similar to how defensive backs play wide receivers in football today, and each guard would defend the forward on their side of the court. If Hough switched from his usual position of forward to guard or stayed at guard but changed his side of the court, someone other than Lew would defend him.

That said, simply changing his side of the court wasn't a perfect solution. While the box score might make it look like Lew defended Hough's counterpart, it could be misleading, because Haverhill started

Chapter 13. Near Misses

switching on defense. According to the William Himmelman, Lew's teammate Scotty Williamson came up with the strategy at about this time:

> Williamson ... revolutionized the game by developing the switch play on defense. Until that time the right guard always covered the left forward and the left guard covered the right forward. [Williamson] decided to take whichever forward the one guard was in position to handle. The other guard adapted by covering the other forward.[2]

So Lew could still guard Hough even if they weren't matched up at the tap and the *Lowell Daily Courier* suggested this did happen. When Haverhill snapped Natick's 13-game winning streak, the paper noted, "The only way to win from Natick is to stop Hough, but that is a proposition that is anything but easy. Haverhill has defeated Natick several times because of Lew's ability to follow the Natick star."[3] The paper suggested Lew played Hough more than anyone else in that game as well as a number of others.

For his part, Lew missed some games against Natick too. While it may just have been because he was hurt, it's also possible there was more to it than that. Haverhill may not have wanted to deal with the drama, or they may have decided to save the matchup for the most important games, such as the streak-ending game or the playoffs.

The shoulder became an issue again in January. According to *Daily Courier*, "Bucky Lew collided with the corner of the cage and injured his left shoulder"[4] at another game at Newburyport. The injury was not described as a dislocation, so it may not have been as severe as the injury he suffered earlier in the season. He did leave the game, and he missed the next one against Natick the following night, but he returned to play a few nights after that.

He exacted his revenge a week later, when he contributed six of his team's 22 points in a 22–15 win over Newburyport. "Three baskets by Lew," the *Daily Courier* reported, "sent his team to the front and from then until the close Haverhill kept the lead."[5] It was a promising performance, but given his willingness to play hurt and his history of returning too quickly from injury, fans couldn't assume it meant he was fully healed.

Regardless of Natick's winning ways, the team said they weren't drawing enough fans to pay their bills. "Natick is barely supporting the team,"[6] the *Daily Courier* reported. So they arranged to play half of their remaining home games in South Framingham, the city they had left in the offseason.

They weren't alone in dealing with attendance issues. As the *Lowell Sun* said, "At present the situation in the league is very unsettled. At Portsmouth the game is experimenting, while Natick ... is really in a dangerous position. The team is without any financial backing, and cannot hold out much longer, owing to the amount of money lost. At Amesbury it is reported that Connie Murphy, disgusted with the support given the team there, has quit, and the players are running the team themselves."[7]

Haverhill was one of the few teams still doing well at the gate, as was typical of Lew's teams. The *Sun* reported that "Haverhill is probably the best paying town in the circuit."[8] Newburyport was doing well too, and that was about it. Even in Lowell, once the league leader in attendance, Gray was struggling. "The season has not been a prosperous one," the *Sun* said.[9]

Why was the league struggling? The *Boston Globe* cited a lack of competitiveness across the board. The paper reported that the game "is in a bad way.... This year's teams were not evenly matched, thus making the games one-sided."[10] In the six-team league, Haverhill and Natick were far ahead of the rest of the pack, with Lowell barely over .500 and the rest of the teams well below that.

So, to the obvious detriment of the rest of the league, Haverhill and Natick dominated the second half of the season just as they had the first. The teams reversed positions this time, though, and Natick finished in first place at 17–4, while Haverhill finished second at 16–8. Regardless, the two teams were set to match up in a seven-game series to decide the league championship.

The Finals Begin

Just as Natick was favored to win the regular season, they were picked to win the finals too. The *Globe* said, "Natick's easy win of the second series makes her a favorite against Haverhill, who, though playing a fast game, is not up to the form it showed in the first series, when it made a runaway race."[11] Even Lew's hometown *Sun* agreed that the smart money was on them: "In the Natick-Haverhill series Lowell sports will place their money on Natick, for there is no doubt that the world's champions can win from Driscoll's men though the latter are capable of putting up a great argument at all times."[12]

In a lengthy article on the team, the *Globe* made it sound like Natick was the best team ever assembled:

Chapter 13. Near Misses

The Natick team is probably the fastest aggregation that has ever played in New England.... The team plays a fast, heady game and for teamwork clearly outranked its opponents throughout the season. A clean passing game is the favorite style, but on a few occasions when the attack was rough they demonstrated their perfect ability to outrough the roughest and pull out the victory on top of it.[13]

It also raved about Hough in particular: "Harry Hough of Trenton, NJ, the little star forward, has been a phenomenal player even among the champions. His dodging and jumping and all-around cleverness, together with a penchant for throwing inconceivable baskets are the bane of opposing teams."[14] Hough was looking to add to an already-impressive resume. He was the leading scorer in the league, which gave him his third scoring title as a pro going back to his National League days, and he already had a championship too, winning the NL title with Bristol in 1901.[15]

Haverhill hosted game one. Lew guarded Hough from the start and held the Natick star scoreless, but Natick won 20 to 15 anyway. The *Globe* called the game "the hottest contest seen on the local surface this season" and said the "team work of Natick was of a spectacular order." Hough may have focused on passing instead of scoring as the reporter credited him with leading "his team mates with remarkable cleverness." The high scorer was Fred Mulliner, the Natick center, who had eight points. Neither Wachter nor Lew scored. Lew played the whole way, and Haggerty played two periods with Williamson coming in to replace him in the third.

The game story ended on an interesting note—while the first game in the series was played on February 25, the next one wouldn't be played until March 2. In basketball today, playoff schedules are often spread out to optimize television ratings, however in those days before TV and even radio, it was unusual to have such a large gap between games.

An Unfortunate Break

So why the pause in the championship series? James Gray arranged for a five-game series between Lowell and Natick before the full finals schedule was set. After squeezing in one game, Haverhill would have to wait for Natick to finish with Lowell before facing them again.

Haverhill was understandably upset about the delay. The *Haverhill Evening Gazette* said their manager "was a sore man last evening." It

Harry "Bucky" Lew

quoted him as saying "'that Natick bunch. Here they are supposed to play Haverhill, but instead they go ahead and get on a series with Lowell. I can see through the whole scheme. They know that Haverhill will wait for them if they have to wait a month.'"[16]

Natick's manager said his hands were tied because his players weren't yet bound to him. His opportunity to reserve them for another year would come at the next league meeting, and it hadn't been held yet, so the players were free agents.

Gray defended his interference in the championship series by saying he needed to make up for his losses from the regular season. So he engaged Natick in a winner-take-all series for $400, roughly $15,000 today. He told the *Sun*, "I have not made any money in the game this year.... I thought I saw a chance to make up some of the lost money and that is why I placed this side bet."[17]

Fans almost had the chance to see Hough and Lew face each other in the series, although it would have taken some gymnastics to get there. As an avid gambler, Gray undoubtedly realized putting money on his team to defeat the team that was favored to win the championship wasn't a smart bet. So he tried to adjust the lineups to better his odds. The *Globe* said Gray signed Wachter, and when Natick objected, he demanded that Hough sit too. When Natick objected to that, Gray said he would add Lew. It may have only been a threat, but that settled things, and Hough, Wachter, Lew sat out the series.[18]

It wasn't surprising that Wachter was looking for someplace to play during the delay, since, like most of Lew's teammates, he was from New York, and they otherwise wouldn't make any money to pay their expenses while they waited. So Haverhill arranged its own series with Newburyport. While Hough rested, Lew played on, returning to the place where he had already injured his shoulder twice that year. It should have been easy for him to skip, however he decided to join his teammates anyway.

Perhaps predictably, Lew hurt his shoulder again in what the *Globe* called a "Rough and One-Sided Game." Haverhill won 35–15, and Lew started, but left early. No injury was disclosed at the time, however, it's obvious he was hurt based on how the rest of the game played out. When Doyle was expelled "for improper talk," the reporter suggested the team would have to play shorthanded as "Haverhill had no substitutes." They brought their usual six players but would be down two players with Doyle and Lew out. So the managers agreed that Doyle could stay to preserve the five-on-five matchup, even after the official "refused

Chapter 13. Near Misses

to referee with Doyle in the game," quit, and went home. Newburyport's manager refereed the remainder of the game instead.[19]

The Finals Resume

Even without Hough, Natick defeated Lowell in four games. As the *Sun* sadly reported about the city's basketball season, "It's all over now."[20] Natick was ready to resume the championship series with Haverhill.

An injured Lew sat out games two and three. Natick won game two 18–16 in what a *Daily Courier* reporter called "a combination pugilistic-basketball encounter" in which "right hooks, left jabs, uppercuts, jolts, biting, kicking, scratching, and tripping fairly describes the actions of the players at times."[21]

The *Berkshire Eagle* provided even more detail on an early scrum:

> Hough started down the floor when Wachter ... tripped him, causing him to fall heavily to the floor. The little forward, much to the surprise of everyone, jumped to his feet, ran down the floor, and landed a heavy right in the back of Wachter's ear, flooring him. Haggerty of Haverhill went after Hough which sent the Natick man on his back. Fogarty, who, by the way, it is stated, is a member of the famous fighting Fogarty family of Philadelphia, went after Haggerty and sent him to the mat.... [Next] the crowd was privileged to see a lively two-minute brush [between Fogarty and Wachter] causing the Haverhill center to drift off to the land of nod.[22]

According to the Newburyport paper, Natick was trying to take Wachter out of the game. Its reporter described their work as "disgraceful doings."[23]

Despite the fistfights, no one was expelled from the game. The referee tried but was overruled by the two managers. Wachter might have benefited from the break, as his injury turned out to be a serious one. About a week after the series concluded, he sought medical treatment for a concussion. After another game against Newburyport, the *Globe* said he "complained of a violent headache ... a physician was summoned and it was found he was suffering from concussion of the brain. He is resting comfortably, although his condition is critical."[24] While the reporter attributed the injury to the Newburyport game, it seems obvious he suffered his first concussion in the Natick one.

Haverhill won game three 24–17 before a capacity home crowd of

Harry "Bucky" Lew

1200. The *Globe* said Lew's backcourt mate Scotty Williamson stepped up and "played Hough to a standstill. The latter not scoring until less than a minute before the close of the game." Haverhill ran the clock down through a passing exhibition and their home fans enjoyed their first win in the series. "Toward the end of the game [they] made little attempt to score baskets, passing the ball among themselves to amuse the crowd."[25]

Lew returned as a starter in game four but was ineffective. The *Sun* said, "the colored lad was of so little use he was taken out of the game."[26] Given the stakes, it seems likely he only played the first period. Natick won easily, 31 to 13, and now had firm control of the series at three games to one.

Despite his struggles, Lew played in the fifth game too, when he came off the bench to replace Haggerty. Haverhill had a significant lead and Lew likely substituted for his more offensive-minded teammate to protect the lead by playing defense and running down the clock. Apparently, it worked as the *Daily News* said "the final period was slow"[27] and Haverhill won 36–23.

Natick had a chance to end it in six games when the series moved to Newburyport. Although it was a neutral site, apparently chosen because of the strong interest the city showed in basketball that year, the *Daily News* said a "record" crowd of 1200 "came prepared to root for Natick." The reporter explained that it was "brought about by Pat Doyle and Bronco Wachter for there are no black looks given the rest of the team, except as a whole and on their account." Apparently, the fans disliked the pair for their rough play since "Natick has always played fair and clean against the Newburyport team."[28]

While Haverhill had some fans in the building, with 100 of them traveling down for the game, the overwhelming majority favored Natick. It seems odd that the fans were rooting against Lew's team in the same city where he had been injured three times. Was racism a factor in the city's treatment of him?

As far as the team goes, the players representing Newburyport were not from the city. Instead, they were mostly the old Marlboro team from Lew's rookie year. They were once again one of the bigger teams in the league, and they always used their size to their best advantage in an already physical game.

The first two times Lew was hurt, he was matched up with Charley Martens. Martens was from Springfield, and interestingly enough, he was the only player other than Lew quoted in Gerry Finn's 1958 story on

Chapter 13. Near Misses

the man. Finn wrote, "One of his rivals was a former Springfield police man, Charley Martens. Martens ... recalls that in four years against Lew he was lucky if he scored 10 baskets."[29] If Martens had a problem with Black players, it would seem unlikely that he would praise Lew in the papers.

The third time Lew was injured he was guarded by Toby Matthews. Matthews was not a regular on the Newburyport team, having played for Lowell the past two seasons. At 6'1" 180,[30] he normally played center, but with Bill Sheridan, at 6'2" 185,[31] taking that spot, Matthews moved to forward instead.

Marlboro played a physical style, and Matthews was known for playing as hard as his new teammates. The *Sun* story lamenting the end of Lowell's season that year featured the subhead "Matthews Tried Hard to Win."[32] When Lowell and Haverhill matched up, Matthews typically played Wachter, and according to Himmelman, "the two friendly rivals engaged in some titanic struggles."[33] Given Matthews' amiable relationship with Wachter, and his likely awareness of Lew's beloved status in Lowell (where he presumably hoped to return for a third season), it seems unlikely he would target him.

Newburyport itself, like Lowell and many other New England cities, had a complicated history when it came to race. A port city with an economy based on shipping, some of its vessels were used to move slaves from Africa to the South. William Lloyd Garrison, an early abolitionist, was born in the city, but he was banned from making anti-slavery speeches there after a poorly-received lecture.[34] Another former resident, Albert Pike, became a Confederate General during the Civil War,[35] and was also rumored to be one of the founding members of the Ku Klux Klan.[36] Then again, the city sent over a thousand volunteers to fight for the Union.[37] And after the war, the city erected statues to honor both Garrison[38] and its Civil War veterans.[39]

Perhaps the simplest explanation is the best one. The fans may have sided with Natick because of their lingering bad feelings about the "rough and one-sided"[40] postseason game between Newburyport and Haverhill a few weeks back.

League Championship

As Lew sat and watched the start of that sixth game, Haverhill opened up an early 12–6 lead. Both Lew and the fans who traveled to support the team would have been happy to see it, but the feeling wouldn't last. Haverhill failed to score a field goal in the second period and, according to the *Daily News*, "Eddie Ferat's long throw that tied the score was the signal for the wildest of celebrations."[41] The two teams were deadlocked, and Natick had all the momentum going into the final period.

At this or some later point, Lew subbed into the game, with the reporter saying, "At near the last, 'Bucky' Lew took Williamson's place."[42] He likely came in as a substitute for the final period, similar to the way he had in the previous game, the only difference being the player he replaced. In the previous game, he subbed for Haggerty, meaning he played next to Williamson, giving the team their best defensive back court. However, in this game, he subbed for Williamson, meaning he played with Haggerty, who was their best offensive guard. With the score tied, the team may have decided to play their best defensive and offensive guards together.

Perhaps Lew provided a spark in game five and they were hoping he could do it again. It wasn't to be. Neither Lew nor Haggerty scored, but Ferat and Hough each had two late baskets, and Natick took the 22–19 win and championship honors. The *Daily News* reporter said Lew "played equal to any of the others,"[43] which he may have appreciated, however losing to Hough like that was adding insult to injury.

The reporter summed up the game as follows:

> The greatest basket ball game ever played in New England is undoubtedly the way to record the Natick-Haverhill game in City Hall court.... Never was there seen more rapid work than was done all through the game and one grew bewildered and filled with excitement in watching the course of the battle, that was like the fury of a cyclone ... Haverhill is every bit as fast as Natick and entitled to equal credit. It was a great game and will long be remembered by local fans.[44]

The teams played a meaningless game seven in Natick, which the home team took 46 to 24. Lew played the whole way for the first time since game one and scored four points. According to the *Globe*, "Lew played his best game here."[45] It wasn't saying much given how limited he was by his shoulder injury. It was only after the season ended that its true condition came to light, when a Newburyport reporter revealed the shoulder wouldn't stay in its socket.

Chapter 13. Near Misses

NEW ENGLAND CHAMPIONS.
Natick Basket-Ball Team Proves Its Superiority Over the Best of Other Teams.

Harry Hough and his Natick teammates from the 1905 *Boston Globe*. Hough stands in the back row at the left. The team tried to force Lew from the league earlier that season. Lew won that battle, however three shoulder dislocations that year, including one after the first game in the series, may have cost him a championship (Newspapers.com).

World Championship

Shortly after the 1905 season ended, and presumably after Wachter recovered from his concussion, he organized a team to go on a midwestern tour. The highlight of the trip was winning the "World's Championship" in Kansas City.

Wachter's team faced the Blue Diamonds of the Kansas City Athletic Club, led by Naismith mentee Phog Allen. (Naismith had relocated from Massachusetts to Kansas by then, and he was coaching basketball at the University of Kansas.) The Blue Diamonds claimed the world title because of their recent victory over the Buffalo Germans, who had won the Olympic trials of basketball in St. Louis the year before. When Wachter's team swept the Blue Diamonds, they assumed the unofficial crown as best in the world.[46]

Harry "Bucky" Lew

Naismith himself watched the game and visited Wachter afterward. Wachter said the man who invented the game found him in the locker room and complimented him on his team's style of play: "You boys play the game of basketball as it was intended to be played, by passing the ball from one player to another until a player reaches an advantageous position to make a try for the basket."[47] Wachter had to be proud to hear he was executing the game exactly as its inventor had envisioned.

Three Haverhill players were on that squad. Besides Wachter, Lew's former teammates Jimmy Williamson and Jimmy Kennedy also appeared on the roster. Lew Wachter, Ed's brother, played too, with the fifth player being Ray Snow from Massachusetts.[48] Snow was a Holyoke man and had played two games with Haverhill the previous year.[49]

Would Lew have joined the team if he were healthy? As someone who had played with Wachter for close to two years, he seemed a more likely choice than Snow. There would be complications, of course. The Jim Crow system of segregation was strictly observed in the Midwest and it's not clear if Lew or his teammates would have tried to challenge that.

At any rate, the question is irrelevant. Lew's shoulder wouldn't remain in its socket, so he wasn't a viable option for the tour. It's unfortunate, because the recurring injury may have cost Lew two championships that year—a formal NEBL title and an unofficial world championship.

Chapter 14

From Allyship to a Championship

After the 1905 season, the New England Basketball League folded, the teams broke up, and the players went their separate ways. Like Wachter and Hough, who returned home and started playing for independent teams, Lew reunited with his old PAC teammates. One frequent stop on the regional independent circuit was Fitchburg, Massachusetts, where Lew met his future wife, Florence Smith. He also played violin and the first time the two saw each other may have been when Lew played with the band in a combined basketball-and-dancing event. After their wedding, he returned to basketball and played a season in Vermont. It was no honeymoon—especially after he was denied a place to stay after an early game—but he persevered and ultimately won his first pro championship.

Playing in the Band

In the early days of pro basketball, promoters would often pair a game with a dance to attract a larger audience. Whether Lew and Florence met at such an event is not clear, however family legend maintains that he first caught her eye when he was playing violin. Their daughter Frances told the *Boston Globe*, "As the story goes—my mother fell in love with my father while he was playing in a band."[1]

The family had a long history with music. Lew's great-great-great-grandfather Primus Lew founded what Eileen Southern called the Lew "musical dynasty."[2] He played the fife with the colonial militia during the French and Indian War.

Lew's great-great-grandfather Barzillai was also a fifer, appearing in the French and Indian War as well as the American Revolution. The *Lowell Courier Citizen* reported that "Barzillai Lew gained wide

Harry "Bucky" Lew

fame as the shrill fifer of Capt. John Ford's company. Several of his children inherited his musical talent and gave concerts which had a wide celebrity."[3]

A simple type of flute used to broadcast military signals, a fife is small and light, and its piercing sound carries far and wide. Made of wood, it features a large open mouthpiece and small finger holes. Fifers play the instrument by holding it sideways to their mouth, and instead of putting their lips on it, they blow air through the mouthpiece while moving their fingers along the holes.

Fifers also directed military life in camp. They alerted soldiers when to wake up, when meals were ready, when work was done for the day, and when to put lights out at night. On the battlefield, they signaled when to attack, when to cease fire, and when to retreat. Fifers were also asked to help with morale during downtime by entertaining soldiers too.

According to Franklin Forman in *Twenty Families of Color in Massachusetts: 1742–1998*, Barzillai may have served as a model for "The Flutist," a portrait which hangs at the State Department in Washington, D.C. Rumored to be painted by Gilbert Stuart or a student of his, the portrait features a young Black man in military dress posing with a fife.

Of course, the family musical interests went beyond military use. Barzillai and his wife Dinah performed in the choir at the Pawtucket Congregational Church. And the family's music extended outside the church too. Forman writes that Dinah also led the family band at elegant parties and college commencements and other engagements up and down the east coast. He wrote that they had so many events in Boston that they lived there over the winter.

Lew playing basketball and in the band was not without precedent. Gil Fitch, a forward for the South Philadelphia Hebrew Association, played the saxophone at dances after the team's games. In *The SPHAs: The Life and Times of Basketball's Greatest Jewish Team*, Douglas Stark says Fitch told him, "Four years after I joined the SPHAs, in 1936, I told Gotty I was going to form a band. He liked the idea and suggested we play after each Saturday night at the Broadwood Hotel. It boosted ticket sales and packed the house."[4] Stark described the scene: "A floor, about 65 feet by 35 feet, greeted the visitors, and two portable baskets were set up on either side. At the far end of the floor was a stage; at times, an overflow crowd sat there and watched the games. Afterward, Fitch's orchestra assembled on the stage, and the dancing commenced on the floor."[5]

Chapter 14. From Allyship to a Championship

Basketball and dancing events were hosted in Lowell and Fitchburg as far back as the mid–1890s. In one early Burkes game in 1896, dancing seemed to be the main attraction. While the concert was rated as "excellent," the game was described somewhat ambiguously as "interesting."[6] The members of the band alone were identified in the story. That said, the YMCA defeated the Burkes by a score of only 2–1, so the writer's ambivalence toward the game is understandable.

White Wedding

Lew made more history when he married Florence in 1906. In a dramatic account that followed the headline "Cured by Marriage," the *Boston Globe* reported that their wedding at the Burbank in Fitchburg was "the first marriage ceremony that has ever been performed in the hospital."[7]

Florence had become sick on a shopping trip to Lowell, and she was so bad off that she was admitted to the hospital when she returned home. It sounded like she was on her death bed. She had been hospitalized for three weeks and "there was little hope for her recovery." Fortunately, the bride-to-be was still clinging to one dream. "The young woman had only one hope—that she might live long enough to get married." When she relayed her hope to her doctor and nurses, they agreed to it, and Lew was summoned, even though "the physician thought that he would become a husband for only a short time."[8]

A local minister performed the marriage ceremony in her room, and it may have been an even whiter wedding than she imagined. She was dressed in her hospital gown and propped up with pillows in her bed; her aunt and the hospital staff served as witnesses. The staff would have been quite familiar with both of them, given her long illness, his frequent visits to her, and his own health issues. He may have gone to the hospital for help when he suffered yet another shoulder dislocation in a game in Nashua the previous week.

According to the *Globe* reporter, physicians had overlooked the "magic of love" in their pessimistic prognosis of Florence's condition, and that seemed to make all the difference. "A few hours after the ceremony, the fever abated and now the physicians think Mrs. Lew will recover."[9] She did indeed, and the couple went on to enjoy over 50 years of marriage.

The wedding made news all over New England. Lowell's *Sun* and

Harry "Bucky" Lew

Daily Courier covered it, as did Boston's *Globe* and *Herald*, and even the *Waterbury Evening Democrat* of Connecticut. The unique circumstances of the event likely contributed to the wide interest, but his fame was a factor too. The *Globe* said, "The groom is the well-known basketball player,"[10] the *Herald* called him a "basket ball hero,"[11] and the *Evening Democrat* called him "the fastest back in New England."[12]

One aspect of the coverage they may not have been as impressed with was the mention of race, such as the last sentence in the *Globe* account: "Both are colored."[13] The writer's motivation for including the fact is unknown, however if readers who were aware that Lew had integrated pro basketball were concerned about him integrating marriage too, they would learn his wife was also Black.

No Honeymoon in Vermont

After the wedding, Lew headed north. He enjoyed no honeymoon up there, however, as he was denied lodging after an early game in Charlestown, New Hampshire.

Lew played his first few games in Vermont with the team he and his old friends put together in early 1907. Then, when he started to attract interest from the locals, he appeared in a game with Vermont's Springfield Athletic Club. Similar to the way the failure of the National League led to an influx of talent joining the NEBL, its collapse gave the Vermont State League the chance to level up. "At least two thirds of the best players in the New England as well as some of the best in the business have been seen on the local floor this season,"[14] the *Springfield Reporter* would say.

After his game with the SAC, Lew was denied a place to stay despite it being a miserably cold winter night. After he scored six points and helped the team to a 34–26 win over their rival Brattleboro squad, he and the Brattleboro players crossed the river from Springfield to Charlestown, presumably to make it easier to catch a train south the next day.

He and his traveling companions were repeatedly denied a place to sleep. At the first inn they tried, the innkeeper said he had only one room with a single bed available. They moved on and the man running the next place they tried said he had no rooms whatsoever. When they returned to the first place, apparently desperate to get some kind of roof over their head, no matter how tight the quarters, the innkeeper rejected

Chapter 14. From Allyship to a Championship

the idea and demanded they leave. The *Brattleboro Reformer* said, "He not only refused them lodging but ordered them from the place."[15]

As a final resort, they tried to stay overnight at the train station. In an early case of racial profiling, the "watchman refused to check their baggage under the impression they were yeggmen,"[16] a term which, in those days, was synonymous with burglar.

Out of options, Lew and the Brattleboro players finally decided to walk to the next town down the line, despite the distance and the weather. "The nearest place of safety was Bellows Falls, 10 long miles away over the frozen hills. The thermometer was hovering way below the zero mark."[17] Why walk to Bellows Falls when they could return to Springfield? At roughly six miles, it was a shorter distance. However, Springfield was north, while Bellows Falls was south, the direction the men wanted to travel, and the train station there had more connections. It was late Saturday night, and as no games were played on Sunday in those days, they were all undoubtedly trying to get home. Once in Bellows Falls, the Brattleboro players could take one train south to home and Lew another southeast to Lowell.

The *Reformer* described the ordeal as "a ten mile walk over the frozen hills of Rock-ribbed Vermont in a ten-below-zero night, after having played a strenuous game of basketball." The reporter didn't say how long it took, but "at last the column made Bellows Falls and bed."[18]

So Lew both faced awful adversity that night and found unexpected allies. The team he played against—whom he helped hand one of their few losses in the season—stayed with him through the entire episode. In that way, it was like Hough's attempted boycott, where the league president reinforced Lew's right to play, and the verbal abuse in Fall River, where the referee refused to let the game go on if the fans continued to insult Lew.

It was the third major racial episode that had made news, and each time, Lew encountered both people who challenged him and people who supported him. It was another unfortunate incident, but once again, Lew was undeterred. A few weeks later, he signed on to join the Springfield Athletic Club for the rest of the season.

State Champion

Lew was a popular player in Vermont from the start. After his independent team lost by three points in Saint Johnsbury, the local paper

Harry "Bucky" Lew

devoted a long story to the game. The reporter from the *Saint Johnsbury Caledonian*, obviously impressed, called it "the closest and most scientific played game as had been seen on the local floor this season" and attributed each basket to "the fastest kind of team work or sensational shots from the center of the hall." Lew's team shocked the locals by opening up an early 18–8 lead. They couldn't hold it, however, and the home team "came back strong" to win in a "dazzling finish." While Lew only scored once, he would have been pleased to learn his defense was appreciated up there too. "Lew was in the lineup, and besides contributing a basket, guarded his man in gilt-edge fashion."[19]

Apparently, the fans took to him as well, because an ad for the team's next appearance in the town specifically called him out and even gave him a new nickname. "The next basket ball game will be played here Friday night when the Lowell Professionals will play Co. D. The players in the visiting team are the original 'Buckey' Lew, J. Fields, E. Cunningham, O. Fields, and H. Tighe."[20] Misspelled or not, that nickname, "The Original Buckey Lew," made him a marquee attraction.

The Vermont State League consisted of only three teams—the Brattleboro Athletics, the Springfield Athletic Club, and Saint Johnsbury's Company D. They played each other as well as other teams that traveled from Massachusetts, New York, and New Hampshire. Despite all those games, the league champion was determined not by overall record or a post-season series—instead it was determined by how the Vermont teams fared against each other.

Lew signed with the SAC in mid–February and with Saint Johnsbury too by the end of the month. It seems odd that he could play for two of three teams in the same league even by the loose standards of those days. However, the *Springfield Reporter* said that since SAC had signed Lew first, Company D dropped out of the race, "agreeing that the state honors should rest between Brattleboro and Springfield."[21]

He was also joined by a former Lowell Textile School player, Charles Church. Church was a member of the class of 1906 so he may have played for Lew when he coached the team in 1903. Even if he didn't, he would have known of him from the press coverage of his playing days in the NEBL. Church excelled at athletics, leading the football and basketball teams as captain, playing soccer, and serving as a member of the athletic council.

Similar to his first game with the SAC, Lew didn't disappoint in his opening game with Company D. "The old axiom that a new broom sweeps clean was clearly demonstrated by the work of the reorganized

Chapter 14. From Allyship to a Championship

company team," the *Saint Johnsbury Caledonian* reported. "The original 'Buckey' Lew was there and he did some original stunts in dribbling and passing that have seldom been surpassed on the local floor."[22]

The highlight of his time with Company D came against Dartmouth College. Company D had never beaten them, and it didn't look good when Church, their center, left the game with an injured ankle. Lew took over, leading the team in scoring, holding his man to a single basket, and scoring a late basket to win it:

> With less than half a minute to play and the score a tie "Buckey" Lew sent the ball squarely through the net ... winning for them one of the closest and most exciting games ever seen in St. Johnsbury.... Lew was the particular star and the idol of the audience. A wonderful player, fast and resourceful. He scored 16 points and his blocking and dribbling was the best seen here in many a day.[23]

Saint Johnsbury did well on the scoreboard and apparently at the gate too, but the season ended on a down note. Lew's traveling companions, the Brattleboro Athletics, and former Haverhill teammates, Flo Haggerty and Pat Doyle, combined to defeat Company D. Haggerty, apparently learning a few things from his games against Natick, knocked Church out cold with a sucker punch. Lew couldn't save Company D that night and Brattleboro went on to a 38 to 19 win.[24]

The Springfield Athletic Club, however, was still in the running for the state championship. According to the *Brattleboro Reformer*, the next time they played. both Haggerty and Lew played well. As for Haggerty, he "played his usual graceful game and did some pretty shooting. His passing was of a high order." Not to be outdone, "Lew played a good game for the visitors."[25] Brattleboro won 38 to 23. As they won an earlier contest without Lew, 40 to 10, Brattleboro led the series two games to one.

The teams would face each other one more time in Springfield. If Brattleboro won, they would claim the state championship, otherwise they would have to share it with the SAC or play a fifth and deciding game.

Church had also joined the SAC, and Haggerty, now "one of the best amateur boxers" around, attempted to knock him out of this game too. The *Brattleboro Reformer* said he gave Church a combination of "three trip-hammer blows" which gave his eye "the appearance of raw beef." When Billy Greene, the SAC manager and referee, tried to separate the fighters, a fan decked him. Greene was "stopped by a straight to the face and went down."²⁶ According to the Brattleboro paper, the perpetrator was a former Brattleboro player.

Once Greene recovered, he expelled Haggerty, but Brattleboro wouldn't accept his ejection unless Church was thrown out too. The team refused to re-take the court. At that point, Greene called the game, making it a forfeit by Brattleboro and a win for the SAC.

Brattleboro was outraged. According to the *Vermont Phoenix*, they "were ready to go on without Haggerty but the referee would not hear it." The reporter blamed Greene for being biased and said, "it was evident from the start that the referee wasn't going to give the Athletics a fair deal."²⁷

The SAC fans could remind them that Greene also refereed an earlier contest, the first one in which Lew appeared, and the Brattleboro players actually praised his work afterward despite their loss. According to the game report from the *Phoenix*, "the Brattleboro boys were warm in their praises of the treatment they received both from the opposing team and the referee."²⁸

The *Springfield Reporter* countered that "after all is said and done, the report of this game in a Brattleboro newspaper has all the appearance of long distance reporting and has very little truth or facts in it."²⁹ The paper seemed to suggest that Brattleboro didn't even have a reporter present at the game.

With the forfeit victory, the SAC tied the series at two games each. The obvious resolution to the controversy was to play one more game for the championship, however, according to the *Brattleboro Reformer*, the team refused: "The Brattleboro management does not consider that it will be necessary to play another game to decide the championship."³⁰ Brattleboro seemed to be satisfied to settle for a share of the championship, so the SAC would have to do the same.

The *Springfield Reporter* was more blunt. They suggested Brattleboro had forfeited their share of the title by refusing to play a deciding game. "The Springfield Athletic club claims the Vermont state championship in professional basket ball, as the Brattleboro management refused to play the fifth and deciding game in a series as agreed." According to the paper, "They evidently did not want the championship question decided. The Springfield team was ready to play the game and the Athletics were not, they therefore lost all hold on anything that looks like championship honors."³¹

Regardless, the SAC had at least a share of the title. They had the right to call themselves the champions and they posed for the picture

Chapter 14. From Allyship to a Championship

BASKET-BALL CHAMPIONS OF VERMONT
Brattleboro Has Refused to Play Off Tie in Series

Bucky Lew with his Springfield Athletic Club teammates from the 1907 *Springfield Reporter.* Lew sits in the back row, at right. The ball reads: "VT. CHAMPS, 06–07" (Newspapers.com).

that proved it, with Greene holding a ball inscribed "VT. CHAMPS 06–07." Lew had won his first professional championship!

The picture also shows how much work Lew had done to build up his body from his earliest days in the game. He was a veteran of five years now, and all the time he spent working out at the YMCA had added a significant amount of muscle to his frame. The extra bulk may have helped him stay healthy that winter, but it wasn't a cure. While the SAC continued to schedule exhibition games, Lew's season soon ended.

In a game against a team from Turners Falls, Massachusetts, the *Brattleboro Reformer* reported that "Bucky Lew was obliged to leave the game in the last period on account of a dislocated shoulder."[32] He was hurt again, but at least the timing of this injury was better than the one in 1905—this time he stayed healthy for the whole championship series!

Chapter 15

Home Again

After Lew's Vermont championship, his life off the court took a more serious turn. Florence made a full recovery, and they settled into married life and started having children. Their happy days were interrupted by tragedy when their first daughter died of scarlet fever. As the needs of his family grew, Lew spent more time on business, and he started managing his own dry-cleaning shop. He wasn't done with basketball, however, and he soon brought his new management skills to the court by running his own team. Then, when he suffered his worst injury yet, a fractured leg, he openly considered calling it quits.

From Triumph to Tragedy

The Lews moved into their own place, a large apartment in a two-family house on Gershom Avenue in Lowell, only a few blocks from his family home on Mount Hope Street. Children soon began to arrive. The Lew's first daughter, Margaret, was born in 1908 and a second, Eleanor, arrived in 1911. A son, William, was born in late 1913.[1]

Margaret died during a scarlet fever epidemic shortly after she turned four.[2] The *Lowell Sun* reported that a "Scarlet Fever Epidemic"[3] broke out in the city in early December 1912 and she fell ill in mid–January. She was seen by a doctor for seven days before she passed late in the month.[4]

Scarlet fever is a bacterial infection most common in children, caused by the same bacteria that leads to strep throat, according to the National Institutes of Health. A contagious disease, it's spread by "bacteria-containing droplets" and transmitted through activities like talking, coughing, and sneezing.[5]

The Board of Health blamed a contaminated milk supply as the primary driver in Lowell's outbreak. In those days, milk dealers delivered milk directly to the homes of their customers and later returned

Chapter 15. Home Again

to collect the used bottles. The pasteurization of milk, heating it to kill germs, was not yet standard practice, and some dealers didn't clean their used bottles thoroughly before re-filling them. Further, the weather had been mild, encouraging children to get together to play and spreading the disease even further.

Today, antibiotics would typically resolve an infection within days. However, they were not available then. Antibiotics would not be invented for another generation and not popularized for another generation after that.

An isolation hospital to provide care for the sick and contain the spread of disease would have helped too. The state had demanded the city build one as far back as 1901. And it was not an outlandish request—by 1899, ten cities in Massachusetts had an infectious disease hospital. However, Lowell did not open one until October 1920.[6]

After little Margaret passed, the Lews buried her under a small marble marker in the Woodbine Cemetery in Pawtucketville. It may have been a source of some comfort to know the cemetery was close to home and not far from Barzillai's old farmstead. What likely did not bring comfort was the fact that the cemetery abutted the land on which the city built its isolation hospital seven years later. Had the hospital been in place as the state requested so long ago, Margaret may never have caught the contagious disease and there would have been no need for a burial at all.

Taking Care of Business

Lew's career in the family's dry-cleaning business took a more serious turn too. Lew is listed as the "manager"[7] of the dye house on 341 Central Street in Lowell's business directory for 1906. His father's name is also associated with it, along with the long-established dry-cleaning shop on John Street, so it appears the son had become a partner in the family business. In contrast, Lew's uncle Fred is listed as running his own, separate shop on Merrimack Street.

The new shop was located on the opposite end of downtown from the first one. Based on its location on Central Street, which was within the business section of the city, and the nature of the advertisements placed in the newspapers to promote it, it appears Lew focused more on the consumer market. One ad read, "Ladies and gentlemen's clothing cleansed, dyed, pressed, and repaired."[8]

Harry "Bucky" Lew

While Lew's endeavors in dry cleaning didn't make the news as often as his exploits in basketball, one day Lew's shop did make the papers when someone stole a coat from him. The *Sun* reported that a man was found "guilty of larceny of a coat from the store of Harry Lew in Central Street."[9] It must have been a nice coat because the man received a sentence of four months in jail!

The Lews running three shops in Lowell is remarkable. Thomas Jennings, the first Black patent holder, received a patent in 1821 for his method of dry scouring, the process of removing stains from clothing using dry chemicals.[10] Like the Lews, Jennings was also active in the pre–Civil War abolitionist cause and post-war civil rights movement. Jennings' example—and perhaps even his shared expertise—may have helped the Lews find their own foothold in the industry.

According to the available business directories, Lew continued to run the shop through at least 1916. Soon after that, he returned to helping his parents with their business, as his name began to appear as manager for the original shop. At that point, they would have been in their sixties and likely in need of his assistance. The city's economy had also turned, and decades of growth would soon become decades of decline.

Back to Basketball

Lew also continued to take care of business on the basketball court. He played for attempted revivals of the New England league in 1906 and 1908, however both proved short-lived, with each iteration only staging a handful of games.[11]

Pro basketball had fallen on hard times. While amateur leagues thrived, pro leagues struggled, and there were many reasons for their decline—a competitive imbalance, the constant movement of players and teams, and the violent nature of the game. Lew experienced each of these firsthand in the NEBL.

Even in Lowell, once a basketball hotbed, and the league leader in attendance, the sport was struggling. A note in the *Lowell Daily Courier* said:

> Speaking of the decline of basketball in Lowell, a former enthusiast has this to say: "Basketball should be given a rest in Lowell. Year after year we have had it, and now it has grown tiresome. The 'newness' has worn off. Ten years ago, the game was a financial winner, everybody was enthusiastic, but time

Chapter 15. Home Again

has produced a big change. This season two games have been played for one admission, and it is little wonder that the public asks for a change. One year without basket ball will do the sport a world of good in this section."[12]

The dominance of Haverhill and Natick in the NEBL and the musical chairs of teams changing cities were certainly factors in its demise. Its extreme physicality was an issue too. In *Cages to Jump Shots*, Peterson cites the roughness of the game as the main culprit for the declining fan interest: "perhaps the most important—was the professional style of play, especially in the East" where "there was only one official to keep order, and when his back was turned there was a good deal of pulling and hauling in the cage.... Fights broke out frequently, and often inflamed fans threatened the referee or the opposing team."[13]

He quotes an unnamed early sportswriter as saying that because of the excessive physicality, "the good old indoor game is falling into disrepute." He continued to say that "gladiatorial combats of the ancient Romans pale into insignificance compared with the rowdyism rampant among some of the fans and some of the players."[14]

While some hard-core fans favored rough play, the rowdiness turned off other fans. According to William Scheffer, an early executive and promoter of the game based in Philadelphia, "The games become regular indoor foot ball contests, players being injured and spectators becoming disgusted. The latter are the ones to look after, as without public support, no sport will last."[15]

Fan support became a problem for the pros when fans began to have more options. While the pro game was stagnating, amateur basketball was exploding. High schools and colleges were rapidly adding teams. The issues present in the pro game didn't exist to the same degree in the amateur one. Players didn't often change schools and schools didn't ever change cities. And the game wasn't as rough. There was no cage to run opponents into and since the double dribble was illegal, a single player couldn't protect their dribble with their hands and elbows on their way down the court. If they wanted to go coast-to-coast, they had to use speed and finesse to do it, not brute force. And players shot free throws in the amateur game!

The managers of the NEBL had it wrong. Casual fans favored offense over defense. The rules and the prevailing philosophy of the amateur ranks led to a more open, cleaner game, and fans responded to it.

Harry "Bucky" Lew

Lew's Lowell Five

With the repeated failures of attempts to restart a New England pro league, Lew continued to play independent ball with his old PAC teammates. Nicknamed the Lowell Five, the team appeared in games all over New England, with regular stops in a number of cities, such as Lowell, Lawrence, and Fitchburg, Massachusetts; Nashua, Portsmouth, and Franklin, New Hampshire; Springfield and Saint Johnsbury, Vermont; and Springvale and Sanford, Maine, too. And they likely played in many more places. Without a regular schedule and familiar opponents, independent games received less attention in the press than the league games had.

Despite his travels, Lew never played outside of New England. When pro leagues started to pop up again after a few years, the ones that stuck were to the west, in New York, New Jersey, and Pennsylvania. But he didn't join them.

Why not? Lew likely stayed close to home because of his young family and the family business. Jim Crow segregation had to be a factor as well. It wasn't easy for him in New England, and it would be even more difficult elsewhere. He couldn't forget how Harry Hough and his teammates from New Jersey and Pennsylvania had treated him, and he could expect more of the same or even worse if he tried to play them out there.

Another top Black player of the day also stayed close to home despite having the talent to travel. Frank "Dido" Wilson integrated the New York State League in 1907 but refused offers to play outside of central New York. In *I Grew Up with Basketball*, Frank Basloe writes, "Fort Plain featured one of the first Negroes to ever play professional basketball. His name was Frank (Dido) Wilson. Frank was offered many contracts with other teams, but he preferred to stay around home." Wilson also appears to have integrated New York's coaching ranks. According to William Himmelman's *Pro Basketball Encyclopedia*, Wilson is listed as Fort Plain's coach in 1915. And while Basloe says Wilson stayed put to play with his brother, it's hard to believe racism wasn't a factor too.[16]

Lew's independent team kept busy, with the *Fitchburg Sentinel* once reporting, "The five men who composed the Lowell team are used to playing four or more games a week."[17] They traveled first by train and later by automobile as cars become common.

Before long, Lew took over management of the team. A *Fitchburg Sentinel* story about the local team traveling to Lowell described the

Chapter 15. Home Again

opponent as "headed by Lew and Tighe."[18] The *Newburyport Daily News* also suggested he was running the show. Under the headline "Bucky Lew Coming," the story read, "Bucky Lew, one of the fast men in the basket ball business, is coming here ... to line his team up against the [Amesbury] Red Sox."[19]

How much players made on independent teams seemed to vary. Teams were most often paid a percentage of the gate, and sometimes they were guaranteed a certain amount to ensure it was worth the trip. At other times, they appeared to be content to play for whatever the fans thought their efforts were worth. Gerry O'Connor, the son of Lew teammate Dan O'Connor, said in an interview they would at times receive what was collected when they passed a hat through the crowd.[20]

One *Concord Enterprise* article promoting an upcoming game said ticket prices would be higher than normal to meet Lew's fee. For what it called "the best basketball attraction of the season," it said, "the admission will be raised a little to help defray the big guarantee the visitors demand."[21] It did not mention the price of tickets or the size of the "big guarantee," however the same story mentioned that a Fitchburg team wanted $50 to come out for a game. The local team concluded they weren't worth it; whether Lew's team was worth that amount is left unsaid.

The Concord game in particular was an interesting one because it included two Lews. The paper mentioned that in addition to Bucky, his brother would also play with the team. The roster rundown featured "Bucky Lew, the only man who is credited with being able to play Harry Hough to a standstill," and his "brother, who is one of the fastest players ever turned out of Lowell."[22]

The unnamed brother, Gerard, was indeed a fast man. While he played basketball at Lowell High School, he was not a standout. He excelled at track, anchoring the school's relay team. The *Boston Sunday Post* called that 1905 team "the champion of New England" and described it as "a team of extremely fast men in the short distance class [that] has never been defeated."[23]

Dan O'Connor said years later they usually made about $7 per game. He told the *Sun*, "Lew was our manager, coach, and paymaster. We would average about $7.00 per night when we played."[24] O'Connor would go on to a lengthy career as a banking executive, so his description of Lew as "paymaster," a position of obvious trust, speaks to his respect for the man.

An editor at the *Nashua Telegraph* who covered Lew late in his career said the players were paid significantly more. Of a Lew team based out of his city, Fred Dobens said, "The players in those days used to get about $25 a night and play six or seven nights a week in many a New England city."[25]

Given the ebb and flow of the popularity of the game during those days, perhaps it's not surprising that reports about the players' earnings differ. Their compensation likely varied according to who, where, and when they played.

The End of the Line?

While the more open college game continued to grow in popularity, the pros continued their physical style. And Lew continued to be known for his toughness, both mental and physical. As O'Connor told the *Sun*:

> I played three years with Bucky Lew on a team known as the Lowell Five.... Bucky, as you know, was a Negro and at times the going was rough for him but he never got ruffled or angry. His one thought was possession of the ball and he usually came up with it after a skirmish.... I recall one night when we were en route to a game in Haverhill and Bucky came up with a toothache.... When we got to Haverhill we stopped at a dentist's office, went upstairs and waited while Bucky had the tooth extracted, a pad of cotton being pressed into the vacated spot. Bucky played the entire game that night, merely biting the cotton pad a little harder in the second half when the Novocain wore off.[26]

As tough as Lew was, it looked like his days in basketball had come to an end one winter night in Franklin, New Hampshire, in 1915, when he fractured a leg. According to the *Sun*, Lew "was going along in great style when last night's deplorable accident occurred."[27]

The *Lowell Courier-Citizen* described what happened:

> Harry Lew, Lowell's fast basketball professional basketball player, known all over New England as "Bucky," met with a bad accident Wednesday night in a scrimmage between the Lowell and Franklin, N.H., teams at Franklin.... The men were both thrown to the floor, during the play, Lew underneath ... the fall resulting in a broken leg below the knee for Lew. The latter was immediately taken to a physician's office, where the fracture was reduced.[28]

Similar to his first shoulder dislocation at the hands of Frank Devlin, Lew was once again injured by another Lowell man, Jimmy Grant, who was playing for Franklin. The *Lowell Sun* said no malice was involved.

Chapter 15. Home Again

"Although it was a fast game there was no unnecessary roughness apparent and 'Bucky's' injury was purely an accident."[29]

The fracture was the worst injury of his career but far from his first. Lew was now past 30 and apparently feeling all of it. The *Sun* added a reflective note in its story, making it sound like Lew's time was up: "In the days when Lowell stood among the leaders in professional basketball, Lew was considered one of the greatest basketball players in the country."[30]

When he returned home in a cast, he indicated to the *Courier-Citizen* that he was indeed retiring. The reporter wrote, "He is 31 years old and has been playing basketball for 15 years, but now declares that he is done with the game."[31]

Chapter 16

Franchise Owner

Lew had second thoughts about his retirement when rumors of a revived New England league started to surface. He applied for entry into the league, which would have made him the first Black owner of an integrated professional sports franchise. His attempt came despite—or perhaps because of—a revival of the Ku Klux Klan after the hit movie *The Birth of a Nation* romanticized the hate group. Now targeting immigrants too, the new Klan went national, and it grew to a reported 400,000 members in New England alone. Lew won his bid for a team and soon assembled a roster of the Klan's enemies. Of course, as a good businessman, he kept costs down by renouncing his retirement and signing himself as a substitute.

Lew Levels Up

Lowell hoops suffered a blow when James Gray died of a heart attack in October of 1914.[1] Gray had dominated the local sports scene, running several pro basketball teams in the city between 1901 and 1908 and its pro baseball team from 1910 to 1914. When Gray took over the Lowell Tigers, Louis Sockalexis' old team, he was so identified with the club that they became known as the Lowell Grays.

So when word spread about an attempt to revive the New England League, there was no obvious candidate to lead a possible Lowell team. Rumors of the city's participation started to appear in the papers in early November, and the *Sun* reported, "Lowell will probably be represented this year by a fast basketball team and arrangements are being made by a prominent local sporting man to fit up one of the halls for the sport. Definite announcement of what the plans will be for the season are promised within a few days."[2] The city was an obvious choice for a franchise given its large population, central location, and long history with the game.

Chapter 16. Franchise Owner

The name of the "prominent local sporting man" was not included in the story. Fred Moore, the owner of the city's Crescent Arena, the biggest venue suitable for basketball, seemed a likely candidate. Lew, of course, would be another, if he wasn't "done with the game"[3] as he had announced after fracturing his leg that winter.

Apparently, he had a change of heart, because he appeared at the next league meeting in Worcester seeking a franchise. "Manager Lew attended the meeting of the league directors and managers," the *Sun* reported. "Two applications from Lowell ... were read and the one from Manager Lew was favorably acted upon."[4] Despite the competition from the Crescent, Lew was awarded the lone Lowell franchise in the eight-team league.

Lew quickly made it known he was moving on from his injury, both physically and mentally. He told the paper he was ending his retirement as a player: "he himself will get into the game."[5] And he also signed the man who broke his leg, local star Jimmy Grant, a "speedy little forward [who shoots] baskets from all angles of the hall."[6]

Instead of retiring, Lew would actually level up and achieve yet another milestone. He had made history again by becoming the first Black owner of an integrated franchise in a pro league.

The opportunity was all the more remarkable considering the revival of the Ku Klux Klan that was underway in the country. *The Birth of a Nation*, a movie that romanticized the Klan as preserving order and the honor of whites in the South after the Civil War, had come out earlier that year and was a huge success at the box office.

Given a boost by the revisionist historical account, the Klan renewed itself by adding recent immigrants to its list of enemies. In addition to Black people, Catholics and Jews would now find themselves targets too. The Klan claimed the immigrants from Ireland and Quebec and elsewhere who were flooding American cities like Lowell threatened the white Protestant character of the country. And they found a receptive population. Klan membership grew into the millions, and even in New England, the hate group boasted 400,000 dues-paying members.[7]

Lew wasn't intimidated by any of it. In fact, he built a roster of players from the Klan's most hated list. That first team would feature many Catholics, including Jim Mulvanity, an Irish cop living and working in Nashua, and Herve Cote, a French Canadian from Lowell. He would later manage a Greek player in Theo Kappala, a German player in Fritz Hansen, and a Jewish player in Nat Hurwitz.

Harry "Bucky" Lew

He even played up these local ties when talking to the *Sun*:

> I feel that Lowell is willing to support a good team and I have made up my mind to give it to them. Of course, the local boys will be given the preference, and you can take it from me that some of the big leaguers will have to step some to oust them from their positions for we've got some really good material in this old town of ours.[8]

Lew may have faced opposition from the Klan, but he had the support of the locals. While everyone wasn't happy with it, Lowell was one of the few cities in the country to ban *The Birth of a Nation*. The *Sun* said, "Mayor Murphy has decided that the picture is 'prejudicial to the colored race'" and "Lowell stands alone in its objection."[9] The paper also wrote glowingly about Lew's leadership abilities. "Harry 'Bucky' Lew," a reporter stated, "a basketball player known in every part of the east where the sport is played is at the head of the project, and this fact alone should make the move a success."[10]

Despite the optimism, the new league didn't do much to differentiate itself from the old one. Once again, there would be no free throws and courts would still be enclosed in a cage. The men running the league apparently thought stopping play for free throws or because a ball went out of bounds was worse than the low scores and roughness that came with the old rules.

Lew's home court was another potential concern. Whether there was lingering resentment from the owner of the Crescent after losing his bid for a team is hard to say, however Lew was unable to use the larger hall for his home games. Instead, he had to rent Associate Hall, which was much smaller, with a capacity of only 700 fans, according to the *Pro Basketball Encyclopedia*.[11] He also had to settle for reserving it on Tuesday nights rather than the more desirable Friday or Saturday evenings.

The league schedule was another issue. While the traditional basketball season typically ran through March, the league only arranged games through New Year's Day. Early pro ball was known for its instability, so the league's hesitance was understandable, however it also set up a lame-duck season of sorts, where teams might look to book their own games if the league didn't provide a full schedule.

A Promising Start

Regardless of any potential concerns, Lew's team got off to a promising start in November. They played three games and each one was

Chapter 16. Franchise Owner

eventful. Lew won his first game at home against South Framingham, 36–20, before 600 fans. It wasn't a sellout, perhaps due to skepticism about the league from a public that hadn't seen a successful one in over 10 years.

The *Sun* covered the game at length. Lew did not play, but his skills as a general manager were praised: "Lew, the well known basketball star and manager of the Lowell team, presented one of the most formidable aggregations ever seen on a local floor." The fans who did attend enjoyed the experience. The reporter said they "applauded and cheered ... continuously from the start until the finish of the game."[12]

Another positive note was that the game was refereed closely: "The game was played in strict accordance with league rules.... Referee Casey commanded the respect of the players throughout, and it goes without saying that the fans warmed up to him the minute he started to work." Casey even called a number of technicals when players complained about his calls. He "silenced any of the offending players who voiced their feelings at his decisions by promptly calling fouls on them."[13] It was an approach to refereeing not seen often and both the reporter and fans responded favorably to it.

The official, William Casey of Northborough, Massachusetts, sounded like a former player. He was described as "a tall thin young man, who ran around the playing surface calling fouls left and right."[14] And he may have well have been, as a Casey (whose first name was apparently not recorded in the papers of the day) appeared on the Marlboro roster in Lew's rookie season according to the *Pro Basketball Encyclopedia*.[15] Casey certainly seemed well aware of the issues that could result from lax refereeing.

Lew won his second game too. This one, against Worcester, was also covered at length in the *Sun*. The reporter wrote that Lew's team "out-played, out-generaled, and oftentimes out-roughed the much heralded Worcester team." While the exact attendance was not included in coverage, the atmosphere harkened back to the golden age of hoops on the city. The hall was described as "packed" with "the most enthusiastic basketball audience seen in this city since the days of the P.A.C.'s-Burke's memorable battles."[16]

It was another strictly officiated affair. "The game started with Referee Gillon calling a brace of fouls ... for holding and pushing," the reporter wrote. "The work of Referee Gillon is to be commended as he was right on the job at all times. The league decision maker showed the players that he was running the game from the start and no disputes resulted"[17] from his calls.

Lew closed out the month with his first road game. The team travelled by car, and this new mode of transportation, while seemingly more convenient than train travel, brought with it a new set of challenges. They got lost on their way, and it took them three and a half hours to cover the 40 miles from Lowell to Milford.

Never mind arriving late, the players also arrived tired from having to seek out directions along the way. The *Sun* said, "The strength of certain members of the team was put to a severe test by their running to farmhouses and other places along the route inquiring the way to Milford."[18]

Lew was finding ownership had its own challenges and he had to pay a fine for arriving late. At least the road crowd of 1700 fans at the Milford Armory seemed happy that he finally made it: "The reputation of Lowell with the fans made up for the delay and when the team arrived at the armory a big cheer went up."

Jimmy Grant was absent, so Lew had to take the court for the first time since he broke his leg. He did start strong ("Lew started off like a racehorse ... his three baskets from the centre of the floor were the prettiest of the game"[19]) but the pause in his playing career and possible pre-game sprints caught up with him and he did not score again. His defense remained steadfast throughout and the man he guarded did not score.

Despite Lew's best efforts, Milford almost doubled up Lowell and won by a score of 43 to 23. Still, he finished the month with two wins and one loss, close to the top of the standings, and his team was generating favorable press and a positive reaction from the fans.

"Weak-Kneed" Officiating

December would be a different story. Lowell started a losing streak as the league moved away from the tight refereeing that had characterized the first month of the season. Referee Casey was fired and rough play returned.

In front of a "record breaking" crowd estimated at 1200, far beyond the official capacity of Associate Hall, Lew experienced his first home loss. The *Sun* reported that "rough house tactics were allowed to prevail" in the second part of a home-and-home series with Milford. "Milford

Chapter 16. Franchise Owner

was a gigantic offender in committing fouls and the holding and pushing of [their] athletes was of a startling order." As opposed to Casey's tight control of the game, the new referee had a different approach: "Fouls were committed every second but either he did not see them or was afraid to make a ruling."[20]

While one might view the report of the excessive crowd or poor refereeing with skepticism, the city's other paper concurred on both points in its coverage. About the crowd, the *Lowell Courier-Citizen* agreed it was a big one: "Tuesday night's crowd in Associate Hall was proof conclusive that basketball has come back." And as for the officiating of Referee Haley, it said, "he forgot his obligations as referee. We don't like constant interruption, but there is such a thing as going to extremes in the rough house business."[21]

The firing of Casey, who had refereed so strictly earlier in the season, was announced shortly thereafter. The *Sun* reporter, who was obviously following the officiating closely, wrote that he was one of "two referees canned by the powers that be" despite being "regarded as one of the best men in the state as a decision maker."[22] It's not clear who made the decision or why, but the impact was obvious.

The *Sun* said officiating was even more of an issue in Lew's next game when he was blasted 52–27 in Marlboro: "Referee Murphy, a new official ... made his first appearance ... and his rulings were decidedly off color." The game featured "football tactics" and "short wrestling matches" with "hammerlocks, half-nelsons, scissor holds, and many other grips known to the wrestling fraternity." The reporter concluded, "The game was certainly the roughest of the year, but one would have to see it to be in a position to judge, for the summary tells nothing, as Referee Murphy was asleep at the switch most of the time."[23] The writer also pointed out that Casey attended the game as a fan and couldn't resist commenting on it: "Casey would have made a much better man on the floor than Murphy."[24]

Despite the blowout, the *Sun* didn't blame Lew:

> "Bucky" Lew ... was the big link in Lowell's chain, and the former star certainly did show great comeback qualities. Lew played the whole game and was in nearly every scrimmage. None of the opposing players were able to stop the Lowell manager when he got the ball, and his speed in going down the floor, dodging and twisting by his opponents, was a revelation. He also showed good judgement in passing the ball, and ... his shots were the most spectacular of the game.[25]

Harry "Bucky" Lew

If fans weren't hearing enough about Lew, they would be treated to coverage of his post-game activities too. The same story continued, "After the game the members of the team visited Doc Forsyth, a former Lowell boy, who is in the optical business in Marlboro. Here lunch was served, after which a short musical program was enjoyed with Manager Lew, Jim Mulvanity, Herve Cote, and Fritz Hansen as chief contributors."[26] With the paper covering his every move, Lew seemed to have achieved celebrity status.

Officiating remained a focus of the *Sun* coverage, and its reporter could not have been more blunt in his assessment of it at the next game: "We do not accuse the official of not knowing the rules, but we do charge him of being weak-kneed and afraid to call fouls when he sees them." The fans didn't like the no-calls either and the referee "was hissed throughout the game."[27]

Lew lost that game to Marlboro, making it four straight defeats. Seven hundred fans attended that one, the official capacity of the small hall. Despite the loss, Lew was again singled out for praise. When he entered the game as a sub for another player, the crowd reaction turned: "With Lew in the lineup the team took a decided brace and a few minutes after his entrance he brought the crowd to its feet with a neat basket."[28]

While Lew didn't take the blame, it didn't mean no one did. The crowd seemed to turn on Jimmy Grant, who, the reporter said, "had been censured recently for individual playing." It's not clear who criticized Grant's play, but the fans took it and ran with it, making him the scapegoat for anything that went wrong afterward. He "was loudly hissed on several occasions by the fans."[29] After the game, Grant quit the team.

After yet another loss, Lowell got a win in front of close-to-capacity crowd of 650 after a visiting Holliston team had their own transportation issues. The *Sun* reported, "They were pitched out after the car had tried to climb a telephone pole." It went on: "The machine ... was traveling at a fair rate of speed when one of the front wheels struck a cog in the electric railway switch, skewing the auto up against the side of the post, and all the occupants were thrown out."[30] The car was disabled and one of the players needed medical assistance. The remaining players took the electric trolley to the game and fought through it.

Chapter 16. Franchise Owner

Stuck in a Klan Stronghold?

Lew had more car trouble on the way to his next game. The *Sun* said the team "could not reach their destination in time on account of the poor condition of the roads and the game was called" despite "a large attendance awaiting the Lowell team in Fitchburg."[31] After four and a half hours of travel, they only made it halfway to their intended destination.

Worse than the car trouble was the team's inability to find a place to stay overnight. The *Sun* reported, "More bad luck attended the team in Ayer where the players found it impossible to get accommodations at the hotels. They were either forced to remain in the machine or sit in the railroad station until 4:30 this morning"[32] and catch the first train home.

Whether Lew and his players were denied lodging due to race or religion is unknown. The area was home to a strong Klan presence and anti-immigrant feeling at the time.

Author William Wolkovich says that as Irish and French-Canadians started to appear in the area, Ayer was the scene of several successful anti–Catholic lectures. He says that "the appearance of number of ex-priests and former Catholics ... found it a lucrative business" to tell "'hair-raising stories and obscene lies'" about the threats caused by the recent immigrants and their religion in the city.[33]

In one pre–Klan incident, the nearby town of Shirley forced out an Irish schoolteacher in 1897. Wolkovich writes that the trouble started when "a young woman bearing a Yankee surname was hired by an unsuspecting school board."[34] He goes on to say that despite her effectiveness as a teacher, once residents learned of Minnie Holden's ethnicity and religion, they protested against her until the school board decided not to renew her contract.

While Ayer itself did not appear to have an active Klan presence, the neighboring town of Groton did. According to the *Boston Globe*,

> Groton was once a Ku Klux Klan stronghold, rife with anti–Catholic and nativist prejudice. In an online database created by author and sociologist James Loewen, Groton is listed as one of 17 possible, though unconfirmed, "sundown towns" that once existed in Massachusetts. Sundown towns, found in states across the country, were all-white jurisdictions that, for decades, excluded or expelled religious and ethnic minorities, usually Black people, sometimes by law and more often through violence and

intimidation. In some of these places, signs posted at the city limits ominously warned Black people that they weren't welcome after dark.[35]

To be fair, neither Lew nor the *Sun* reporter who followed the team so closely that season ever commented on a possible racial angle to the story. That said, given the temperature of the times, it seems irresponsible to ignore the possibility.

Lame Duck Finish

Lew's team returned to Lowell and defeated Northborough to earn their fourth win of the season. Attendance was not announced, but those that were there enjoyed a return to clean play. "The contest was … the cleanest of the season," the *Sun* reported, "and this fact made a big hit with the spectators as was evidenced by the applause that greeted the players at the end of each period." While Casey had been fired, the other top official remained in the league. "Referee Gillon was on duty … and he gave complete satisfaction…. He called fouls left and right the minute he saw them and his impartiality was a feature of his work."[36]

It may have been the last highlight of the season. The fact that the league owners had not planned games beyond January 1 seemed to cause trouble as December drew to a close. Teams started to take some liberties with Marlboro, for example, announcing it was taking a week off from league action to do a barnstorming tour of New Hampshire.

It was bad timing for Lew and he told the papers he was operating at a deficit. The *Sun* reported, "The team has been playing but a little over a month, still Manager Lew has lost considerable money. It costs something to run a team in the new league."[37]

His financial losses became even worse when Maynard skipped an appearance in Lowell without notice and played a game at home instead. Lew was left with an arena full of fans and no team to play. As the *Sun* said, it was "no way the fault of the local management" but Lew had "some expense on his hands."[38] As owner, the loss was all on him. He had to issue refunds to the fans while remaining on the hook for player salaries and all of the other expenses involved in hosting a game.

The growing absences were an issue for Lew because he had played a lopsided schedule. The *Sun* said the team "has not played a home game for nearly two weeks [and] Lowell has had twice as many games on the road as at home and consequently the team has lost considerable

Chapter 16. Franchise Owner

money. Out-of-town games don't begin to pay expenses when traveling expenses and the salaries of the respective players are taken into consideration."[39]

Lew wasn't the only one to have financial issues. According to another *Sun* report, "There's trouble ahead for the ... league if the reports we've heard are true. Northboro has dropped out and there are two other teams on the verge of calling for assistance."[40]

When Worcester, the team led by the president of the league, refused to come to Lowell before Lew brought his team to that city, he decided to cut his losses. Despite news on the sinking of the *Lusitania* and World War I and everything else happening that day, his decision made the front page of the *Sun*:

> Announcement was made today by Harry H. Lew, manager of the Lowell basketball team, that he will withdraw his quintet.... Worcester's action in refusing to appear in Lowell next Tuesday night and other happenings which have taken place in the last few weeks were given as the reason for the local team dropping out. In the future the team will play strictly professional basketball and no league will be entered under any consideration.[41]

The league officially suspended operations the same day.[42]

A Fresh Start

Lowell finished at four wins and eight losses, just good enough for fourth place in the eight-game league. It was a disappointing finish, but it wasn't all bad news. The team did post a winning record at home and presumably that would have continued to do so if its opponents had kept coming out.

Lew also showed he could still handle himself on the court. As the *Sun* reporter who apparently followed him all season wrote, "The Lowell manager has proven conclusively ... that he can still play the game."[43] That assessment was backed up by the limited statistics available in those days. According to the *Pro Basketball Encyclopedia*, Lew led the team in scoring by averaging 6.9 points a game. One of the league's top 10 scorers, he finished fourth in total points and seventh in average points per game.[44]

On top of that, Lew saw there was still a measure of interest in pro basketball in the area. The *Sun* said the team had "drawn large crowds, and the fans have given the team support of the superior order."[45] It also

Harry "Bucky" Lew

reported that "basketball is red hot at the present time."[46] Regardless of how the league turned out, he had reasons for staying in the game.

Lew acted on it immediately. He kept his team together and scheduled a home-and-home series against nearby Lawrence for early January. Lew and his Lowell Five were back!

CHAPTER 17

Back to School

IN 1922, LEW RETURNED TO COACH at Lowell Textile School (now the Division 1 University of Massachusetts Lowell). It was not his first time leading a college team. He had already coached at the school in 1903 before Gray moved him to Haverhill and then at Lowell Commercial College in 1906 after the NEBL disbanded. In contrast to those roles, however, this one received significant press attention. College sports had become a much bigger deal, and the papers were all over Textile's attempts to overcome their regional rivals. After a Textile victory over Boston College gave the team a 5–1 start, some speculated it might be their best team ever.

Early Coaching

As discussed previously, Lew's first coaching role was noted by a lone one-liner in the *Lowell Daily Courier*. Its "Textile School Notes" of early 1903 ends with the line "The coach of the team is Harry H. Lew of the P.A.C."[1] Lew was finishing up his rookie season as a pro.

Coaching a college team in 1903 put Lew well ahead of his time. As Claude Johnson has pointed out, the majority of the YMCAs in the country were segregated and the few Ys available to Black athletes did not have appropriate facilities for basketball. And the Amateur Athletic Union, which had taken control of the game from the YMCA when it got too big for the Y to handle, barred Black participation.

Lew's role as a basketball authority came before several better-known pioneers had even been introduced to the game. Edwin Henderson, the grandfather of Black basketball, and Bob Douglas, the founder of the New York Renaissance, would only be exposed to it in the years that followed.

Henderson first learned the game at Harvard in 1904 then brought it back to Washington, D.C.'s segregated school system after earning his degree. According to Douglas Stark, he organized the Public School Athletic League in 1905, making "basketball part of the physical education curriculum in the public school system."[2] Claude Johnson says Henderson formed the "Inter-Scholastic Athletic Association of Middle-Atlantic States"[3] in 1906 to organize amateur Black athletics. Johnson also says 1906 was the same year Bob Douglas "discovered basketball" for the first time when he saw some men playing at a park "throwing a round ball through a hoop."[4] Douglas started putting professional Black teams together in the 1910s and founded the Rens in the 1920s. They would remain one of pro basketball's dominant teams up to the start of the NBA.

If Lew's role as coach was such a significant landmark, why did it receive so little attention? There are a number of reasons.

Lowell Textile School, now known as the University of Massachusetts Lowell, was in its infancy at the time. The school was trying to level up when Lew joined them. It had just moved from a few rented rooms in an office building downtown to its own dedicated campus and the newly constructed Southwick Hall. The distinctive yellow brick building still dominates the campus today.

The site for the campus and the funds for the construction of the school's flagship building were donated by a millionaire businessman with roots in the city, Frederick Ayer. According to the school yearbook, the *Pickout*, "his continuing contributions which amount in the aggregate to the great sum of $150,000 have enabled the Trustees to add extensively to the grounds and buildings of the institution."[5] It was a major contribution—$150,000 then is roughly $5 million today.

Southwick Hall was designed with a high-ceilinged top floor suitable for basketball and space for both a court and stands for hundreds of fans. The students at the *Pickout* credited those involved for designing it with basketball in mind. The space now hosts UML's robotics labs, and its refinished floors still retain some of the markings for the center court jump circle and free throw arc today.

The game itself was also relatively new, and most colleges did not have teams. Textile mostly played area high schools, YMCAs, and some colleges, like Dartmouth and Dean. Not surprisingly, given their small talent pool, they weren't very good, and while reports are limited, they don't appear to have won a game.

Lew's stint was also brief. He only coached the one year before James Gray "loaned" him to the NEBL's Haverhill franchise for the 1904 season. The distance may have made the role impractical.

Chapter 17. Back to School

He wasn't done coaching college hoops, however. After the NEBL failed, he coached at the Lowell Commercial College in 1906. The paper again noted his role with a one-liner: "The Commercial College team managed by Harry Steves and coached by Skip Field and Harry Lew should make a much better showing this year than last."[6]

While Harry Steves remains an unknown, Field was an old friend and teammate. The pair played together at the YMCA, the PAC, and on some independent teams. Field too wanted to be more than a player. A few years later, the *Sun* reported that he had moved to Grand Rapids, Michigan, where "he was given a berth as physical director of the Y.M.C.A."[7] in 1908.

Lowell Commercial College was a vocational school of sorts, focused on helping students achieve positions as "office help" in "business and banks."[8] It offered day and night courses in shorthand, typewriting, bookkeeping, accounting, and so on. The basketball team played a schedule similar to Textile's, and they also received little press attention.

As mentioned briefly earlier, Lew was able to coach college while continuing to play in the pros because the coaching position wasn't as demanding as it is today. The three primary roles involved in running a team—coach, captain, and manager—all shared some of the responsibilities in leading a team. In 1922, Lew partnered with team captain Carlton Lombard and faculty manager Lester Cushing to run the team. (Cushing was at times also called "faculty coach" and would be known by the more familiar term of "athletic director" today.)

Roaring in 1922

Lew's coaching stint in 1922 received far more attention than his earlier ones. College sports and college basketball were more established then, and Lew was a more established authority. He also may have made more of an effort to promote the team. By this point, Lew had another child, Eleanor, born in 1920.[9] With three children at home to provide for, and with close to two decades as a pro behind him, he may have been looking ahead to another, more permanent role in the game.

The first mentions of Lew's role with the team came as soon as he took the job. With the opening game a few days away, the *Sun* reported, "Harry (Bucky) Lew, the newly appointed coach, took charge of the team and immediately started to iron out the rough places in the teamwork."[10]

Harry "Bucky" Lew

Readers who were aware of the Lew family business would likely have noted the dry (cleaning) humor in the statement.

The *Sun* also broke down the roster. Four of five starters from the previous season would return, while the fifth spot was still up in the air:

> Captain Lombard and Matthews ... played strong guard positions last year.... Smith and Schneider took care of the forward positions last season and are the most logical choices for the places this season, although [two other players] are going hot for the regulars ... the pivot position is still undecided.... Marshall ... having a finer knowledge of the game. On the other hand, Farwell rises up some six feet or more and his ability to get the jump on his opponent would be instrumental in starting combination work.[11]

The *Daily Courier* also ran a similar story on the coming season featuring Lew: "The captain of the red and black quintet turned the squad over to the new coach, Harry 'Bucky Lew,' the well known local professional basketball player ... he is expected to build up a fast team at the school."[12] Similar to the run up to his 1915 pro team, coverage from both papers was positive and hopeful.

The *Courier-Citizen* ran another complimentary story just before opening day:

> Coach "Bucky" Lew put the Textile basketball squad through a fast practice yesterday afternoon and practically picked the team that will represent Lowell tonight.... In a fast scrimmage played against the second five yesterday afternoon this quintet easily ran up a high score and developed a fast passing game.[13]

There was a lot of enthusiasm for basketball going into the season. The previous one was the first Textile had played since 1906. While the 1921 season had included several YMCAs on the schedule, this time would be different. The *Pickout* said, "It is the first year that Textile could boast of a real schedule."[14] Also, the previous season, the team "had no financial support from the Athletic Association and the team was without an outfit."[15] The school was once again looking to level up in hoops and it hoped Lew was the man to get them there.

In another echo from 1915, the Fitchburg college team got in an accident and totaled their car on the way to the opening game at Southwick Hall. In a lengthy report on the game, which was delayed an hour, the *Sun* said, "Several players were cut and bruised and the machine wrecked."[16] The team acquired another vehicle and eventually made it to Southwick Hall. Lew tried to let them off the hook, but they insisted on playing. It was a close game, but the home team prevailed 22–21.

Chapter 17. Back to School

Lew's team won the game, but they had to work for it. In what must have been a nightmare scenario for the banged-up Fitchburg squad, the game was tied at the end of regulation and required an overtime session to decide the outcome. It led to a dramatic finish: "With only 30 seconds of this period left, Matthews, Tech's leftback, looped a long shot from the middle of the floor which swished through the cotton netting"[17] for the win.

While he may not have been running up and down the sidelines, Lew was certainly watching the game closely. "Matthews, by the way, demonstrated to Coach 'Bucky Lew' that he can be counted on as a running back who carried a triple threat inasmuch as he can shoot, block, and pass with a smoothness approaching perfection."[18] While Mat Matthews finished with eight points on four field goals, the team's high scorer was Ken Smith, who had 10 points, six of which came on three throws.

Foul shots were one of a number of differences between the college and pro games. College players shot free throws for fouls and Smith took all of them that night for Textile. (His accuracy is unknown, since makes, and not misses, were recorded that night.) A second difference between the two games was its duration. The teams played two 20-minute halves instead of the three, 15-minute periods observed by the pros. Another difference was the length of the season. The college basketball season was shorter, starting in January and ending in mid–March.

Boston College Looms

The positive vibes around Textile continued in the papers a few days later as the team looked forward to more games. The *Sun* reported the team was continuing to put in the work: "The team is pretty confident of victory after downing the fast Fitchburg Normal Five and has showed much improvement during practice sessions this week."[19]

Textile continued to improve on the court too. They hosted Providence and dominated them, 51–19, then lost a tight one in New Hampshire by a score of 30–28. They returned home and defeated Northeastern 31–20 then doubled up New Bedford 42–21 to close out the first month of the season with a record of four wins and one loss.

The *Sun* credited Lew for his players' progression. "Smith and Matthews of the Lowell Textile team are developing into a wonderful pair of scorers. Between this pair, they divide the majority of the points scored in every game."[20] And the *Courier-Citizen* was even more direct in praising the coach's work: "Lew has been coaching Textile team this season and with results very apparent. Textile never has had the team that it has the present season."[21] It was still early, but the team seemed headed for a historic season on a number of levels.

Boston College was next up on the Textile schedule, and everyone had marked their calendars. With its Irish Catholic origins, BC had a special place in the hearts and minds of Lowell's large Irish community.

In the run-up to the game, the *Sun* said:

> The Lowell Textile team will engage in its first test of the year when it plays the strong Boston College team in the Moody Street gymnasium Friday night. The local five has turned in four victories out of five games this season, losing to New Hampshire state by one point in a hotly contested game.
>
> The coming of the Boston collegians will be received here with much enthusiasm as there are many alumni from that school living in Lowell and vicinity. Added to this the visitors always present a scrappy team and one that seldom suffers defeat.[22]

Another *Sun* reporter even tied the enthusiasm for the game back to Lew's first team, the PAC, and their epic battles with the Burkes:

> In the days of the P.A.C.-Burkes combats many a fan forgot all about supper, so anxious was he to get to the hall and land a seat. By game time the hall was generally packed to its capacity. And the games were among the most bitterly contested ever seen in this city.
>
> One player who was in those games and is still at it and going along as well as ever. He is "Bucky" Lew.... Bucky Lew's Textile team is ready for its game with Boston College, which is to be played here tomorrow night. The local boys have pointed toward the game and want to win it more than any other one on the schedule.[23]

He also quoted Lester Cushing talking about the matchup. While BC won by a score of 33–22 the previous season, Cushing had a good feeling about the two games the teams would play this year:

> At the close of the football season the subject of basketball was brought up in Faculty Manager Cushing's presence. He immediately became interested and almost the first thing he said was: "Well we are out to win the Boston College games anyway. I think we will have a team to turn the trick this coming season." And it seems he was right. Seldom has the local institution been so well represented on the local basketball floor.[24]

Textile scored the first four points of the game, then BC stormed back, opening up a 14–4 lead eight minutes into the game. Then Textile

Chapter 17. Back to School

worked to methodically erase the deficit and reclaim a one-point lead by halftime at 19–18. They opened it up further in the second half and won 33–24.

The *Courier* said, "fast drilling and clever passing ... enabled Textile to run up the score."[25] The *Sun* noted that "the fast floor work of Textile was a revelation to the packed gymnasium. Boston was outclassed in this respect and unable to follow the ball as well as Lowell."[26]

The *Sun* reacted as if the team had won a championship:

> Lowell Textile's cup of joy was filled to overflowing last night when its sturdy, fighting basketball quintet earned a 33 to 24 victory over the Boston college basketball five.... If the local team fails to win another contest this season, it can consider the schedule a success, for it achieved what it set out to do at the first of the season—give Boston College a trimming.[27]

The win made Lew's team 5–1, and even though the team was only halfway through its season, the *Sun* had declared the season a success already.

Insight into Lew's Approach

As Textile prepared for a three-game tour of Vermont, a 500-mile round trip, the team was introduced to that state's basketball fans through a lengthy write-up in the *Burlington Daily News*.

The article provided a detailed analysis of the team's approach and thus Lew's basketball philosophy. They had played enough games under his leadership by now to demonstrate his basketball philosophy—with its focus on conditioning, physicality on defense, and sophistication on offense.

Conditioning was one of the team's defining traits. The article noted that the team had the "ability to come from behind and kick through in the pinches,"[28] which helped them overcome early deficits in their wins over Providence and Boston College. After the BC game, the *Sun* noted, "Textile was in much better condition than its opponents and kept up a fast pace throughout the game."[29]

Lew had demonstrated his own commitment to maintaining his conditioning as a player. He said he stayed in running shape 10 months out of the year and it undoubtedly helped his longevity. He had played twenty years in the pro game by that point, and he was still going strong.

Physicality was another hallmark of the team. As the *Daily News* noted:

Harry "Bucky" Lew

> Four of the five regular players on the team are football players who do not seem to mind in the least when the opponents start to rough it up a bit. In fact, the textile five plays a pretty rough and tumble brand of the game, just enough smoothness and science being coupled with its hardy play to give the five a shifty running attack.[30]

Given the rough style of play in the pro game of Lew's era, the emphasis on physicality was no surprise. And while the writer does describe the team as rough-and-tumble, he doesn't accuse them of dirty play or fighting. Like Lew, they appeared to play a physical but clean game.

The team also appeared to run a sophisticated offense. The story describes "clever combination plays" that "mixed a running back combination with a series of forward shifts."[31] It's important because it speaks to a part of Lew's game as a player which hadn't received much consideration. Lew had been credited anecdotally as a skilled passer, but since assists on made baskets were not tracked in those days, it's impossible to quantify that part of his game.

The only real statistics from Lew's playing days are games played, and field goals made. Games played attests to his durability—he was always one of the leaders on his teams in appearances, despite a long history of injuries and chronic shoulder problems. If it's true that the best ability is availability, as legendary football coach Bill Parcells is reported to have said, Lew was a key contributor to his team's successes.

Field goals made, however, only provides limited insight into a player's contributions on offense. Lew's approach seemed to emphasize forwards getting most of the scoring chances. For example, in the big win over BC, his forwards, Smith and Matthews, scored 29 of Textile's 33 points. Of course, the other players on the team had roles in creating those opportunities, indirectly through player movement and picks and more directly through passing. While statistics are available to track these contributions today, in the form of screen assists and the more traditional "leading-someone-to-the-basket" assists, they weren't in Lew's day. His philosophy of setting up forwards to score suggests that as a player he had more of an impact on offense than is otherwise known.

Chapter 18

All Things Considered

THE TEXTILE BASKETBALL TEAM headed north, but their fortunes on the court went south. Only six players took the trip to Vermont, and their star forwards, Ken Smith and Mat Matthews, would have been better off staying home. Smith dislocated a shoulder in the first game and Matthews caught the flu. Lew does not appear to have made the trip, and it's not clear that Manager Cushing did either, making Captain Lombard the adult in the train car. With time on his hands, Lew agreed to play a city championship series with a revived Lowell Five. When a new player appeared on Lew's Five with the same last name as one of his college players, a national scandal over pros leading college athletes astray appeared to take a local angle. Despite it all, Textile's season was a success, with the team taking home what one paper called a "textile league championship" after they swept the other textile engineering schools on their schedule.

Pivot Point

The three day, 500-mile round trip Vermont trek was always going to be a challenging one. The schedule called for Textile to play three games on consecutive days in three different cities—February 9 in Northfield, February 10 in Burlington, and February 11 in Winooski. It turned out to be even more challenging than expected.

Ken Smith dislocated a shoulder playing in the first game and Mat Matthews caught the flu.[1] The traveling party only included six players so they had to try to play through it as best they could. Not surprisingly, the team dropped all three games.

Textile lost to Norwich 19–14, Vermont 37 to 12, and St. Michael's 32 to 20. Their offensive output in the three games represented their three lowest scores of the season. While they averaged 34.5 points per contest over their first six games, they averaged only 15.3 points per on the trip.[2]

Lew doesn't appear to have traveled with the team. He hadn't traveled with the team on their first road trip to New Hampshire either, so it may have been standard practice. On the earlier trip, Cushing accompanied the team,[3] but he may not have made the Vermont one. A *Lowell Sun* blurb on the team's departure only mentioned traveling party of six players.[4] It's possible the budget was a factor. The team hadn't had any financial support the previous season, so the 1922 budget was probably not overly generous either.

After the trip, the team limped home, but the players didn't have much time to rest and recover. They were set to face Boston College for the second time only a few days later. At least the game was at home. BC typically played in Boston Arena, but it wasn't available that year as it was undergoing renovation. So Textile would get a second home game against the team.

The game started as poorly as the Vermont trip. The *Sun* reported that "Boston started in whirlwind style and ran up 10 points before Lowell scored." Textile slowly clawed their way back into the game, took a late lead, and hung on for another comeback win. It was a low-scoring and "rough but clean" 22–20 contest. Once again, conditioning seemed to be the difference between the teams. "Textile won because it had more stamina," the reporter said. "The visitors were ... drooping and wilting" at the end.[5]

While "Ken Smith and Mat Matthews were not quite up to their game," they played well enough to give the team a chance. The pair scored all of the team's first half points—six—then matched that number in the second half. That's when Lombard and Schneider stepped up. They combined for the team's other 10 points, including its last four field goals, and they helped the team pull away and then preserve their lead.[6]

Despite the team's sweep of BC, newspaper coverage suggested the victory was anticlimactic. Their enthusiasm may have been tempered by Textile's disastrous Vermont trip and ongoing health issues. The *Sun* said, "Smith, who is generally reliable at a short distance, was way out of form. Too much playing with a bad shoulder has thrown this boy off his stride."[7] The comment sounded fatalistic, as if Smith needed the off-season to rest, recover, and rebuild his shooting form. While Textile was 6–4 with four games remaining, it seemed the team had already peaked.

Chapter 18. All Things Considered

Textile School Championship

Textile wasn't quite done yet. The offense continued to struggle, and the team still only averaged 24.6 points the rest of the way, almost 10 points—and 30 percent less—than their total of 34.5 over the first six games.[8] They would win only one of their remaining four games, but it was a big one.

Textile defeated Fall River 31–17, assuring the team at least a .500 season, and earning them "the textile school championship."[9] The *Courier-Citizen* said the textile engineering schools of Lowell, New Bedford, and Fall River made up an informal league and Lowell's sweep of the others made them champions.

Textile did have an open date late in the season, however instead of scheduling another game, they left it that way. Apparently, the team needed rest more than another win or loss.

Overall, the season was a success, in spite of the adversity the team faced. And it may have helped two of the three leaders of the team gain induction into the UML Athletic Hall of Fame. Lester Cushing, the team's faculty manager, and later the school's athletic director, served in a variety of academic and administrative roles over a 49-year career. The school's athletic complex is named in his honor. Carlton Lombard, the captain, starred on several basketball and football teams and also served as class president. His Hall of Fame bio notes the role he played in bringing basketball back to the school the previous season and the team's .500 record in 1922.[10] Lew's own candidacy will be considered soon.

The *Courier-Citizen* crisply summarized the season after it ended, saying that the "Textile school basketball team has played a strong game this season, and its record has been very satisfactory, all things considered."[11] The last phrase was an interesting one—and it was likely a reference to a list of potential "considerations" too lengthy to fill the small space available.

"All things considered"?

So what did the reporter mean with that "all things considered"? Likely a lot.

Two of those "things" were clearly Smith's injury and Matthew's flu. Each had a significant impact on the team's leading scorers and there

Harry "Bucky" Lew

wasn't enough time left in the short season for them to recover and return to their previous form. And coming at the outset of the ambitious Vermont trip with its three road games in three days, the health issues couldn't have happened at a worse time.

Another was the declining interest in the team. With Textile's poor second half, a flurry of activity on the pro front recaptured the attention of the fans. The Crescent Arena was under new management, and the men running it were eager to fill the biggest hall in town with basketball. And they asked Lew to help.

With the team on the road without him, Lew revived the Lowell Five to play for a city championship. With the Crescent as host, Lew agreed to a five-game city championship for a pot of $200, roughly $4000 today, with the Lowell Five playing another team from the city, the Catholic Young Men's Lyceum. The CYML started as an Irish Catholic organization with the same mission as the YMCA.

Lew also reconstituted his "roadsters," a team he ran based out of Nashua, New Hampshire, and they played some games at the Crescent too. The *Courier-Citizen* said they were a talented team: "It will take some team to defeat Lew's road outfit.... It possesses speed and strength combined. Individually the players are star athletes; collectively they play fine basketball. Team work is there. Few teams in New England have anything on the Lew outfit."[12]

While it may seem strange, coaching college and playing pro was not unusual in those days. Aided by rules that limited a coach's involvement during games, Lew's old friend Ed Wachter, and another star of the era, Nat Holman, were coaching at Harvard and City College of New York respectively without any interruption to their pro careers.

Murry Nelson describes how Holman did it. He said he scheduled his college and pro games so they didn't conflict with each other, and if he was unable to avoid both teams playing on the same night, he staggered the game times. Since he couldn't coach during games anyway, Holman would talk to the team before the game and at halftime, then head out for his own game.[13] Lew appeared to follow the same model, with ads showing Textile games starting at 7:45 and Lowell Five games starting at 8:15.[14]

That said, a student playing college and pro games would be unusual. And the possibility that a Textile player may have done so is likely another of those "things considered."

Chapter 18. All Things Considered
College Scandal Hits Close to Home

After the college football season of 1921 ended, a handful of players from Notre Dame and the University of Illinois appeared in an annual football matchup between two rival towns in central Illinois. Players on Notre Dame and Illinois had relatives in the towns, Taylorville and Carlinville, and they recruited friends to join them. While they were not paid to play, their involvement did have a financial impact. When word got out about the ringers, interest in the game increased, fan confidence soared, and a reported $100,000[15] was gambled on the event, an astonishing $2 million today.

Authorities learned of the event after the season, and it became headline news in late January. Notre Dame, one of the top football programs in the country, barred eight players as a result. Whether the players were paid or not did not matter—the school didn't allow its athletes to represent any another organization and remain eligible.[16]

When the news broke, Notre Dame football coach Knute Rockne railed about the influence of pros on the amateur game, declaring, "Professionalism is the biggest menace to college athletics."[17] He took the affair personally, saying, "It is a regrettable affair, because it hurts the game, the college, and the coaches, even more than the men. After years of effort in training players to become proficient at some particular sport, the lure of the professional promoter undoes all the work."[18]

Rockne didn't say why professionalism was such a menace, so another well-known coach, University of Chicago football coach Alonzo Stagg, may have felt it necessary to fill in the details. Stagg compared the character of pro athletes to that of movie stars: "They have a tendency toward laxness of morals" and feel "they are entitled to special privileges." He concluded "professional athletes are a poor class to have in a university."[19] The message was clear—the college and pro games had to be kept separate, or college athletes would become similarly corrupted.

The scandal hit the papers just as the Textile basketball team was getting unprecedented press attention. In fact, pictures of the suspended players appeared in the *Sun* the same day—and on the same page—as the story raving about the team's first win over BC.[20]

Things got more interesting when a new player with the same last name as one of Textile's stars appeared on Lew's pro team. Lew had added several new players for the second game of the city series after a number of players (including himself) were injured in the first and the additions helped him even the series. The *Sun* reported that "two new players, named Smith and Jones appeared in the Lowell Five lineup, and both figured prominently in the result."[21]

Smith scored six points and Jones had 10 in helping Lew's team to the 23–21 win. Both players were only identified by their last names, but Smith sounded and played a lot like Textile's Ken Smith. And Jones played like he had partnered with Smith before. Could Jones have been Matthews, perhaps slightly less bold than Smith, playing under a false name?

The potential for controversy only grew when Lew declined to identify where he found the new players. "Where Bucky Lew dug 'em up he did not say," the *Courier-Citizen* reported, "but he did say he had a perfect right to strengthen his team."[22] Lew took it a step further a few days later when he bragged to the paper about all the players at his disposal. "'You haven't seen half my talent,' said Bucky Lew yesterday. 'I've got a dozen players eligible to take part in games.'"[23] Was he saying he had two teams from which to draw players? If so, was the second Textile?

Yes and no. The true identities of Smith and Jones came out a few days later, and they were, in fact, from another one of Lew's teams—but it wasn't Textile. It was his Nashua team. A *Courier-Citizen* reporter said two of the Nashua players, "Winn and Ryan, were known as Smith and Jones in the battle."[24] When Lew described them as "eligible," he meant it. They were pros, not amateurs.

Winn and Ryan undoubtedly gave false names to avoid any controversy about expanding the Lowell Five team in the middle of a series. But the unfortunate decision of Winn to call himself Smith may have scared Textile. At the same time college football was going through a national scandal, for a few days anyway, it appeared their coach and a star player may have crossed the line too.

Lew Steps Back

After the incident, Lew's visibility with the Textile team faded. For example, after the win over Boston College, a picture of the team with Cushing and without Lew appeared in the *Courier* that day.[25]

While at first this might seem unusual, to be fair, Lew never appeared in a photo with any team he coached. This was true as late as 1935 when he coached his last known team, the Springfield Visitations. When a photo of the team appeared in the *Springfield Republican*, the team's owner and manager, Bill Donovan, was in it, but their coach, Lew, wasn't.

Chapter 18. All Things Considered

Why? Wendy Johnson, Lew's granddaughter, has said he did not like having his picture taken. This is further evidenced by the fact that both Lowell papers ran the same picture of Lew for his entire amateur and pro career. It was obviously taken when he was a young man. Apparently, Lew never posed for either one of them again.

At any rate, Lew's name, which had been closely linked with the Textile team, was now associated more with his pro teams and less with the college team.

So what changed? Lew was a known commodity, and he had been involved in the pro game for 20 years, but the college football scandal was a new event. The Textile administration may have asked Lew or the papers to ease up a bit because it feared that a pro player leading its team would reflect poorly on its emerging program.

It's also possible the press simply moved on. Lew's role with the team may have received less attention because Textile got less space in the papers. In the "Basketball" column the day after the second BC win, a *Sun* writer talked about the "robust revival of the game here,"[26] but instead of raving about another win over BC, he only discussed the pro game.

The column reviewed the city series, discussed Lew's "road team"—the one team that played out of Nashua—and mentioned that "many of the famous quintets in the state are anxious to come here" and play.[27] And with the new management in the Crescent Arena eager to fill their hall, they had a first-class place to do it.

Chapter 19

Partnerships

William and Joseph Sullivan purchased the largest hall in Lowell, the Crescent Arena, in January 1922. If the Sullivan name sounds familiar, it's because William Sullivan, Jr., better known as Billy, was the man who started one of the premier franchises in pro sports. He founded the original Boston Patriots of the American Football League and continued to run the team for decades after the AFL merged with the National Football League. Despite a continued Klan resurgence and several cross burnings in the area, Billy's father and uncle partnered with Lew to bring basketball to the Crescent. Then the economy tanked, Lew's father died, and he moved on. He retired from basketball and refocused on his initial partnership with Florence. He stepped back and she stepped up, taking on a number of leadership roles in various church, charity, and social justice efforts.

Partnering with the Sullivans

A longtime *Lowell Sun* employee, William Sullivan started at the bottom as an office boy and worked his way to a top role at the editing desk. In between, he worked as a sports reporter, writing about a number of sports, including basketball at the time Lew was running his Massachusetts league franchise.[1]

It's impossible to say with certainty exactly what William wrote about Lew. There were no bylines in those days, so reporters' names didn't accompany their stories. That said, as the *Sun* coverage that season was characterized by an appreciation of Lew's achievements and the importance of strict refereeing, and since Sullivan was known for deep knowledge of local sports history and strong sense of fairness, it's likely many of those words were his.

When the Sullivans purchased the Crescent Arena, it was the biggest arena in the city, capable of holding 1500 fans for basketball.[2] A

Chapter 19. Partnerships

capacity crowd of that size might seem small today, but it was respectable in those days. As Peterson writes, "eastern promoters were delighted with a crowd of 1,000."[3]

The refreshed Crescent had three floors, 17 bowling alleys, and a large hall for boxing and basketball. The Sullivans ran large ads in the papers announcing their ambitious plans for it. "We plan to make the establishment one of the best and biggest amusement centers in New England," they said, "where only clean entertainment, conducted under the proper supervision, will be countenanced."[4]

The Sullivans soon partnered with Lew to add pro basketball to the schedule. They hosted both the Lowell Five, who

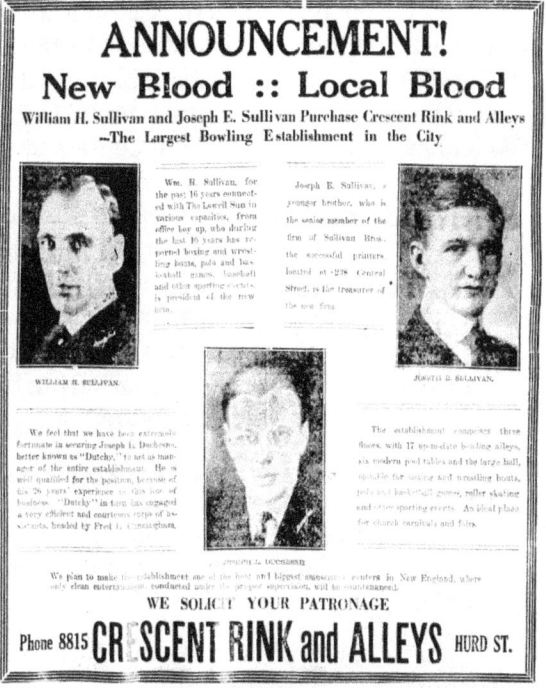

Ad announcing the Sullivan brothers purchase of the Crescent Arena from 1922 *Lowell Sun*. Among other events, the Sullivans hosted basketball and they partnered with Lew to bring the pro game to what was the largest hall in the city. William may have been the reporter who so closely covered Lew's 1915 franchise (NewspaperArchive).

would play other teams from the city, as well as Lew's "Roadsters," a team based in Nashua who played other outside teams. A "Sportometer" ad in the papers often announced the week's events, which typically featured one or two games a week.[5]

Lew's Roles

Lew's first attempt to fill the Crescent was the five-game city championship that began as Textile was preparing to go to Vermont. In previewing the series, the *Sun* said it was "the first to be held here in several years."[6]

Harry "Bucky" Lew

Lew's opponent was the Catholic Young Men's Lyceum, or CYML, an Irish Catholic organization with the same mission as the YMCA. The CYML were serious about basketball too, and they featured a clubhouse with all the amenities. As historian David McKean says, "The 'clubhouse' opened in 1902. It contained a basketball court, showers, a library, meeting space and space for other sporting events."[7]

While they were a few years behind the Burkes, CYML basketball also started as an amateur pursuit then moved toward professionalism. Players weren't paid salaries, but they could make money by participating in winner-take-all tournaments for cash prizes.

According to the *Sun*, this version of the CYML was one of the best teams around. Of course, in previewing the matchup, it acknowledged Lew could put together a team too:

> The Lyceum team will depend on its star lineup, which for many years has been regarded as one of the best in this vicinity. Lew, himself one of the greatest players ever developed in this section of the country, who has been playing the game for many years, has assembled a team of well known players.[8]

In its coverage of the opening game, the *Sun* indicated fans were supportive of more pro ball: "The enthusiasm that greeted the return of basketball here the other night is considered a good omen for a robust comeback of the game so popular here in the old days."[9] The *Courier-Citizen* also noted a "Growing interest shown in basketball this year."[10]

The city series observed the old pro rules of New England basketball, such as physical play and a lack of free throws. Not surprisingly, scores stayed low, with both teams only scoring in the teens most games. The *Courier-Citizen* said, "Play ... has been fast and at times, rough. In their anxiety to make gains, players have forgotten the rules now and then."[11]

The series was a tight one, with CYML taking the first game and the teams alternating wins until it came down to a deciding game five. Lew demonstrated both his basketball and leadership skills in getting a big win in the finale. The *Sun* reported that "Lowell's big basketball 'serious' is over and the Lowell Five holds the title."[12]

On the court, Lew played center in that last game. He must have had some hops left in his legs even in his late thirties. The game still featured a jump ball after every score so winning the tap was one of a center's key responsibilities.

Chapter 19. Partnerships

Off the court, he played strategist. One of his forwards, Richard Ryan, got off to a hot start, then when the defense adjusted, Lew used him as a decoy to get his other forward, Jimmy Keenan, going at critical moment: "In the final period, Manager Lew shifted his attack.... He awakened Keenan to the task of taking passes, and instructed the other four men in feeding Keenan and blocking the opposition. The maneuver worked out quite successfully."[13] Keenan had three consecutive field goals to open up a commanding 17–10 lead in the third period. While the reporter may have oversimplified the strategy, Lew was clearly running the show.

The second team Lew brought to the Crescent was alternately known as his "Roadsters," "All Stars," or "Professionals." (The last nickname, which appeared in a few ads, may have been an attempt to differentiate them from his college team.[14])

The roster was made up of mostly Nashua men, like Winn and Ryan, who had recently appeared as Smith and Jones in game two of the city series. A *Nashua Telegraph* story on the team featured a headline announcing "Bucky Lew Heads Nashua Star Aggregation," and the story reinforced the message: "'Bucky' Lew ... one of the best known basket ball players in New England will lead the five this year." It also praised the team he put together, saying they "will be able to compete with the best of teams."[15]

The Sullivans would have to be pleased to see a *Sun* report saying Lew was receiving many offers from teams eager to face him at the Crescent. "Bucky Lew has received about a dozen challenges during the past few days from teams in and round Boston who desire to come to Lowell for games."[16] Lew played host to teams from Lawrence, Lynn, Clinton, Watertown, Bunker Hill, and Pere Marquette (a South Boston club named for a Jesuit missionary).

In their second season running the arena, the Sullivans helped Lew achieve yet another integration milestone when they hired him to referee games. If it wasn't already obvious, it was another sign that he was an authority on the game and held in high regard as a player and a leader. Of course, refereeing games didn't mean he stopped playing in them. The *Courier-Citizen* wrote about one game that had to be rescheduled because he was supposed to coach, play, and officiate at the same time: "Bucky Lew, who coaches and plays on the CMAC team, is signed up as referee."[17] He was a true triple threat!

Harry "Bucky" Lew

A New New England League?

Their earliest efforts hosting games must have been a success, because the Sullivans and Lew partnered to revive a regional pro league the next year. The *Fitchburg Sentinel* reported that "the league mainly started through the efforts of Bucky Lew of Lowell who thought [it] would pay."[18] Lew had already made history as the first owner of an integrated pro basketball franchise. Was he now trying to make history as its first magnate?

The Sullivans were also there from the very beginning. According to the *Sun*, the first league meeting, held, of course, at the Crescent, resulted in "William H. Sullivan of Lowell being chosen president." Their partnership continued despite the Ku Klux Klan presence in the area. That summer, in a tell-tale sign of Klan activity, a large cross was burned at midnight at Fort Hill Park, a prominent city landmark. The *Sun* reported that "as the K.K.K. symbol, outlined against the night sky in tongues of flame, burned fiercely, the entire neighborhood was thrown into consternation."[19] Authorities dismissed the event as a prank, however when police in Lawrence interfered with another attempted cross burning in nearby West Andover later that August, the *Courier-Citizen* reported that it reinforced "the belief of many that Klan members have actually started operations in this vicinity."[20]

Regardless, the partners were undeterred. Sullivan was also "empowered to bring in a set of by-laws"[21] for a vote by the league. His interest in fair play was an echo of his possible coverage of Lew's franchise in 1915, where the reporter who followed Lew's team described in no uncertain terms the difference strict versus lax refereeing made on the quality of play.

Sullivan had been around the game a long time, and he codified his ideas to correct the problems he had seen. If the league followed his by-laws, they would be running a tight ship. Players would be fined for "tardiness, too much argument with the referee, fighting" and so on. "Basketball will be played promptly and to purpose, in striking contrast to" recent leagues which "marred the basketball picture by conduct generally unsatisfactory."[22] The league would also be more scoring-friendly than the previous failures, by following the more open college rules, including free throws.

Lew would run Lowell's team with the Crescent as his home floor. The *Courier-Citizen* reported that "Bucky Lew, veteran of the game, will have charge of the local outfit. More than 20 years have passed since he

Chapter 19. Partnerships

first donned a uniform and entered fast company, yet he remains today one of the best backs in the business."[23] Old friend Ed Wachter was rumored to be running the Haverhill franchise.[24]

Similar to his efforts in 1915, Lew attempted to balance local interest and competitiveness by leveraging both homegrown talent and imported stars. Of a seven-man roster, Lew included men from Lowell (including, of course, himself) and others from Nashua, Cambridge, and Boston.

Unfortunately, the league was beset by bad news before it even started. While it originally hoped for eight teams, it had to settle for six as opening day approached. Then Haverhill and Maynard, cities who had hosted successful pro franchises in past years, dropped out too. Despite the early enthusiasm, the league would start with only four teams.

The rest didn't last much longer. The league began play on November 21 and called it quits on December 10. Lew had played six games, three at home and three on the road, and the *Courier-Citizen* said "attendance grew smaller each week."[25]

It was early to pull the plug, but bigger forces were at work. The region was at the beginning of a dramatic economic decline. Old northeast mill cities like Lowell relied on a textile industry that was no longer committed to them. After workers' lives improved in 1912, with a workweek reduced to 54 hours as a result of a new state law and a 10 percent raise due to a widespread strike, mill owners stopped investing in their aging plants. They diverted the funds to build new facilities in the South where labor costs were cheaper, and the cotton was closer.[26] Lowell's population dropped as mills closed, and jobs disappeared. The city lost over 10 percent of its population, roughly 12,500 people, between 1920 and 1930.[27]

League play would continue to struggle to gain a foothold in New England for decades. The Boston Whirlwinds joined the 1925 American Basketball League, the first true national league, but not for long, as they left at the conclusion of the first half of season. A New England pro team wouldn't make it through a full season until the Boston Trojans did it in the American Basketball League 10 years later. Even then, they didn't return for a second season. Overall, William Himmelman says, "Major-league basketball in New England did not take hold ... until after World War II."[28]

So Lew returned to playing, and the Sullivans to hosting, independent basketball. The *Courier-Citizen* wrote about another series at the

Harry "Bucky" Lew

Crescent in 1924: "Bucky Lew, the grand old master of local basketball, is still in the harness in his 25th year at the game."[29] While there is no known record of Lew playing in 1925, his partnership with the Sullivans took a new turn the next year.

Head Referee

The Sullivans and Lew next partnered on a plan that was slightly less ambitious than their previous one. While the region wasn't ready for a regional pro league, there might be still enough interest in the city for a league of its own. So they organized a city-wide pro league for the Crescent, with two to three games a week from January through April.

This time it was Joseph Sullivan's turn to serve as a league executive. He was named the Lowell Pro League's treasurer, a perfect choice for the man who starred in his own rags-to-riches story. Joseph began by selling newspapers as a kid, running both a paper route and a busy newsstand. He also missed school Friday mornings so he could work on the "fish wagon." Obviously not afraid to get his hands dirty, he started a printing business with another brother, Daniel, in a one-room office. The office was on Central Street, not far from where Lew ran his dry-cleaning shop.

The print shop grew from a one-room affair to a 150,000-square-foot facility and just one of seven plants Joseph would run nationwide. And he was about much more than just business. He played a leading role in a large number of religious, fraternal, and social organizations and was famous for his fundraising efforts. He donated altars and stained-glass windows to a dozen or so churches and raised millions for hospitals and colleges.[30]

In a sign of the brothers' wide influence, when they ultimately passed, their funerals were star-studded affairs. The most notable attendees at William Sr.'s funeral were the Patriots of New England and those at Joseph's were the Cardinals of the Catholic Church.

Lew would also play a prominent role in the city league. He was named its head referee and also appeared to be the face of the league. When the papers announced the news, only one man's picture accompanied the stories, and it was his. The *Sun* featured his role in a subhead, "Bucky Lew Chosen League Referee,"[31] and included his photo. Not to be outdone, in reporting on the first night of games a few days later, the *Courier-Citizen* included a version of the same photo (but flipped it so

Chapter 19. Partnerships

he was facing right instead of left) and included the caption "Bucky Lew, League Referee."[32]

As the season got underway, Lew's performance received positive reviews. After the first game, the *Courier-Citizen* said, "Bucky Lew, a living monument of basketball history in Lowell, was on the job as referee and turned in a fine game as arbiter. To handle two such teams, with feeling as it is, is no easy task but Bucky carried it off to perfection."[33]

A few days later, a *Courier-Citizen* columnist agreed:

> Bucky Lew made a good referee. He has the right idea with reference to the use of the whistle. He employs it only when it is actually needed. Some officials think they are bigger than the game or the basketball public, and by too frequent use of the whistle they spoil the sport.[34]

Lew's role certainly wasn't an easy one. The *Courier-Citizen* also reported that the players kept him busy in one early game. "'Bucky' Lew had his hands full as a referee. Frequently he was called upon to quell disturbances among the contestants."[35]

As a man with a reputation for being a gentleman, Lew seemed well-suited for officiating. If he remembered George Hepbron's early instruction manual on the game, *How to Play Basketball*, he would have been familiar with its "Competent Officials" chapter. In a lengthy list of attributes, Hepbron called for officials to have "a strong purpose to follow the rules in letter and spirit" and employ "kindness and courtesy to all and the maintenance of a level head under trying circumstances."[36]

Unfortunately, some teams didn't think he called enough fouls. While no criticism of his performance appeared in the papers, apparently there had been some complaints. The *Sun* reported that, at one league meeting, "it was agreed that Referee Bucky Lew would enforce all rules without exception in the future."[37] One wonders what William Sullivan, a Bucky Lew fun and stickler for strict officiating, thought about it!

Lew did not referee the league championship. Instead, a referee from outside the city was brought in. "Dick Roberts of Fitchburg ... will be in charge of the game," the *Sun* reported, and it went on to suggest why: "all violations will be called and no partiality will be shown."[38]

Given the importance of gambling in the game, the league may have wanted to make sure there was no doubt that it was on the level. The same story confirmed that gambling was a factor. "Several side bets, it is understood, have been wagered on the outcome of the big event."[39] Since a number of the participants in the game had played with Lew, the appearance of bias had to be avoided. Free throws were now standard and one of Lew's calls might put one of them in position for an easy score at a critical moment. While the influence of gambling may have helped Lew get into his first game as a player, it may have hurt his career as an official.

Regardless, Lew's continuing partnership with the Sullivans, his election as head referee, and his portrayal as the face of a league all reinforced his status as a recognized basketball authority. The fact that his accomplishments took place in an otherwise white game makes them all the more remarkable.

Lew's First Partnership

Lew took over as manager of the dry-cleaning shop after his father William died in July 1922. The *Sun, Courier,* and *Globe* all noted his passing and described his long and respectable career. The *Sun* said he was "well and favorably known in business circles."[40]

Lew assumed management of the business during the same economic decline that sunk the most recent attempt to build another New England league. Over 10 percent of the city's residents were on their way out of the city and many of those who remained had less money to spend on what might be deemed a luxury. After all, people could take care of their clothes at home.

A larger great migration was underway in the country, with Black men and women fleeing the South for northern cities. But they weren't headed to the struggling textile cities. Instead, they moved to growing cities, ones that were adding jobs, like New York, Chicago, Pittsburgh, and even Springfield, Massachusetts.

Springfield was a unique Massachusetts city because it had a diverse manufacturing base. It was able to pull through the textile slowdown due to new factories that cranked out firearms, automobiles, motorcycles, and even random machine parts.[41] Lew retired from play and the Lews moved there in the late 1920s. He and Florence had another daughter, Frances, who was born in Springfield in 1929.[42]

Lew didn't entirely give up on the game, however. He did coach at least one team in Springfield. An article in the *Springfield Republican* from 1935 announced that an independent pro team was holding their first practice that night and he was their coach: "The Visitation basketballers ... coached by 'Bucky' Lew, former Lowell professional hoopster, will

Chapter 19. Partnerships

stage their first workout of the season."[43] Lew did not manage the team and it's not clear if he was associated with them for more than that one season. One interesting fact about this team is that it featured the only Black player known to play for Lew, besides his brother Gerard. Harry Fitch was described in the article as a "crack Negro athlete."[44]

At any rate, once they were settled, Lew did step back, and Florence stepped up. With him home more often, she could do more outside of the house. After sacrificing so much for so long so he could pursue his basketball dreams, she was ready for her moment. She took on a number of leadership roles in various church, charities, and social justice efforts.

Florence was featured in the Springfield newspapers several times and may have been more widely known in the city than he was. Her resume was also a long one; she led the Missionary Society and Women's Fellowship at Saint John's Congregational Church, served on the board of the Springfield YWCA, worked with the Prevention of Cruelty to Children and the Protestant Guild for the Blind, and taught Sunday school for 25 years.

Perhaps her most impressive achievement was when she became

Brings Cheer to Others

(Sunday Republican Staff Photo)
Mrs. Harry Lew of Lebanon St., this city is one of the busiest of women and still finds a bit of time to work at her hobby of making hook rugs. Mrs. Lew, now 78, is a member of St. John's Congregational Church, and for many years has been admirably active in church and civic affairs. To be of service to the ill and the needy, that's Mrs. Lew's greatest wish, and the happiness such work brings is her most cherished reward.

Photograph of Florence Lew from the 1958 *Springfield Union*. Florence served in a number of leadership roles in various church and charity efforts (Newspapers.com).

Harry "Bucky" Lew

"the first Negro woman to hold a high position in the United Church Woman of Massachusetts."[45] Florence was vice president of the state-wide nondenominational group and president of its Springfield chapter.[46]

The *Springfield Union* ran profiles of her in 1955 and 1963. In the earlier story, she explained the philosophy of teamwork that drove her. "'No one person or no one church can do the work that [we] all can do together,'" she told the reporter.[47]

Together more than 50 years, the couple shared a remarkable partnership. And Lew's willingness to match Florence's earlier sacrifices might say as much about him as any of his accomplishments on the court.

Chapter 20

Lew Circles the Bases

If Louis Sockalexis' success in baseball eased Lew's path in basketball, he returned the favor. When the Dodgers sought a place to host a farm team for their first Black players in the U.S., one man raised his hand to tell them his city would welcome an integrated baseball team. How did a newspaper editor in Nashua, New Hampshire, know? The man, Fred Dobens, had shared a court with Lew, playing with his high school teammates at halftime of Lew's games. Dobens assured the Dodgers their Black players would be accepted because he remembered what a beloved figure Lew had been. And once the Dodgers integrated their organization, the rest of the dominoes started to fall, and all of major league sports soon followed.

Lew Gets an Assist

When Branch Rickey decided to integrate his Dodgers organization, he signed Jackie Robinson to play in Montreal then looked for a place for Black players in the U.S. The Dodgers struggled until they reached Fred Dobens. Dobens, a newspaper editor for the *Nashua Telegraph*, assured the Dodgers that his city would welcome their efforts based on Lew's success there. A former high school basketball player whose team entertained fans at halftime of Lew's games, he saw firsthand the depth of the respect fans, peers, and press held for the man.

Lew had a long history in Nashua and the *Telegraph* covered the full arc of his basketball career. He first visited the city for a Christmas game during his rookie season in 1902, when he held his man scoreless in Lowell's victory over the local team. The *Telegraph* said that despite the "attendance [being] the largest of the season" the Nashua fans left disappointed: "The fans who had brought cow bells, etc. just stowed them away in their pockets and took a sneak out the back door when the game was over."[1]

Harry "Bucky" Lew

When the NEBL league folded, Lew continued to visit the city, playing on an independent team with his old PAC teammates. The *Telegraph* recognized him as a star in another win: "Bucky Lew, the Spindle City wonder, was in the main responsible for the victory earned by his team."[2] By the next season, he was playing for a Nashua team. "Bucky Lew, the colored whirlwind of the locals," the *Telegraph* said, "played a strong, heady game" and his "teamwork was of a sensational order."[3] Lew continued to level up and by 1922 he was running the team.

It was about this time that Dobens and his high school teammates played at halftime of Lew's games, with the high schoolers entertaining the fans while the pro players took a break. Dobens was a star in his own right, and the scoring records he established at Nashua High lasted for years. Once he graduated, he started his career with the *Telegraph*, and he had a ready answer when the Dodgers came looking for a city to host their integrated farm team decades later.

Bucky Lew in formal dress in his retirement years from the 1958 *Springfield Union*. The occasion is unknown (Newspapers.com).

Dobens had a front seat to history, and he would not forget it. He said Lew's team played all over New England and matched up with the top teams of the era, such as the Original Celtics of New York. He would write that Lew's team, "a bunch of real pros, was known all over New England."[4]

After Lew passed in 1963, Dobens reflected on him in an *Around the Town* column. "Out of state papers the other day reported the death of Bucky Lew, one-time great for the … basketball team for this city, back in the early Twenties," he wrote. "He lived in Lowell but used to come up here for the games."[5]

Chapter 20. Lew Circles the Bases

Dobens said when the team played at home, they "used to sell out every game."⁶ He also said while Lew experienced racism on the road, he had no trouble in Nashua: "Bucky was a Negro and in those days they didn't like to see Negroes playing on white teams and many is the time the fans refused to let him play—not in this city though."⁷

Dobens further wrote,

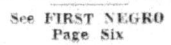

HARRY LEW

Bucky Lew obituary from the 1963 *Springfield Union*. Newspapers around the country highlighted his historic achievements at the time of his passing (Newspapers.com).

> He was a great favorite with the hundreds who used to jam their way into O'Donnel Hall to watch their local favorites play some of the great pro teams in the New England area. They even played the famed Celtics one night at that small hall and could those games get rough. But the rougher they were the more the fans came back.... He was one of the greats in those days.⁸

And all of this was not just speculation, as Dobens makes clear: "We saw every game because we played on the team that kept the crowd quiet between the halves when we were in high school."⁹

Overlooked History

Neither Nashua's role in integrating baseball nor Dobens' influence on it has received much attention, but it has been well documented. In *Dem Little Bums: The Nashua Dodgers*, Steve Daly writes,

> Dobens' role in helping pave the way for the Dodgers arrival ... is one that has never been truly appreciated ... [Dodgers representative Buzzie] Bavasi placed a call to Dobens to get a feel for what Nashua's reaction would be if the Dodgers had sent the Black ballplayers to the city to begin their

professional career. Dobens told Bavasi that all Nashua wanted was a winning team, and that local baseball fans wouldn't care what they looked like as long as they were good ballplayers. It was the answer Bavasi and Rickey were looking—and hoping—for.[10]

In the foreword to Daly's book, written by Bavasi himself, he says,

> Mr. Rickey summoned me to New York.... He was having difficulty finding a city for Roy Campanella and Don Newcombe to play in.... I was then asked to find a city where the young men would be welcome. After talking to Fred Dobens.... I knew that Nashua was the place. Thus came the Nashua Dodgers.... The choice of Nashua turned out to be perfect. The citizens of Nashua fell in love with Newk and Campy, and they in turn loved playing there. I'd have to say that Fred Dobens made it all possible.[11]

Dobens had a continuing role in ensuring the success of the Dodgers. He was offered—and accepted—a position as president of the Dodgers. (Besides his inside knowledge, his role at the *Telegraph* certainly didn't hurt.) And his support was validated. As Daly writes, "Campanella and Newcombe recall few problems during their stay in Nashua."[12] He quotes Bavasi as saying, "By the end of that 1946 season, either one of those guys could have run for mayor and won easily."[13]

While the Dodgers' choice of Nashua as the place to integrate baseball in the U.S. has often been described as an accident, Charlie Bevis suggests differently in *The New England League: A Baseball History, 1885–1949*. He says Rickey may have targeted the city all along: "[T]he selection of Nashua was very likely part of a well-planned maneuver orchestrated by Rickey to serve as the base for the newly signed Black players in 1946 ... Rickey had already determined months earlier that Nashua would be the location for the next group of blacks signed after Robinson."[14]

Bevis contends that New England League president Claude Davidson met with Rickey during minor league meetings in November after it was decided Robinson was going to Montreal. Then Bavasi and Dobens talked early the next month, just after Robinson signed but before any other Black players did. A story in the *Telegraph* noted "Branch Rickey's personal representative"[15] was in town, and Bevis suggests it was Bavasi who had come to meet with Dobens.

Why Nashua?

At first glance, Nashua was a surprising choice because the city had struggled to host minor league baseball for years. Bevis writes,

Chapter 20. Lew Circles the Bases

Nashua, located 40 miles northwest of Boston, Massachusetts, was a poor candidate for minor league baseball in 1946. The small city last had a minor-league team for an entire season in 1929. Its more recent attempt at supporting a team had been in 1933, when the franchise had been a miserable failure and had become an orphan team within weeks, playing all of its games on the road. During the war years, even with a new WPA-financed ball park in Holman Stadium, Nashua failed to field a team....[16]

Daly says the South was out after some Florida teams objected to Robinson reporting there for spring training, a league in Illinois had already rejected the players, and "more calls to different clubs were answered with apprehension and outright refusal."[17] Lowell wasn't a serious option because of the sharp decline of the city. By then, Lew himself had been gone more than a decade.

Nashua's economy was in reasonable shape, and it had a relatively new ballpark. Also, with only one newspaper, communicating with the public would be simpler. Daly said Dobens was the "primary voice of the local newspaper" and "the *Nashua Telegraph* had virtual saturation coverage of the city's homes."[18]

Dobens provided more clarity on the Dodgers' interest years later. When Bavasi was elevated to the role of general manager for the Brooklyn Dodgers in 1950, Dobens wrote at length about their first meeting. As a longtime observer of failed baseball teams in Nashua, and his own brief stint as an owner in 1933, Dobens had legitimate concerns about the viability of the enterprise. When he shared them, he was surprised to hear Bavasi counter that the Dodgers would bankroll the whole operation. All the city needed to do was welcome their players and provide a place to play. Dobens wrote, "This was going to be wonderful if it was true but we asked the stranger to pardon us is we were a bit skeptical. Then Bavasi unburdened the whole story, what Brooklyn would do and what it expected."[19]

While Dobens does not detail the Dodgers' expectations, offering only "that was good enough for us,"[20] Bevis writes that considering the context, those expectations were clear:

> Unfortunately, Dobens never explains in the column what "the whole story" was, as if the story was obvious and thus did not need explanation five years later.... While Dobens does not overtly refer to trailblazing racial integration as "the whole story," it seemingly is inferred. What other desperate motivation ... could the Brooklyn Dodgers possibly have had then to place a club in Nashua?[21]

Harry "Bucky" Lew

The experiment was a success, and beyond their positive minor league experience, Robinson, Newcombe, and Campanella soon progressed all the way to the majors. The Dodgers' integrated organization gave them an obvious competitive edge and other teams in Major League Baseball and even the National Football League followed their lead.

The NBA Rebuilds the Wall

Unfortunately, despite the fact that MLB and the NFL had integrated before the creation of the NBA, the latest pro basketball league began by excluding Black players. The decision came despite the example set by Lew and others that followed:

- Frank "Dido" Wilson integrated the New York State League as a player in 1907[22] and a coach in 1915.[23]
- Two Jewish players, Abraham Tischinsky[24] and Irving Rose,[25] played on Black Fives teams in the 1910s.
- Bob Douglas created the New York Renaissance, "the first Black-owned, all Black, openly professional team in history"[26] in 1923.
- Howard Ross integrated the Central Basketball League with Lorain in 1926.
- Hank Williams integrated the Midwest Basketball Conference with the Buffalo Bisons in 1935.
- Chicago's World Professional Basketball Tournament included integrated games, integrated teams, and even integrated all-tournament teams starting in 1939 and running for 10 years.
- The NBA's early rival, the National Basketball League, included several integrated teams and an all–Black team in the 1940s.

Douglas even sought a place for his Rens in the early NBA. He met with league officials in 1947 and brought Joe Lapchick, a former star player and then-coach of the New York Knicks, to support him. It didn't help. Douglas' bid was rejected. Stark says league owners had "financial concerns."[27]

When seven of nine the NBL teams were absorbed into the NBA, the Rens were again snubbed, even though it meant the league would start with a scheduler's nightmare, an odd number of 17 teams. According to Claude Johnson, "For the NBA, the Rens card was never even in the deck."[28]

To be fair, the NBA did feature some diversity. In *The Birth of the*

Chapter 20. Lew Circles the Bases

Modern NBA: Pro Basketball in the Year of the Merger, 1949–1950, Josh Elias writes that a Japanese American player, Wat Misaka, played with the Knicks in 1947, a Native American player, Bob Harrison, played with the Lakers for several seasons, and a number of Jewish players participated in the league.

In fact, the NBA was actually an integrated league before it knew it. Elias also writes that "Leroy Chollet, the rookie small forward for Syracuse ... was multiracial but passed for white during his career."[29] Chollet appeared in the NBA from 1949 to 1951.

The Rest of the Dominoes Fall

Finally following the example of MLB and the NFL, the NBA added Black players in 1950. That year, the Celtics drafted Chuck Cooper, the Capitols Earl Lloyd, and the Knicks Nat Clifton.

Like Dobens, Walter Brown, the co-owner and president of the Celtics, grew up in Lew's orbit. While a hockey man, he also helped his father manage the Boston Garden and Boston Arena, so basketball was on his radar too. He was one of the NBA's original owners, helping to start the league to fill otherwise-empty nights in their arenas when their NHL teams were out of town.

Although research has found no direct connection between Brown and Lew, Brown attended schools in Hopkinton, Massachusetts, 30 miles from Lowell, and Exeter, New Hampshire, 30 miles from Nashua. Like Dobens, he was a sports mad high schooler when Lew was still playing. So it's reasonable to assume Brown was aware of his accomplishments. (Interestingly, Brown was president of the Bruins when they brought in their first Black player, Willie O'Ree, in 1958.)

While the NFL integrated as early as 1946, the pace accelerated with the start of a rival American Football League. When Billy Sullivan started the Patriots in 1959, the AFL was far more open to Black players than the NFL had been. According to football historian Charles Ross, the AFL was able to match the talent level of the more-established league surprisingly soon because it drafted more Black players, gave them opportunities to play traditionally white positions, and looked for skilled players in places the NFL had not, such as historically Black college and universities. One of the Patriots' early stars was Black athlete Ron Burton, known as the "First Patriot,"[30] who was as beloved off the field as he was on it.

Lew's granddaughter, Wendy Johnson, and great-granddaughter, Kiah Jamille, posing at Lew Family Square in Lowell, Massachusetts (photograph by the author).

Chapter 20. Lew Circles the Bases

It's clear that Sullivan knew Lew. While a generation apart, both were born and raised in Lowell. Billy's father, William Sr., had been a sports reporter in the city and was an expert on its sports history. As a sportswriter who knew him said after his passing, "If anyone could have written a history of sports in Lowell, it was [him]. He so amazed me with great names of athletes and events he made me realize what little knowledge I had in comparison."[31] And of course, Billy was a child when his father and uncle partnered with Lew in the 1920s.

Lew's influence on Dobens and the integration of baseball is clear. While his influence on men like Walter Brown and Billy Sullivan, Jr., and the continued integration of major league sports, is more indirect, the fact is that all three men grew up in an environment where an integrated professional game existed, and Lew was the man who provided that example.

As the man whose assist set the integration of all major league sports in motion, Lew has not received the recognition he deserves. Fortunately, renewed interest in the length and breadth of his career—and his true legacy—promises to change that.

Chapter Notes

Chapter 1

1. William Himmelman, "1900–1901," *Pro Basketball Encyclopedia*, https://probasketballencyclopedia.com/seasons/1900-1901/.
2. "Annual Banquet of the Y.M.C.A. Basket Ball Team," *Lowell Sun*, May 10, 1902, 2.
3. "Season Ended," *Lowell Daily Courier*, March 28, 1902, 5.
4. "Another Defeat: Burkes Could Score Only Two Points," *Lowell Sun*, November 29, 1902, 14.
5. George Hepbron, *How to Play Basketball* (American Sports Publishing Company, 1904), 21.
6. George Hepbron, *How to Play Basketball* (American Sports Publishing Company, 1904), 47.
7. "Two Teeth Gone from Tighe's Set—Devlin's Blow Loosens Ivories," *Lowell Daily Courier*, January 7, 1903, 4.
8. "Fatal Boxing Bout," *Lowell Sun*, August 16, 1901, 2.
9. Ed Rice, *Baseball's First Indian: Louis Sockalexis: Penobscot Legend, Cleveland Indian* (Tide-Mark, 2013), Kindle, Location 1652.
10. "Sockalexis Once More," *Boston Globe*, May 2, 1902, 4.
11. "Batting Streak," *Lowell Sun*, May 9, 1902, 23.
12. "Pencil Snapshots," *Lowell Sun*, May 9, 1902, 23.
13. "An Easy Thing: Lowell Defeats Nashua," *Lowell Sun*, May 10, 1902, 25.
14. "The Indians Fall," *Cincinnati Commercial Tribune*, April 27, 1897, 3.
15. "The Indians Fall," *Cincinnati Commercial Tribune*, April 27, 1897, 3.
16. "Poor Sockalexis," *Lowell Sun*, April 6, 1900, 24.

Chapter 2

1. "Lowell, Story of an Industrial City: Seeds of Industry," National Park Service, https://www.nps.gov/articles/lowell-handbook-seeds-of-industry.htm.
2. "History of Lowell: Pawtucketville," UMass Lowell Library Guides, https://libguides.uml.edu/pawtucketville.
3. David Vermette, *A Distinct Alien Race: The Untold Story of Franco-Americans: Industrialization, Immigration, Religious Strife* (Baraka Books, 2018), 49.
4. "Anti-Slavery in Lowell," National Park Service, https://www.nps.gov/lowe/learn/historyculture/anti-slavery-in-lowell.htm.
5. "Southern Ties: Lowell Manufacturing Company," National Park Service, https://www.nps.gov/lowe/learn/historyculture/southern-ties-northern-gospels.htm.
6. "Split Interests & Signed Statements," National Park Service, https://www.nps.gov/lowe/learn/historyculture/split-interests-signed-statements.htm.
7. "Lowell History: African Americans in Lowell," UMass Lowell Library, https://libguides.uml.edu/c.php?g=520711.
8. Arthur Eno, Jr., et al., *Cotton Was King: A History of Lowell, Massachusetts* (New Hampshire Publishing Company in Collaboration with the Lowell Historical Society, 1976), 128.
9. "Mrs. Elizabeth Lew: Observing Her 91st Birthday Today," *Lowell Sun*, March 1, 1912, 2.

Notes—Chapter 3

10. Barbara York, "Hub Woman, 100, Is Firm Pacifist After Four Wars," *Boston Traveler*, July 16, 1951, 14.
11. "Freedom's Cost & Black Business," National Park Service, https://www.nps.gov/lowe/learn/historyculture/freedom-s-cost-black-business.htm.
12. "Zimri Lew—55th Massachusetts Infantry," African American Civil War Memorial Museum, https://afroamcivilwar.org/soldier/lew-zimri-age-36-year-1865-55th-massachusetts-infantry-jones-macofee/.
13. Douglas Egerton, *Thunder at the Gates: The Black Civil War Regiments That Redeemed America* (Basic Books, 2016), 271.
14. Barbara York, "Hub Woman, 100, Is Firm Pacifist After Four Wars," *Boston Traveler*, July 16, 1951, 14.
15. Elizabeth Leonard, *Benjamin Franklin Butler: A Noisy, Fearless Life* (University of North Carolina Press, 2022), 66.
16. "Teresa Garland Lew," UMass Lowell Library, https://libguides.uml.edu/c.php?g=1125577&p=8222675.
17. Ian Webster, "CPI Inflation Calculator," https://www.in2013dollars.com/us/inflation/1850?amount=200.
18. "Caroline Van Vronker," Lowell Stories: Black History, UMass Lowell Library, https://libguides.uml.edu/c.php?g=1125577&p=8210381.
19. "Caroline Van Vronker," Lowell Stories: Black History, UMass Lowell Library, https://libguides.uml.edu/c.php?g=1125577&p=8210381.

Chapter 3

1. "The Nutone Club: Held Its Second Successful Meeting Last Evening," *Lowell Sun*, May 10, 1899, 13.
2. "The Nutone Club: Held Its Second Successful Meeting Last Evening," *Lowell Sun*, May 10, 1899, 13.
3. "The Nutone Club: Held Its Second Successful Meeting Last Evening," *Lowell Sun*, May 10, 1899, 13.
4. "Boxing Gossip: Supt. Moffat's Experience with Young Starlight," *Lowell Sun*, June 19, 1901, 45.
5. "Boxing Gossip: Supt. Moffat's Experience with Young Starlight," *Lowell Sun*, June 19, 1901, 45.
6. "Some Cycle News," *Lowell Sun*, April 22, 1901, 42.
7. "Major Taylor: Champion Colored Bicycle Sprinter in Lowell," *Lowell Sun*, March 6, 1899, 14.
8. "Major Taylor Established New Track Record," *Lowell Sun*, September 25, 1899, 18.
9. "Major Taylor Established New Track Record," *Lowell Sun*, September 25, 1899, 18.
10. "Iver Johnson Sponsored Major Taylor," *Fitchburg Historical Society*, August 2024 Newsletter, 1.
11. Andrew Ritchie, *Major Taylor: The Extraordinary Career of a Champion Bicycle Racer* (Johns Hopkins University Press, 1988), 146.
12. Marshall Taylor, *The Fastest Bicycle Rider in the World* (Commonwealth Press, 1928), 421.
13. "Yellow Racing," *Lowell Sun*, October 8, 1900, 23.
14. "Some Cycle News," *Lowell Sun*, April 22, 1901, 42.
15. "Two Lowell Men Disqualified in the Medfield Race," *Lowell Sun*, May 2, 1901, 23.
16. "Some Cycling News," *Lowell Sun*, August 16, 1901, 7.
17. "Keegan Won," *Lowell Sun*, August 19, 1901, 19.
18. "Amateur Base Ball," *Lowell Sun*, April 22, 1902, 12.
19. Charlie Bevis, *The New England League: A Baseball History, 1885–1949* (McFarland, 2007), 20.
20. Josh Elias, *The Birth of the Modern NBA: Pro Basketball in the Year of the Merger, 1949–1950* (McFarland, 2024), Kindle, Location 7074.
21. Josh Elias, *The Birth of the Modern NBA: Pro Basketball in the Year of the Merger, 1949–1950* (McFarland, 2024), Kindle, Location 7083.
22. Robert Peterson, *Only the Ball Was White: A History of Legendary Black Players and All-Black Professional Teams* (Oxford University Press, 1992), 29.
23. "Color Line in Baseball," *Boston Globe*, September 12, 1887, 2.

24. "Diamond Points," *Boston Globe*, September 17, 1887, 11.
25. Charlie Bevis, *The New England League: A Baseball History, 1885–1949* (McFarland, 2007), 54.
26. Charlie Bevis, *The New England League: A Baseball History, 1885–1949* (McFarland, 2007), 59.
27. Charlie Bevis, *The New England League: A Baseball History, 1885–1949* (McFarland, 2007), 76.
28. Ed Rice, *Baseball's First Indian: Louis Sockalexis: Penobscot Legend, Cleveland Indian* (Tide-Mark, 2003), Kindle, Location 351.
29. Charles Scoggins, *Bricks and Bats* (Lowell Historical Society, 2002), 36.

Chapter 4

1. Claude Johnson, *The Black Fives: The Epic Story of Basketball's Forgotten Era* (Abrams Press, 2022), Kindle, 45.
2. Claude Johnson, *The Black Fives: The Epic Story of Basketball's Forgotten Era* (Abrams Press, 2022), Kindle, 45.
3. "James Naismith on Basketball," Britannica.com, https://www.britannica.com/biography/James-Naismith-on-basketball-2215550.
4. Robert Peterson, *Cages to Jumpshots: Pro Basketball's Early Years* (Oxford University Press, 1990), 21.
5. Robert Peterson, *Cages to Jumpshots: Pro Basketball's Early Years* (Oxford University Press, 1990), 22
6. Claude Johnson, *The Black Fives: The Epic Story of Basketball's Forgotten Era* (Abrams Press, 2022), Kindle, 84.
7. Claude Johnson, *The Black Fives: The Epic Story of Basketball's Forgotten Era* (Abrams Press, 2022), Kindle, 86.
8. Claude Johnson, *The Black Fives: The Epic Story of Basketball's Forgotten Era* (Abrams Press, 2022), 87.
9. "A Game New to Lowell Played at the Y.M.C.A. Gymnasium," *Lowell Daily Courier*, December 10, 1892, photocopy from UML Center for Lowell History Archives.
10. "A Game New to Lowell Played at the Y.M.C.A. Gymnasium," *Lowell Daily Courier*, December 10, 1892, photocopy from UML Center for Lowell History Archives.
11. "A Game New to Lowell Played at the Y.M.C.A. Gymnasium," *Lowell Daily Courier*, December 10, 1892, photocopy from UML Center for Lowell History Archives.
12. "A Game New to Lowell Played at the Y.M.C.A. Gymnasium," *Lowell Daily Courier*, December 10, 1892, photocopy from UML Center for Lowell History Archives.
13. "A Game New to Lowell Played at the Y.M.C.A. Gymnasium," *Lowell Daily Courier*, December 10, 1892, photocopy from UML Center for Lowell History Archives.
14. "Basket Ball at the Burkes Gym Last Evening," *Lowell Sun*, January 11, 1896, 1.
15. "At Basket Ball: The Burkes Defeat the YMCA at Basket Ball," *Lowell Sun*, May 15, 1896, 1.
16. "Harry Haskell Bucky Lew," UMass Lowell Library, https://libguides.uml.edu/c.php?g=1125577&p=8215152.
17. "Annual Banquet of the Y.M.C.A. Basket Ball Team," *Lowell Sun*, May 10, 1902, 2.
18. "Victor M. Meister: New Physical Director of the Y.M.C.A.," *Lowell Sun*, September 21, 1900, 24.
19. "Lowell Y.M.C.A. Defeated Lawrence at Basket Ball," *Lowell Sun*, January 31, 1902, 36.
20. "Basket Ball: YMCA Teams Winners in Two Games," *Lowell Sun*, November 22, 1901, 19.
21. "Lowell Beaten," *Lowell Sun*, March 12, 1902, 16.
22. "Y.M.C.A. Wins," *Lowell Daily Courier*, January 3, 1902, 2.
23. "Bucky Lew Clinches Victory with Phenomenal Goal," *Lowell Daily Courier*, December 12, 1901, 2.
24. "Basket Ball," *Lowell Daily Courier*, December 2, 1902, 2.

Chapter 5

1. "Elms 10, P.A.C. 9," *Lowell Sun*, July 10, 1902, 15.

Notes—Chapter 6

2. Charles Scoggins, *Bricks and Bats* (Lowell Historical Society, 2002), 38.
3. Charles Scoggins, *Bricks and Bats* (Lowell Historical Society, 2002), 93.
4. Charles Scoggins, *Bricks and Bats* (Lowell Historical Society, 2002), 38.
5. Jimmy Stamp, "A Brief History of the Baseball," *Smithsonian Magazine*, June 28, 2013, https://www.smithsonianmag.com/arts-culture/a-brief-history-of-the-baseball-3685086.
6. Charles Scoggins, *Bricks and Bats* (Lowell Historical Society, 2002), 46.
7. "Weekly Hoodoo," *Lowell Sun*, June 3, 1902, 17.
8. "Weekly Hoodoo," *Lowell Sun*, June 3, 1902, 17.
9. "Rain Everywhere," *Lowell Sun*, May 20, 1902, 53.
10. "For First Place," *Lowell Sun*, June 14, 1902, 16.
11. "For First Place," *Lowell Sun*, June 14, 1902, 16.
12. Ed Rice, *Baseball's First Indian: Louis Sockalexis: Penobscot Legend, Cleveland Indian* (Tide-Mark, 2003), Kindle, Location 2883.
13. Ed Rice, *Baseball's First Indian: Louis Sockalexis: Penobscot Legend, Cleveland Indian* (Tide-Mark, 2003), Kindle, Location 2976.
14. "Lowell Captures Two Games from Nashua," *Lowell Sun*, May 31, 1902, 7.
15. "Base Ball Notes," *Lowell Daily Courier*, May 2, 1902, 9.
16. "Base Ball News," *Waterbury Democrat*, June 13, 1902, 7.
17. "Base Ball Notes," *Lowell Daily Courier*, June 13, 1902, 4.
18. "Diamond Notes," *Lowell Sun*, June 13, 1902, 7.
19. "League Gossip," *Lowell Daily Courier*, August 18, 1902, 3.
20. "How Yesterday's Game Impressed the Citizen Artist," *Lowell Daily Courier*, August 14, 1902, 3.
21. "The Diamond," *Lowell Daily Courier*, March 5, 1903, 3.
22. "Decline of Baseball in New England," *Lowell Daily Courier*, July 29, 1905, 9.
23. "The Diamond," *Lowell Daily Courier*, May 27, 1903, 3.
24. "Indian Blood," *Lowell Daily Courier*, January 26, 1903, 10.
25. "Ragged Game," *Lowell Sun*, June 16, 1902, 7.
26. Ed Rice, *Baseball's First Indian: Louis Sockalexis: Penobscot Legend, Cleveland Indian* (Tide-Mark, 2003), Kindle, Location 3100.
27. Charles Scoggins, *Bricks and Bats* (Lowell Historical Society, 2002), 38.
28. "Crippled Team," *Lowell Sun*, July 19, 1902, 15.
29. "Crippled Team," *Lowell Sun*, July 19, 1902, 15.
30. Charles Scoggins, *Bricks and Bats* (Lowell Historical Society, 2002), 39.
31. Ed Rice, *Baseball's First Indian: Louis Sockalexis: Penobscot Legend, Cleveland Indian* (Tide-Mark, 2003), Kindle, Location 3152.
32. "1902 Lowell Tigers Statistics," Stats Crew, https://www.statscrew.com/minorbaseball/stats/t-lt12692/y-1902.
33. "Wise Move," *Lowell Daily Courier*, January 17, 1903, 3.

Chapter 6

1. William Himmelman, "1900–1901," *Pro Basketball Encyclopedia*, 2022, https://probasketballencyclopedia.com/seasons/1900-1901/.
2. Leonard Koppett, et al., *Total Basketball: The Ultimate Basketball Encyclopedia* (Sportclassic Books, 2003), 321.
3. "Of Basket Ball: Teams Ready to Open Season," *Lowell Sun*, October 7, 1902, 51.
4. "Of Basket Ball: Teams Ready to Open Season," *Lowell Sun*, October 7, 1902, 51.
5. "Basket Ball," *Lowell Sun*, October 17, 1902, 6.
6. "Basket Ball," *Lowell Sun*, October 17, 1902, 6.
7. William Himmelman, "Early Years," *Pro Basketball Encyclopedia*, https://probasketballencyclopedia.com/early-years/.
8. William Himmelman, "Early Years," *Pro Basketball Encyclopedia*, https://probasketballencyclopedia.com/early-years/.
9. Frank Basloe, *I Grew Up with Basketball: Twenty Years of Barnstorming*

Notes—Chapter 7

with Cage Greats of Yesterday (University of Nebraska Press, 2022), 27.

10. Robert Peterson, *Cages to Jumpshots: Pro Basketball's Early Years* (Oxford University Press, 1990), 186.

11. Robert Peterson, *Cages to Jumpshots: Pro Basketball's Early Years* (Oxford University Press, 1990), 32–36.

12. Robert Peterson, *Cages to Jumpshots: Pro Basketball's Early Years* (Oxford University Press, 1990), 37.

13. Frank Basloe, *I Grew Up with Basketball: Twenty Years of Barnstorming with Cage Greats of Yesterday* (University of Nebraska Press, 2022), 27.

14. William Himmelman, "1898–1899," *Pro Basketball Encyclopedia*, https://probasketballencyclopedia.com/seasons/1898-1899/.

15. Murry Nelson, *The Originals: The New York Celtics Invent Modern Basketball* (Bowling Green University Popular Press, 1999), 24.

16. Murry Nelson, *The Originals: The New York Celtics Invent Modern Basketball* (Bowling Green University Popular Press, 1999), 25.

17. William Himmelman, "1900–1901," *Pro Basketball Encyclopedia*, https://probasketballencyclopedia.com/seasons/1900-1901/.

18. "Burke Institute Taking on Another Boom or Prosperity," *Lowell Sun*, October 4, 1899, 15.

19. "Notice is hereby given...," *Lowell Daily Courier*, March 21, 1898, 4.

20. William Himmelman, "1904–1905," *Pro Basketball Encyclopedia*, https://probasketballencyclopedia.com/seasons/1904-1905/.

21. William Himmelman, "1901–1902," *Pro Basketball Encyclopedia*, https://probasketballencyclopedia.com/seasons/1901-1902/.

22. "Basketball," *Lowell Sun*, February 2, 1922, 28.

23. William Himmelman, "1904–1905," *Pro Basketball Encyclopedia*, https://probasketballencyclopedia.com/seasons/1904-1905/.

24. "PAC Champions: They Won the Title Fairly Last Night," *Lowell Sun*, April 18, 1902, 35.

25. "Game Ended in Fight," *Lowell Sun*, April 1, 1902, 55.

26. "Game Ended in Fight," *Lowell Sun*, April 1, 1902, 55.

27. "Sawyer Beaten: Webster Took the First Game," *Lowell Sun*, March 21, 1902, 47.

28. "$200 Challenge," *Lowell Sun*, March 24, 1902, 44.

29. "$200 Challenge: Manager Gray Will Post Money," *Lowell Daily Courier*, March 25, 1902, 10.

30. "P.A.C. 14; Burkes 7: First Game Played in Championship Series," *Lowell Sun*, April 3, 1902, 30.

31. "PAC Champions: They Won the Title Fairly Last Night," *Lowell Sun*, April 18, 1902, 35.

32. "Basket Ball Teams Celebrated Their Victories at Their Managers Homes," *Lowell Sun*, April 24, 1902, 5.

33. "Basket Ball Notes," *Lowell Daily Courier*, April 19, 1902, 2.

Chapter 7

1. "Basket Ball," *Lowell Daily Courier*, October 27, 1902, 2.

2. "Lowell Defeats Lawrence," *Lowell Sun*, October 13, 1902, 19.

3. "Lowell Defeats Lawrence," *Lowell Sun*, October 13, 1902, 19.

4. "Basket Ball On," *Lowell Sun*, October 13, 1902, 19.

5. "Burke Victory," *Lowell Sun*, November 5, 1902, 12.

6. "Tuesday's Game," *Lowell Sun*, November 6, 1902, 14.

7. "Basket Ball," *Lowell Sun*, October 30, 1902, 18.

8. "Get Your Seats," *Marlboro Daily Enterprise*, November 5, 1902.

9. Murry Nelson, *The Originals: The New York Celtics Invent Modern Basketball* (Bowling Green University Popular Press, 1999), 25.

10. "Large Crowd," *Marlboro Daily Enterprise*, November 6, 1902, 1.

11. Gerry Finn, "Bucky Lew First Negro in Pro Basketball," *Springfield Union*, April 2, 1958, 35.

12. Gerry Finn, "Bucky Lew First Negro in Pro Basketball," *Springfield Union*, April 2, 1958, 35.

Notes—Chapter 8

13. Gerry Finn, "Bucky Lew First Negro in Pro Basketball," *Springfield Union*, April 2, 1958, 35.
14. Gerry Finn, "Bucky Lew First Negro in Pro Basketball," *Springfield Union*, April 2, 1958, 35.
15. Gerry Finn, "Bucky Lew First Negro in Pro Basketball," *Springfield Union*, April 2, 1958, 35.
16. Gerry Finn, "Bucky Lew First Negro in Pro Basketball," *Springfield Union*, April 2, 1958, 35.
17. "Lost the Game," *Lowell Sun*, November 7, 1902, 7.
18. "Marlboro's First," *Marlboro Daily Enterprise*, November 7, 1. AU: Year?
19. "Large Crowd," *Marlboro Daily Enterprise*, November 6, 1. AU: Year?
20. "P.A.C. Lost," *Lowell Daily Courier*, November 7, 1902, 3.
21. "Marlboro's First," *Marlboro Daily Enterprise*, November 7, 1. AU: Year?
22. "Lost the Game," *Lowell Sun*, November 7, 1902, 7.
23. "Basket-Ball Results," *Boston Globe*, November 7, 1902, 5.
24. "P.A.C. Lost," *Lowell Daily Courier*, November 7, 1902, 3.
25. Gerry Finn, "Bucky Lew First Negro in Pro Basketball," *Springfield Union*, April 2, 1958, 35.
26. Gerry Finn, "Bucky Lew First Negro in Pro Basketball," *Springfield Union*, April 2, 1958, 35.
27. Lee Williams, "Dear Miss Lew," letter to Lew family, Naismith Memorial Basketball Hall of Fame, January 25, 1978.

Chapter 8

1. William Himmelman, "Lowell—1901–1902," *Pro Basketball Encyclopedia*, https://probasketballencyclopedia.com/team-standings-by-year/?y=1901-1902&t=LOWELLPAC.
2. Robert Peterson, *Cages to Jumpshots: Pro Basketball's Early Years* (New York: Oxford University Press, 1990), 4
3. Leonard Koppett, et al., *Total Basketball: The Ultimate Basketball Encyclopedia* (Sportclassic Books, 2003), 375.
4. Leonard Koppett, et al., *Total Basketball: The Ultimate Basketball Encyclopedia* (Sportclassic Books, 2003), 376.
5. Robert Peterson, *Cages to Jumpshots: Pro Basketball's Early Years* (Oxford University Press, 1990), 49.
6. Robert Peterson, *Cages to Jumpshots: Pro Basketball's Early Years* (Oxford University Press, 1990), 49.
7. Frank Basloe, *I Grew Up with Basketball: Twenty Years of Barnstorming with Cage Greats of Yesterday* (University of Nebraska Press, 2022), 25.
8. Robert Peterson, *Cages to Jumpshots: Pro Basketball's Early Years* (Oxford University Press, 1990), 49.
9. "Basket Ball," *Lowell Daily Courier*, December 7, 1904, 2.
10. Murry Nelson, *The National Basketball League: A History 1935 to 1949* (McFarland, 2009), Kindle, Location 592.
11. Murry Nelson, *The National Basketball League: A History 1935 to 1949* (McFarland, 2009), Kindle, Location 1492.
12. Todd Gould, *Pioneers of the Hardwood: Indiana and the Birth of Professional Basketball* (Indiana University Press, 1998), Kindle, 170.
13. "Winning Streak," *Lowell Daily Courier*, February 4, 1903, 3.
14. "Time That Hudson Won Hoop Tilt, Minus One to Minus Two," *Springfield Union*, February 5, 1953, 2.
15. "Time That Hudson Won Hoop Tilt, Minus One to Minus Two," *Springfield Union*, February 5, 1953, 2.
16. "Hudson's Game," *Lowell Sun*, January 6, 1903, 18.
17. "Basket Ball," *Lowell Daily Courier*, December 2, 1902, 2.
18. Robert Peterson, *Cages to Jumpshots: Pro Basketball's Early Years* (Oxford University Press, 1990), 40.
19. Robert Peterson, *Cages to Jumpshots: Pro Basketball's Early Years* (Oxford University Press, 1990), 7.
20. "Danny Recalls Bucky Lew," *Lowell Sun*, November 1, 1963, 16.
21. Robert Peterson, *Cages to Jumpshots: Pro Basketball's Early Years* (Oxford University Press, 1990), 4.
22. Robert Peterson, *Cages to Jumpshots: Pro Basketball's Early Years* (Oxford University Press, 1990), 4.
23. Robert Peterson, *Cages to Jump-*

shots: *Pro Basketball's Early Years* (Oxford University Press, 1990), 9.
24. Gerry Finn, "Bucky Lew First Negro in Pro Basketball," *Springfield Union*, April 2, 1958, 35.
25. George Hepbron, *How to Play Basketball* (American Sports Publishing Company, 1904), 81.
26. William Himmelman, "1898–1899," *Pro Basketball Encyclopedia*, https://probasketballencyclopedia.com/seasons/1898-1899/.
27. Murry Nelson, *The Originals: The New York Celtics Invent Modern Basketball* (Bowling Green University Popular Press, 1999), 49.
28. Robert Peterson, *Cages to Jumpshots: Pro Basketball's Early Years* (Oxford University Press, 1990), 27.
29. George Hepbron, *How to Play Basketball* (American Sports Publishing Company, 1904), 73.
30. William Himmelman, "The War Years," *Pro Basketball Encyclopedia*, https://probasketballencyclopedia.com/the-war-years/.

Chapter 9

1. "Basket Ball," *Lowell Daily Courier*, November 13, 1902, 3.
2. "P.A.C. Victory," *Lowell Sun*, November 12, 1902, 19.
3. "P.A.C. Victory," *Lowell Sun*, November 12, 1902, 19.
4. "Allard's Work," *Lowell Daily Courier*, November 12, 1902, 3.
5. "Oscar McFarland," *Lowell Sun*, November 13, 1902, 57.
6. "P.A.C. Victory," *Lowell Sun*, November 12, 1902, 19.
7. "Marlboro Leads: P.A.C. Stand in Second Place," *Lowell Sun*, November 18, 1902, 12.
8. "Easy Money," *Lowell Daily Courier*, November 14, 1902, 3.
9. "Marlboro Leads: P.A.C. Stand in Second Place," *Lowell Sun*, November 18, 1902, 12.
10. "Tighe Injured," *Lowell Sun*, November 22, 1902, 25.
11. "Four Straight," *Lowell Sun*, November 25, 1902, 42.
12. "A Bad Defeat," *Lowell Sun*, November 26, 1902, 15.
13. "P.A.C. Players Easy for Marlboro," *Lowell Daily Courier*, November 26, 1902, 2.
14. Robert Peterson, *Cages to Jumpshots: Pro Basketball's Early Years* (Oxford University Press, 1990), 140.
15. Robert Peterson, *Cages to Jumpshots: Pro Basketball's Early Years* (Oxford University Press, 1990), 142.
16. "P.A.C. Went Down," *Lowell Sun*, November 28, 1902, 26.
17. "Basket Ball," *Lowell Daily Courier*, November 29, 1902, 2.
18. "Basket Ball," *Lowell Daily Courier*, December 2, 1902, 2.
19. "Nashua Swamped, PAC Ran Up 45 points," *Lowell Sun*, December 4, 1902, 46.
20. "Game Was Fast," *Lowell Sun*, December 10, 1902, 13.
21. "Game Was Fast," *Lowell Sun*, December 10, 1902, 13.
22. "Game Was Fast," *Lowell Sun*, December 10, 1902, 13.
23. William Himmelman, "Harry Hough," *Pro Basketball Encyclopedia*, https://probasketballencyclopedia.com/player/harry-hough/.
24. "Down They Go," *Lowell Sun*, December 20, 1902, 29.
25. "Game Was Fast," *Lowell Sun*, December 10, 1902, 13.
26. "Both Teams Won," *Lowell Sun*, December 13, 1902, 29.
27. "Burkes Won," *Lowell Daily Courier*, December 13, 1902, 2.
28. "Tables Turned," *Lowell Sun*, December 16, 1902, 13.
29. "Basket Ball," *Lowell Daily Courier*, March 19, 1903, 2.
30. "Can't Stop Them," *Lowell Sun*, December 19, 1902, 31.
31. "Beaten at Last," *Lowell Sun*, December 27, 1902, 19.
32. "Basket Ball," *Lowell Daily Courier*, December 26, 1902, 2.
33. "Basket Ball," *Lowell Daily Courier*, December 26, 1902.
34. "Basket Ball," *Lowell Daily Courier*, December 26, 1902.
35. "Three Victories," *Lowell Sun*, December 26, 1902, 19.

Notes—Chapter 10

36. "Hough Absent," *Lowell Sun*, January 1, 1903, 42.
37. "Mighty Hough," *Lowell Sun*, January 2, 1903, 36.
38. "Hough's Colors," *Lowell Daily Courier*, January 2, 1903, 4.
39. "Hough's Colors," *Lowell Daily Courier*, January 2, 1903, 4.
40. "Mighty Hough," *Lowell Sun*, January 2, 1903, 36.
41. "Mighty Hough," *Lowell Sun*, January 2, 1903, 36.
42. "Mighty Hough," *Lowell Sun*, January 2, 1903, 36.
43. "Basket Ball," *Lowell Daily Courier*, January 3, 1903, 2.

Chapter 10

1. "Two Teeth Gone from Tighe's Set," *Lowell Daily Courier*, January 7, 1903, 4.
2. "Once More the P.A.C. Boys Lose," *Lowell Daily Courier*, January 31, 1903, 3.
3. "Beaten at Last," *Lowell Sun*, December 27, 1902, 19.
4. "Beaten at Last," *Lowell Sun*, December 27, 1902, 19.
5. "In Rough Game," *Lowell Sun*, January 21, 1903, 26.
6. "Two Teeth Gone from Tighe's Set," *Lowell Daily Courier*, January 7, 1903, 4.
7. "Bag of Gold," *Lowell Sun*, January 31, 1903, 20.
8. "Two Teeth Gone from Tighe's Set," *Lowell Daily Courier*, January 7, 1903, 4.
9. "Two Teeth Gone from Tighe's Set," *Lowell Daily Courier*, January 7, 1903, 4.
10. "Marlboro Won," *Lowell Daily Courier*, January 9, 1903, 5.
11. "Marlboro Won," *Lowell Daily Courier*, January 9, 1903, 5.
12. "Marlboro on Top," *Lowell Sun*, January 9, 1903, 10.
13. "Marlboro on Top," *Lowell Sun*, January 9, 1903, 10.
14. "Marlboro on Top," *Lowell Sun*, January 9, 1903, 10.
15. "Marlboro Men Have Jumped to Chicopee," *Lowell Daily Courier*, January 13, 1903, 2.
16. "Basket Ball Notes," *Lowell Sun*, January 23, 1903, 31.
17. "Old Burkes Won," *Lowell Sun*, January 20, 1903, 76.
18. "Down They Go," *Lowell Sun*, December 20, 1902, 29.
19. "In Rough Game," *Lowell Sun*, January 21, 1903, 26.
20. "P.A.C. Went Down," *Lowell Daily Courier*, January 17, 1903, 3.
21. "P.A.C. Weak," *Lowell Sun*, January 17, 1903, 30.
22. "Old Burke Team," *Lowell Sun*, February 18, 1903, 7.
23. "P.A.C. Weak," *Lowell Sun*, January 17, 1903, 30.
24. "Healey Ignored in the Marlboro Basket Ball Deal," *Lowell Sun*, January 14, 1903, 44.
25. "Bag of Gold," *Lowell Sun*, January 31, 1903, 20.
26. "Bag of Gold," *Lowell Sun*, January 31, 1903, 20.
27. "Large Score," *Lowell Sun*, February 17, 1903, 30.
28. "Large Score," *Lowell Sun*, February 17, 1903, 30.
29. "Down They Go," *Lowell Sun*, March 3, 1903, 44.
30. "Never in It," *Lowell Daily Courier*, March 8, 1903, 3.
31. "Down They Go," *Lowell Sun*, March 11, 1903, 23.
32. "Hissed the Referee," *Lowell Sun*, March 17, 1903, 14.
33. "Hissed the Referee," *Lowell Sun*, March 17, 1903, 14.
34. "PAC-Burke: Final Game Schedule for Tonight," *Lowell Sun*, March 27, 1903, 89.
35. "Burke Victory," *Lowell Sun*, March 21, 1903, 32.
36. "Got Revenge," *Lowell Sun*, March 28, 1903, 22.
37. "Basket Ball," *Lowell Daily Courier*, March 21, 1903, 2.
38. "Basket Ball," *Lowell Daily Courier*, April 2, 1903, 2.
39. "Textile School Notes," *Lowell Daily Courier*, February 10, 1903, 10.
40. Kenneth Johnson, *Kansas University Basketball Legends* (History Press, 2013), Kindle, 18.

Notes—Chapters 11 and 12

Chapter 11

1. "Game Was Fast," *Lowell Sun*, December 10, 1902, 23.
2. "In Basket Ball," *Lowell Sun*, September 5, 1903, 26.
3. "For Basket Ball," *Boston Sunday Globe*, September 6, 1903, 57.
4. "Basket Ball," *Lowell Sun*, October 17, 1904, 18.
5. "Basket Ball," *Lowell Sun*, October 30, 1903, 18.
6. "Concord Easy," *Lowell Sun*, December 29, 1903, 10.
7. "Manchester Leads," *Lowell Sun*, November 16, 1903, 17.
8. "Close Game," *Lowell Daily Courier*, November 23, 1903, 2.
9. "Strong League," *Lowell Daily Courier*, November 23, 1903, 2.
10. "Basketball Notes," *Lowell Sun*, December 3, 1903, 5.
11. "Great Contest," *Lowell Sun*, December 1, 1903, 32.
12. "Fast Game," *Lowell Daily Courier*, November 19, 1903, 2.
13. "Basketball Notes," *Lowell Daily Courier*, November 12, 1903, 2.
14. "Gray Got Back," *Lowell Sun*, December 31, 1903, 26.
15. "Lowell on Top," *Lowell Sun*, December 2, 1903, 27.
16. "Allard Absent," *Lowell Sun*, December 17, 1903, 13.
17. "Basketball Notes," *Lowell Sun*, February 4, 1904, 12.
18. "Basketball Notes," *Lowell Daily Courier*, November 18, 1904, 14.
19. William Himmelman, "Pat Doyle," *Pro Basketball Encyclopedia*, https://probasketballencyclopedia.com/player/pat-doyle/.
20. Leonard Koppett, et al., *Total Basketball: The Ultimate Basketball Encyclopedia* (Sportclassic Books, 2003), 15.
21. Robert Peterson, *Cages to Jumpshots: Pro Basketball's Early Years* (Oxford University Press, 1990), 64.
22. William Himmelman, "Ed Wachter," *Pro Basketball Encyclopedia*, https://probasketballencyclopedia.com/player/eddie-wachter/.
23. "Great Playing," *Lowell Sun*, February 17, 1904, 27.
24. "Wachter Injured," *Lowell Sun*, February 20, 1904, 29.
25. "Basketball," *Lowell Daily Courier*, February 23, 1904, 8.
26. "Haverhill Won: Bucky Lew Equal to Hough," *Lowell Sun*, February 29, 1904, 4.
27. "Tessie Failed," *Lowell Sun*, March 4, 1904, 4.
28. "Tessie Failed," *Lowell Sun*, March 4, 1904, 4.
29. "Tessie Failed," *Lowell Sun*, March 4, 1904, 4.
30. "Basket Ball Notes," *Lowell Sun*, March 7, 1904, 5.
31. "Basket Ball Notes," *Lowell Sun*, March 7, 1904, 5.
32. "Haverhill Won," *Lowell Sun*, March 11, 1904, 14.
33. "PAC Lost," *Lowell Sun*, March 14, 1904, 7.
34. "Haverhill 72, South Framingham 23," *Lowell Daily Courier*, March 18, 1904, 10.
35. "Haverhill 72, South Framingham 23," *Lowell Daily Courier*, March 18, 1904, 10.
36. "Haverhill 72, South Framingham 23," *Lowell Daily Courier*, March 18, 1904, 10.
37. "An Easy Victory," *Lowell Sun*, March 24, 1904, 18.
38. "Lowell Beaten," *Lowell Sun*, March 26, 1904, 4.
39. "Final Standing," *Lowell Sun*, March 21, 1904, 4.
40. "Basketball," *Lowell Sun*, March 21, 1904, 4.

Chapter 12

1. William Himmelman, "1904–1905," *Pro Basketball Encyclopedia*, https://probasketballencyclopedia.com/seasons/1904-1905/.
2. "Haverhill Basketball Team Leading the New England League," *Boston Globe*, December 15, 1904, 8.
3. William Himmelman, "Jimmy Williamson," *Pro Basketball Encyclopedia*, https://probasketballencyclopedia.com/player/Jimmy-Williamson/.

Notes—Chapter 13

4. "Still Sliding Down," *Newburyport Daily News*, December 1, 1904, 8.
5. "First Home Game," *Newburyport Daily News*, November 17, 1904, 1.
6. "Haverhill," *Boston Daily Globe*, November 18, 1904, 6.
7. "Driblets," *Newburyport Daily News*, March 21, 1905, 8.
8. "Basket Ball," *Fall River Daily Globe*, November 26, 1904, 8.
9. "Lew Barred," *Lowell Daily Courier*, November 28, 1904, 8.
10. "Lew Barred," *Lowell Daily Courier*, November 28, 1904, 8.
11. "Drawing the Color Line," *Newburyport Daily News*, November 29, 1904, 8.
12. "Drawing the Color Line," *Newburyport Daily News*, November 29, 1904, 8.
13. "Drawing the Color Line," *Newburyport Daily News*, November 29, 1904, 8.
14. "Color Line Is Drawn," *Waterbury Evening Democrat*, November 30, 1904, 9.
15. "League Stands Back of Bucky Lew," *Lowell Daily Courier*, November 28, 1904, 8.
16. "Haverhill Easily Leads New England Basket-Ball League," *Boston Globe*, December 30, 1904, 17.
17. "Natick Trimmed," *Lowell Sun*, November 29, 1904, 18.
18. "Basket Ball," *Haverhill Evening Gazette*, Tuesday, November 29, 1904.
19. "Natick Drew the Color line," *Boston Journal*, November 29, 1904, 5.
20. "Drawing the Color Line," *Newburyport Daily News*, November 29, 1904, 8.
21. "League Stands Back of Bucky Lew," *Lowell Daily Courier*, November 28, 1904, 8.
22. "League Stands Back of Bucky Lew," *Lowell Daily Courier*, November 28, 1904, 8.
23. "Quits League," *Lowell Daily Courier*, December 7, 1904, 8.
24. "Quits League," *Lowell Daily Courier*, December 7, 1904, 8.
25. "Basket Ball," *Haverhill Evening Gazette*, Tuesday, November 29, 1904.
26. "Still Sliding Down," *Newburyport Daily News*, December 1, 1904, 8.
27. "Still Sliding Down," *Newburyport Daily News*, December 1, 1904, 8.
28. "Basketball Notes," *Lowell Daily Courier*, December 5, 1904, 8.
29. "Basketball Notes," *Lowell Daily Courier*, December 5, 1904, 8.
30. "Bucky Lew Has Been Signed by Manager Gray," *Lowell Sun*, December 1, 1904, 5.
31. "Basketball Notes," *Lowell Daily Courier*, February 6, 1905, 8.
32. "Basketball Notes," *Lowell Daily Courier*, January 24, 1905, 8.
33. "Basket Ball," *Haverhill Evening Gazette*, December 5, 1904.
34. "Basket Ball," *Haverhill Evening Gazette*, December 5, 1904.
35. "Basketball Notes," *Lowell Daily Courier*, December 5, 1904, 8.
36. "Split Even," *Lowell Daily Courier*, December 5, 1904, 8.
37. "Snowed Under," *Lowell Daily Courier*, December 7, 1904, 8.

Chapter 13

1. "Defeat at Last," *Lowell Sun*, February 6, 1905, 12.
2. William Himmelman, "Jimmy Williamson," *Pro Basketball Encyclopedia*, https://probasketballencyclopedia.com/player/Jimmy-Williamson/.
3. "Basketball Notes," *Lowell Daily Courier*, February 6, 1905, 8.
4. "Lowell Lost," *Lowell Daily Courier*, January 27, 1905, 8.
5. "Trimmed Us," *Lowell Daily Courier*, February 8, 1905, 8.
6. "Basket Ball Notes," *Lowell Daily Courier*, January 31, 1905, 8.
7. "Defeat at Last: Natick's String of Victories Broken," *Lowell Sun*, February 6, 1905, 12.
8. "Defeat at Last," *Lowell Sun*, February 6, 1905, 12.
9. "Basketball Notes," *Lowell Sun*, February 27, 1905, 4.
10. "Its Last Week," *Boston Daily Globe*, February 13, 1905, 11.
11. "Its Last Week," *Boston Daily Globe*, February 13, 1905, 11.
12. "Basketball Notes," *Lowell Sun*, February 27, 1905, 4.

13. "New England Champions," *Boston Globe*, March 18, 1905, 8.
14. "New England Champions," *Boston Globe*, March 18, 1905, 8.
15. William Himmelman, "Harry Hough," *Pro Basketball Encyclopedia*, https://probasketballencyclopedia.com/player/harry-hough/.
16. "Natick Victory," *Lowell Sun*, February 22, 1905, 7.
17. "Tonight's Game May Decide the Series," *Lowell Sun*, February 24, 1905, 9.
18. "Lowell and Natick Match," *Boston Daily Globe*, February 18, 1905, 16.
19. "Rough and One Sided," *Boston Daily Globe*, February 28, 1905, 5.
20. "Natick's Series," *Lowell Sun*, February 25, 1905, 17.
21. "Rough Game," *Lowell Daily Courier*, March 3, 1905, 10.
22. "Big Center Went Down," *Berkshire Evening Eagle*, March 4, 1905, 12.
23. "Locals Beaten," *Newburyport Daily News*, March 7, 1905, 6.
24. "Wachter Seriously Ill," *Boston Daily Globe*, March 18, 1905, 22.
25. "Haverhill's First Win," *Boston Globe*, March 5, 1905, 76.
26. "Haverhill Easy," *Lowell Sun*, March 8, 1905, 4.
27. "Basketball Games," *Newburyport Daily News*, March 10, 1905, 1.
28. "Basketball Games," *Newburyport Daily News*, March 10, 1905, 1.
29. Gerry Finn, "Bucky Lew First Negro in Pro Basketball," *Springfield Union*, April 2, 1958, 35.
30. William Himmelman, "Toby Matthews," *Pro Basketball Encyclopedia*, https://probasketballencyclopedia.com/player/Toby-Matthews/.
31. William Himmelman, "Bill Sheridan," *Pro Basketball Encyclopedia*, https://probasketballencyclopedia.com/player/Bill-Sheridan/.
32. "Natick's Series," *Lowell Sun*, February 25, 1905, 17.
33. William Himmelman, "Toby Matthews," *Pro Basketball Encyclopedia*, https://probasketballencyclopedia.com/player/Toby-Matthews/.
34. William Hallett, *Newburyport and the Civil War* (History Press, 2012), Kindle, Location 138.
35. William Hallett, *Newburyport and the Civil War* (History Press, 2012), Kindle, Location 928.
36. William Hallett, *Newburyport and the Civil War* (History Press, 2012), Kindle, Location 994.
37. William Hallett, *Newburyport and the Civil War* (History Press, 2012), Kindle, Location 1535.
38. William Hallett, *Newburyport and the Civil War* (History Press, 2012), Kindle, Location 183.
39. William Hallett, *Newburyport and the Civil War* (History Press, 2012), Kindle, Location 1516.
40. "Rough and One Sided," *Boston Daily Globe*, February 28, 1905, 5.
41. "Basketball Games," *Newburyport Daily News*, March 10, 1905, 1.
42. "Basketball Games," *Newburyport Daily News*, March 10, 1905, 1.
43. "Basketball Games," *Newburyport Daily News*, March 10, 1905, 1.
44. "Great Basketball," *Newburyport Daily News*, March 11, 1905, 1, 6.
45. "Natick 46, Haverhill 24," *Boston Globe*, March 12, 1905, 84.
46. Frank Basloe, *I Grew Up with Basketball: Twenty Years of Barnstorming with Cage Greats of Yesterday* (University of Nebraska Press, 2022), 82.
47. Robert Peterson, *Cages to Jumpshots: Pro Basketball's Early Years* (New York: Oxford University Press, 1990), 64.
48. Frank Basloe, *I Grew Up with Basketball: Twenty Years of Barnstorming with Cage Greats of Yesterday* (University of Nebraska Press, 2022), 82.
49. William Himmelman, "Ray Snow," *Pro Basketball Encyclopedia*, https://probasketballencyclopedia.com/player/Ray-Snow/.

Chapter 14

1. "A Binding Chord," *Boston Globe*, February 23, 1999, 28.
2. Eileen Southern, *The Music of Black Americans: A History* (W.W. Norton, 1997), 249.
3. "Lowell's Own Story," *Lowell Courier-Citizen*, January 15, 1926, 11.
4. Douglas Stark, *The SPHAs: The Life

Notes—Chapter 15

and Times of Basketball's Greatest Jewish Team (Temple University Press, 2011), 96.

5. Douglas Stark, *The SPHAs: The Life and Times of Basketball's Greatest Jewish Team* (Temple University Press, 2011), 98.

6. "Stroud Testimonial: Successful Concert and Basketball Game," *Lowell Sun*, April 1, 1896, 1

7. "Cured by Marriage," *Boston Globe*, December 13, 1906, 2.

8. "Cured by Marriage," *Boston Globe*, December 13, 1906, 2.

9. "Cured by Marriage," *Boston Globe*, December 13, 1906, 2.

10. "Cured by Marriage," *Boston Globe*, December 13, 1906, 2.

11. "Married in Hospital," *Boston Herald*, December 14, 1906, 9.

12. "Married in Hospital," *Waterbury Evening Democrat*, December 15, 1906, 11.

13. "Cured by Marriage," *Boston Globe*, December 13, 1906, 2.

14. "Basket-Ball Champions of Vermont," *Springfield Reporter*, March 22, 1907, 1.

15. "A Ten Mile Walk by Night," *Brattleboro Reformer*, February 1, 1907, 1.

16. "A Ten Mile Walk by Night," *Brattleboro Reformer*, February 1, 1907, 1.

17. "A Ten Mile Walk by Night," *Brattleboro Reformer*, February 1, 1907, 1.

18. "A Ten Mile Walk by Night," *Brattleboro Reformer*, February 1, 1907, 1.

19. "Co. D 35, Lowell 32," *Saint Johnsbury Caledonian*, January 23, 1907, 8.

20. Advertisement, *Saint Johnsbury Caledonian*, January 16, 1907, 2.

21. "Basket-Ball Champions of Vermont," *Springfield Reporter*, March 22, 1907, 1.

22. "Basket Ball," *Saint Johnsbury Caledonian*, February 27, 1907, 5.

23. "Basket Ball: Co. D Wins from Dartmouth," *Saint Johnsbury Caledonian*, March 6, 1907, 5.

24. "Athletics State Champions: Took Deciding Contest in Basketball Series from Saint Johnsbury Tuesday Evening. Score 38 to 19," *Brattleboro Reformer*, March 8, 1907, 6.

25. "Take Another from Springfield," *Brattleboro Reformer*, February 22, 1907, 4.

26. "Game Ended with a Slugging Match," *Brattleboro Reformer*, March 1, 1907, 6.

27. "Game Ended in Fight: Athletics Were in the Lead 28–21 at Springfield When Haggerty Used His Fists on Church," *Vermont Phoenix*, March 1, 1907, 3.

28. "Springfield 34, Athletics 26," *Vermont Phoenix*, February 1, 1907, 3.

29. "'Gentlemanly' Haggerty," *Brattleboro Reformer*, March 22, 1907, 7.

30. "Game Ended with a Slugging Match," *Brattleboro Reformer*, March 1, 1907, 6.

31. "Basket-Ball Champions of Vermont," *Springfield Reporter*, March 22, 1907, 1.

32. "Sporting Notes," *Brattleboro Reformer*, March 22, 1907, 7.

Chapter 15

1. Martha Mayo, "Harry (Bucky) Haskell Lew," Ancestry.com, https://www.ancestry.com/family-tree/person/tree/10876273/person/-564384895/facts.

2. "Standard Certificate of Death: Margaret F. Lew," Commonwealth of Massachusetts, January 19, 1913.

3. "Scarlet Fever Epidemic May Close Schools and Playhouses," *Lowell Sun*, December 9, 1912, 1.

4. "Standard Certificate of Death: Margaret F. Lew," Commonwealth of Massachusetts, January 19, 1913.

5. "Overview: Scarlet Fever," NIH: National Library of Medicine, September 21, 2023, https://www.ncbi.nlm.nih.gov/books/NBK279620/.

6. "The Necessities of the Many," UMass Lowell Library, https://libguides.uml.edu/early_lowell/neccessities_of_the_many.

7. "The Lowell Directory: 1906," Internet Archive, https://archive.org/details/lowellma-directory-1906/page/n11/mode/2up.

8. "National Dye House," *Lowell Sun*, Friday, July 3, 1908.

Notes—Chapter 16

9. "Larceny Cases," *Lowell Sun*, July 28, 1910, 12.
10. Nick Manos, "Thomas L. Jennings (1791–1856)," BlackPast.org, February 2, 2009, https://www.blackpast.org/african-american-history/jennings-thomas-l-1791-1856/.
11. William Himmelman, "Bucky Lew," *Pro Basketball Encyclopedia*, https://probasketballencyclopedia.com/player/bucky-lew/.
12. "Catch All," *Lowell Daily Courier*, February 23, 1905, 8.
13. Robert Peterson, *Cages to Jumpshots: Pro Basketball's Early Years* (Oxford University Press, 1990), 80–81.
14. Robert Peterson, *Cages to Jumpshots: Pro Basketball's Early Years* (Oxford University Press, 1990), 81.
15. Robert Peterson, *Cages to Jumpshots: Pro Basketball's Early Years* (Oxford University Press, 1990), 53.
16. Frank Basloe, *I Grew Up with Basketball: Twenty Years of Barnstorming with Cage Greats of Yesterday* (University of Nebraska Press, 2022), 68.
17. "Centrals Outclassed," *Fitchburg Sentinel*, March 19, 1906, 4.
18. "Basketball Notes," *Fitchburg Sentinel*, February 21, 1907.
19. "Bucky Lew Coming," *Newburyport Daily News*, January 28, 1909, 3.
20. Gerry O'Connor interview with author, August 4, 2022.
21. "P.A.C.s Saturday," *Concord Enterprise*, January 30, 1907, 3.
22. "P.A.C.s Saturday," *Concord Enterprise*, January 30, 1907, 3.
23. "Lowell Track Team in Active Training," *Boston Sunday Post*, April 30, 1905, 14.
24. "Danny Recalls Bucky Lew," *Lowell Sun*, November 1, 1963, 1.
25. "FHD's Around the Town," *Nashua Telegraph*, December 10, 1958, 16.
26. "Danny Recalls Bucky Lew," *Lowell Sun*, November 1, 1963, 1.
27. "Bucky Lew Injured," *Lowell Sun*, January 21, 1915, 37.
28. "Leg Broken in Basketball Game," *Lowell Courier-Citizen*, January 23, 1915, 11.
29. "Bucky Lew Injured," *Lowell Sun*, January 21, 1915, 37.
30. "Bucky Lew Injured," *Lowell Sun*, January 21, 1915, 37.
31. "Leg Broken in Basketball Game," *Lowell Courier-Citizen*, January 23, 1915, 11.

Chapter 16

1. "James J. Gray Dies Suddenly," *Lowell Sun*, October 27, 1914, 1.
2. "Lowell Basketball Possible," *Lowell Sun*, November 3, 1915, 23.
3. "Leg Broken in Basketball Game," *Lowell Courier-Citizen*, January 23, 1915, 11.
4. "Lowell in the League," *Lowell Sun*, November 16, 1915, 10.
5. "Big League Game," *Lowell Sun*, November 10, 1915, 19.
6. "Basketball Notes," *Lowell Sun*, November 11, 1915, 9.
7. Mark Paul Richard, "Not a Catholic Nation," *Historical Journal of Massachusetts*, Vol. 47, Winter 2019, Institute for Massachusetts Studies, Westfield State University, 5.
8. "Big League Game," *Lowell Sun*, November 10, 1915, 19.
9. "Getting the Colored Vote," *Lowell Sun*, September 4, 1915, 20.
10. "Big League Game," *Lowell Sun*, November 10, 1915, 9.
11. William, Himmelman, "Lowell PAC 1901–1902," *Pro Basketball Encyclopedia*, https://probasketballencyclopedia.com/team-standings-by-year/?y=1901-1902&t=LowellPAC.
12. "Lowell Victory," *Lowell Sun*, November 17, 1915, 9.
13. "Lowell Victory," *Lowell Sun*, November 17, 1915, 9.
14. "Lowell Victory," *Lowell Sun*, November 17, 1915, 9.
15. William Himmelman, "### Casey," *Pro Basketball Encyclopedia*, https://probasketballencyclopedia.com/player/casey/.
16. "Lowell Victory," *Lowell Sun*, November 24, 1915, 21.
17. "Lowell Victory," *Lowell Sun*, November 24, 1915, 21.
18. "Lowell Team Defeated," *Lowell Sun*, November 26, 1915, 24.

Notes—Chapter 17

19. "Lowell Team Defeated," *Lowell Sun*, November 26, 1915, 24.
20. "Milford Victory," *Lowell Sun*, December 1, 1915, 9.
21. "You Must Hand It to Milford," *Lowell Courier-Citizen*, December 2, 1915, 9.
22. "Basketball Comment," *Lowell Sun*, December 4, 1915, 23.
23. "Lowell Beaten," *Lowell Sun*, December 6, 1915, 9.
24. "Basketball Comment," *Lowell Sun*, December 7, 1915, 11.
25. "Lowell Beaten," *Lowell Sun*, December 6, 1915, 9.
26. "Lowell Beaten," *Lowell Sun*, December 6, 1915, 9.
27. "Lowell Five Lost," *Lowell Sun*, December 8, 1915, 11.
28. "Lowell Five Lost," *Lowell Sun*, December 8, 1915, 11.
29. "Lowell Five Lost," *Lowell Sun*, December 8, 1915, 11.
30. "Victory for Lowell," *Lowell Sun*, December 15, 1915, 9.
31. "Lew's Basketball Luck," *Lowell Sun*, December 18, 1915, 10.
32. "Lew's Basketball Luck," *Lowell Sun*, December 18, 1915, 10.
33. William Wolkovich, "The Ku Klux Klan in the Nashoba Valley, 1840–1933," *Historical Journal of Massachusetts*, Vol. 18, No. 1 (Winter 1990), 65.
34. William Wolkovich, "The Ku Klux Klan in the Nashoba Valley, 1840–1933," *Historical Journal of Massachusetts*, Vol. 18, No. 1 (Winter 1990), 68.
35. Dianna Pan, "Once a Ku Klux Klan Stronghold, Groton Fights Its Reputation as a 'Sundown Town,'" *Boston Globe*, October 7, 2020, https://www.bostonglobe.com/2020/10/07/metro/once-ku-klux-klan-stronghold-groton-rejects-its-reputation-sundown-town/.
36. "Lowell Five Won," *Lowell Sun*, December 22, 1915, 13.
37. "Basketball Comment," *Lowell Sun*, December 24, 1915, 15.
38. "No Basketball Game," *Lowell Sun*, December 29, 1915, 19.
39. "League May Disband," *Lowell Sun*, January 7, 1916, 5.
40. "Basketball Comment," *Lowell Sun*, December 30, 1915, 15.
41. "Lowell Quits League," *Lowell Sun*, January 7, 1916, 1.
42. William Himmelman, "Central Massachusetts Basketball League," *Pro Basketball Encyclopedia*, https://probasketballencyclopedia.com/league/central-massachusetts-basketball-league/.
43. "Basketball Comment," *Lowell Sun*, December 7, 1915, 11.
44. William Himmelman, "Central Massachusetts Basketball League," *Pro Basketball Encyclopedia*, https://probasketballencyclopedia.com/league/central-massachusetts-basketball-league/.
45. "League May Disband," *Lowell Sun*, January 7, 1916, 5.
46. "Basketball Comment," *Lowell Sun*, January 6, 1916, 11.

Chapter 17

1. "Textile School Notes," *Lowell Daily Courier*, February 10, 1903, 10.
2. Douglas Stark, *Breaking Barriers: A History of the Integration of Basketball* (Rowman & Littlefield, 2019), 11.
3. Claude Johnson, *The Black Fives: The Epic Story of Basketball's Forgotten Era* (Abrams Press, 2022), Kindle, 114.
4. Claude Johnson, *The Black Fives: The Epic Story of Basketball's Forgotten Era* (Abrams Press, 2022), Kindle, 102.
5. "Frederick Fanning Ayer," *Pickout 1906: Year Book of the Lowell Textile School*, https://archive.org/details/pickout1906/page/n11/mode/2up.
6. "Basketball Notes," *Lowell Daily Courier*, November 25, 1906.
7. "'Skip' Field," *Lowell Sun*, November 6, 1908, 5.
8. "Lowell Commercial College," *Lowell Sun*, September 2, 1916, 3.
9. Martha Mayo, "Harry (Bucky) Haskell Lew," Ancestry.com, https://www.ancestry.com/family-tree/person/tree/10876273/person/-564384895/facts.
10. "Lowell Textile Basketball Team," *Lowell Sun*, January 4, 1922, 25.
11. "Lowell Textile Basketball Team," *Lowell Sun*, January 4, 1922, 25.
12. "Textile Resumes Basketball Work," *Lowell Courier-Citizen*, January 4, 1922, 5.

Notes—Chapter 18

13. "Textile Meets Team from Fitchburg Normal," *Lowell Courier-Citizen*, January 7, 1922, 10.
14. "Basketball," *The 1922 Pickout: The Year Book of Lowell Textile School*, https://archive.org/details/pickout1922/page/n145/mode/2up.
15. "Basketball," *The 1921 Pickout: The Year Book of Lowell Textile School*, https://archive.org/details/pickout1921/page/n125/mode/2up.
16. "Wins Overtime Contest," *Lowell Sun*, January 9, 1922, 21.
17. "Wins Overtime Contest," *Lowell Sun*, January 9, 1922, 21.
18. "Wins Overtime Contest," *Lowell Sun*, January 9, 1922, 21.
19. "Textile Team Keeps Busy," *Lowell Sun*, January 12, 1922, 14.
20. "Basket Ball," *Lowell Sun*, January 30, 1922, 8.
21. "Basketball Revival Tonight at Crescent," *Lowell Courier-Citizen*, January 31, 1922, 11.
22. "Basketball," *Lowell Sun*, February 1, 1922, 10.
23. "Basketball," *Lowell Sun*, February 2, 1922, 28.
24. "Basketball," *Lowell Sun*, February 2, 1922, 28.
25. "Textile Winner Over Boston College," *Lowell Courier-Citizen*, February 4, 1922, 10.
26. "Lowell Textile Wins," *Lowell Sun*, February 4, 1922, 9.
27. "Lowell Textile Wins," *Lowell Sun*, February 4, 1922, 9.
28. "Lowell Tech Has Lost but One Contest," *Burlington Daily News*, Wednesday, February 8, 1922, 1.
29. "Lowell Textile Wins," *Lowell Sun*, February 4, 1922, 9.
30. "Lowell Tech Has Lost but One Contest," *Burlington Daily News*, Wednesday, February 8, 1922, 1.
31. "Lowell Tech Has Lost but One Contest," *Burlington Daily News*, Wednesday, February 8, 1922, 1.

Chapter 18

1. "Boston College to Seek Its Revenge," *Lowell Courier-Citizen*, February 14, 1922, 11.
2. "Basketball Schedule: 1922," *The Text*, March 20, 1922, https://archive.org/details/textvol4no9.
3. "Textile Plays New Hampshire Tonight," *Lowell Courier-Citizen*, January 16, 1922, 23.
4. "Textile Basketball Team Off Today," *Lowell Sun*, February 9, 1922, 32.
5. "Victory for Home Five," *Lowell Sun*, February 15, 1922, 10.
6. "Victory for Home Five," *Lowell Sun*, February 15, 1922, 10.
7. "Textile Loses Game," *Lowell Sun*, February 18, 1922, 6.
8. "Basketball Schedule: 1922," *The Text*, March 20, 1922, https://archive.org/details/textvol4no9.
9. "Fall River Team Against Textile," *Lowell Courier-Citizen*, February 24, 1922, 17.
10. "Carlton J. Lombard," *UML Athletics Hall of Fame*, https://goriverhawks.com/honors/umass-lowell-athletics-hall-of-fame/carlton-j-lombard/94.
11. "C.Y.M.L. vs Y.M.C.I.," *Lowell Courier-Citizen*, March 3, 1922, 21.
12. "Here and There Along the Old Sport Pike," *Lowell Courier Citizen*, March 9, 1922, 11.
13. Murry Nelson, *The Originals: The New York Celtics Invent Modern Basketball* (Bowling Green: Bowling Green University Popular Press, 1999), 71–72.
14. *Lowell Sun*, February 10, 1922, 14.
15. "The Carlinville-Taylorville Scandal of 1921," *Football Archaeology*, August 22, 2023, https://www.footballarchaeology.com/p/the-taylorville-carlinville-scandal.
16. "Rockne of Notre Dame Says College Players Must Be Severely Dealt with for Violating Rules" *Lowell Sun*, February 4, 1922, 9.
17. "Eight Players Make Confession," *Lowell Courier-Citizen*, January 31, 1922, 11.
18. "Eight Players Make Confession," *Lowell Courier-Citizen*, January 31, 1922, 11.
19. "Says 'Pro' Athletes Are Like Movie Stars," *Lowell Sun*, February 14, 1922, 11.
20. "College Athletes Suspended," *Lowell Sun*, February 4, 1922, 9.

21. "Great Game of Basketball," *Lowell Sun*, February 8, 1922, 10.
22. "Lowell Five Evens Series with C.Y.M.L.," *Lowell Courier-Citizen*, February 8, 1922, 11.
23. "Here and There Along the Old Sport Pike," *Lowell Courier-Citizen*, February 10, 1922, 21.
24. "Here and There Along the Old Sport Pike," *Lowell Courier-Citizen*, February 10, 1922, 21.
25. "Textile Winner Over Boston College," *Lowell Courier-Citizen*, February 4, 1922, 10.
26. "Basketball," *Lowell Sun*, February 15, 1922, 10.
27. "Basketball," *Lowell Sun*, February 15, 1922, 10.

Chapter 19

1. "Announcement," *Lowell Courier-Citizen*, January 20, 1922, 29.
2. John Kenney, "The Lookout," *Lowell Sun*, January 22, 1934, 44.
3. Robert Peterson, *Cages to Jumpshots: Pro Basketball's Early Years* (Oxford University Press, 1990), 83.
4. "Announcement," *Lowell Courier-Citizen*, January 20, 1922, 29.
5. "Sportometer: At Crescent Rink," *Lowell Courier-Citizen*, March 6, 1922, 9.
6. "Basket Ball," *Lowell Sun*, January 30, 1922, 8.
7. David McKean, *Lowell Irish* (History Press, 2016), 94.
8. "Plans Made for Big Basketball Series," *Lowell Sun*, January 25, 1922, 25.
9. "Basketball," *Lowell Sun*, February 2, 1922, 12.
10. "Boston College vs Textile Tonight," *Lowell Courier-Citizen*, February 3, 1922, 17.
11. "Lew's Road Outfit Against Lawrence," *Lowell Courier-Citizen*, February 20, 1922, 11.
12. "Lowell Five Wins Title," *Lowell Sun*, February 25, 1922, 18.
13. "Lowell Five Wins Title," *Lowell Sun*, February 25, 1922, 18.
14. "Basketball," *Lowell Courier-Citizen*, February 22, 1922, 11.
15. "Profs Open Court Games Next Week," *Nashua Telegraph*, December 28, 1922, 6.
16. "Basketball," *Lowell Sun*, February 16, 1922, 28.
17. "Here and There Along the Old Sports Pike," *Lowell Courier-Citizen*, January 25, 1923, 13.
18. "Lowell a Member of New England Basketball League," *Lowell Sun*, October 22, 1923, 10.
19. "Fort Hill Illuminated by Burning Cross at Midnight Hour," *Lowell Sun*, August 15, 1923, 4.
20. "K.K.K. Invades West Andover," *Lowell Courier-Citizen*, August 25, 1923, 4.
21. "New Basketball League," *Lowell Sun*, October 29, 1923, 24.
22. "Lowell and Clinton Meet in Basketball Revival," *Lowell Courier-Citizen*, November 21, 1923, 12.
23. "Lowell and Clinton Meet in Basketball Revival," *Lowell Courier-Citizen*, November 21, 1923, 12.
24. "Well-Known Net Stars Interested in N.E. League," *Lynn Daily Item*, October 25, 1923, 4
25. "New England Basketball League Out of Business," *Lowell Courier-Citizen*, December 10, 1923, 10.
26. Arthur Eno, Jr., et al., *Cotton Was King: A History of Lowell, Massachusetts* (New Hampshire Publishing Company in Collaboration with the Lowell Historical Society, 1976), 146.
27. "Population of Lowell, MA," Population.us, https://population.us/ma/lowell/.
28. William Himmelman, "Bucky Lew," *Pro Basketball Encyclopedia*, https://probasketballencyclopedia.com/player/bucky-lew/.
29. "Cadets and Y.M.C.I. Play Monday Night," *Lowell Courier-Citizen*, January 12, 1924, 12.
30. "A Great Lowellian: Joseph E. Sullivan, Philanthropist, Dies at 77," *Lowell Sun*, August 15, 1972, 1.
31. "Lowell Basketball League Formed," *Lowell Sun*, January 11, 1926, 8.
32. "Sacred Hearts and CMYL to Clash," *Lowell Courier-Citizen*, January 15, 1926, 17.
33. "Sacred Hearts Take the C.Y.M.L.,

Notes—Chapter 20

24 to 20," *Lowell Courier-Citizen*, January 20, 1926, 11.

34. "Here and There Along the Old Sport Pike," *Lowell Courier-Citizen*, January 21, 1926, 11.

35. "Sacred Hearts Defeat C.Y.M.L. in Fast Basketball Game," *Lowell Sun*, January 20, 1926, 28.

36. George Hepbron, *How to Play Basketball* (New York: American Sports Publishing Company, 1904), 56.

37. "League Meeting," *Lowell Sun*, January 27, 1926, 28.

38. "Big Basketball Series Gets Underway Tonight," *Lowell Sun*, April 16, 1926, 44.

39. "Big Basketball Series Gets Underway Tonight," *Lowell Sun*, April 16, 1926, 44.

40. "Deaths: Lew," *Lowell Sun*, July 25, 1922.

41. Robert Forrant, "The Rise and Demise of the Connecticut River Valley's Industrial Economy," *Historical Journal of Massachusetts*, Vol. 46, No. 1, Winter 2018, 2–21, Institute for Massachusetts Studies and Westfield State University.

42. Martha Mayo, "Harry (Bucky) Haskell Lew," Ancestry.com, https://www.ancestry.com/family-tree/person/tree/10876273/person/-564384895/facts.

43. "Visitation Five Lists Opening Drill Tonight," *Springfield Republican*, November 21, 1935, 8.

44. "Dowd Will Play with Visitations," *Springfield Union*, December 6, 1935, 27.

45. "Mrs. Harry Lew Served Church, Civic Groups," *Springfield Union*, December 14, 1966, 24.

46. "Mrs. Harry Lew Finds Cheer in Work That Helps Others," *Springfield Union*, 1955, January 24, 2.

47. "Mrs. Harry Lew Finds Cheer in Work That Helps Others," *Springfield Union*, January 24, 1955, 2.

Chapter 20

1. "Basketball," *Nashua Daily Telegraph*, December 26, 6. AU: Year?

2. "PACs of Lowell Defeat the Montcalms," *Nashua Telegraph*, February 26, 1906, 7.

3. "An Easy Win from Haverhill," *Nashua Telegraph*, December 14, 1906, 8.

4. "FHD's Around the Town," *Nashua Telegraph*, April 7, 1967, 4.

5. "FHD's Around the Town," *Nashua Telegraph*, October 29, 1963, 4.

6. "FHD's Around the Town," *Nashua Telegraph*, April 7, 1967, 4.

7. "FHD's Around the Town," *Nashua Telegraph*, October 29, 1963, 4.

8. "FHD's Around the Town," *Nashua Telegraph*, October 29, 1963, 4.

9. "FHD's Around the Town," *Nashua Telegraph*, April 7, 1967, 4.

10. Steve Daly, *Dem Little Bums: The Nashua Dodgers* (Plaidswede, 2002), 20–21.

11. Steve Daly, *Dem Little Bums: The Nashua Dodgers* (Plaidswede, 2002), x.

12. Steve Daly, *Dem Little Bums: The Nashua Dodgers* (Plaidswede, 2002), 20–21.

13. Steve Daly, *Dem Little Bums: The Nashua Dodgers* (Plaidswede, 2002), xiii.

14. Charlie Bevis, *The New England League: A Baseball History, 1885–1949* (McFarland, 2007), 257–258.

15. Charlie Bevis, *The New England League: A Baseball History, 1885–1949* (McFarland, 2007), 263.

16. Charlie Bevis, "Fortuitous Event or Planned Action? Nashua Dodgers, the Second Front of Baseball Integration in 1946," *Black Ball 10: New Research in African American Baseball History*, edited by Leslie Heaphy (Jefferson: McFarland, 2021).

17. Steve Daly, *Dem Little Bums: The Nashua Dodgers* (Plaidswede, 2002), 12.

18. Steve Daly, *Dem Little Bums: The Nashua Dodgers* (Plaidswede, 2002), 20.

19. "Around the Town," *Nashua Telegraph*, November 6, 1950, 10.

20. "Around the Town," *Nashua Telegraph*, November 6, 1950, 10.

21. Charlie Bevis, "Fortuitous Event Or Planned Action? Nashua Dodgers, the Second Front of Baseball Integration in 1946," *Black Ball 10: New Research in African American Baseball History*, edited by Leslie Heaphy (Jefferson: McFarland, 2021).

22. Frank Basloe, *I Grew Up with Basketball: Twenty Years of Barnstorming*

Notes—Chapter 20

with Cage Greats of Yesterday (University of Nebraska Press, 2022), 68.

23. William Himmelman, "Dido Wilson," *Pro Basketball Encyclopedia*, https://probasketballencyclopedia.com/coach/DIDO-WILSON/.

24. Claude Johnson, *The Black Fives: The Epic Story of Basketball's Forgotten Era* (Abrams Press, 2022), Kindle, 235.

25. Claude Johnson, *The Black Fives: The Epic Story of Basketball's Forgotten Era* (Abrams Press, 2022), Kindle, 240.

26. Claude Johnson, *The Black Fives: The Epic Story of Basketball's Forgotten Era* (Abrams Press, 2022), Kindle, 346

27. Douglas Stark, *Breaking Barriers: A History of the Integration of Basketball* (Rowman & Littlefield, 2019), 132.

28. Claude Johnson, *The Black Fives: The Epic Story of Basketball's Forgotten Era* (Abrams Press, 2022), Kindle, 410.

29. Josh Elias, *The Birth of the Modern NBA: Pro Basketball in the Year of the Merger, 1949–1950* (McFarland, 2024), Kindle, Location 6055.

30. "The First Patriot, Ron Burton," The Sports Museum, https://www.sportsmuseum.org/curators-corner/the-first-patriot-ron-burton/.

31. "Bill Sullivan, Sr., Well Respected," *Lowell Sun*, January 30, 1972, C1.

Bibliography

Basloe, Frank. Introduction by Michael Antonucci. *I Grew Up with Basketball: Twenty Years of Barnstorming with Cage Greats of Yesterday.* University of Nebraska Press, 2022.
Bavasi, Buzzie, and John Strege. *Off the Record.* Contemporary Books, 1987.
Bayne, Bijan. *Sky Kings: Black Pioneers of Professional Basketball.* Franklin Watts, 1997.
Bevis, Charlie. *The New England League: A Baseball History, 1885–1949.* McFarland, 2007.
Boucher, Chris. *The Original Bucky Lew: Basketball's First Black Professional.* Wings ePress, 2023.
Daly, Steve. *Dem Little Bums: The Nashua Dodgers.* Plaidswede, 2002.
Egerton, Douglas. *Thunder at the Gates: The Black Civil War Regiments That Redeemed America.* Basic Books, 2016.
Elias, Josh. *The Birth of the Modern NBA: Pro Basketball in the Year of the Merger, 1949–1950.* McFarland, 2024.
Eno, Arthur, Jr., et al. *Cotton Was King: A History of Lowell, Massachusetts.* New Hampshire Publishing Company in Collaboration with the Lowell Historical Society, 1976.
Forman, Franklin. *Twenty Families of Color in Massachusetts: 1742–1998.* The New England Historic Genealogical Society, 1998.
Gill, Joel Christian. *Strange Fruit, Volume I: Uncelebrated Narratives from Black History.* Fulcrum Publishing, 2014.
Gould, Todd. *Pioneers of the Hardwood: Indiana and the Birth of Professional Basketball.* Indiana University Press, 1998.
Hallett, William. *Newburyport and the Civil War.* History Press, 2012.
Heaphy, Leslie, ed. *Black Ball 10: New Research in African American Baseball History.* McFarland, 2021.
Henderson, Edwin. *The Grandfather of Black Basketball: The Life and Times of Dr. E.B. Henderson.* Rowman & Littlefield, 2024.
Hepbron, George. *How to Play Basketball.* American Sports Publishing Company, 1904.
Holman, Nat. *Scientific Basketball.* Herald Square Press, 1922.
Johnson, Claude. *The Black Fives: The Epic Story of Basketball's Forgotten Era.* Abrams Press, 2022.
Johnson, Kenneth. *Kansas University Basketball Legends.* History Press, 2013.
Koppett, Leonard, et al. *Total Basketball: The Ultimate Basketball Encyclopedia.* Sportclassic Books, 2003.
Kuska, Bob. *Hot Potato: How Washington and New York Gave Birth to Black Basketball and Changed America's Game Forever.* University of Virginia Press, 2006.
Lang, Arne. *Sports Betting and Bookmaking: An American History.* Rowman & Littlefield, 2016.
Leonard, Elizabeth. *Benjamin Franklin Butler: A Noise, Fearless Life.* University of North Carolina Press, 2022.
Maraniss, Andrew. *Games of Deception: The True Story of the First U.S. Olympic Basketball Team at the 1936 Olympics in Hitler's Germany.* Philomel Books, 2019.

Bibliography

McKean, David. *Lowell Irish*. History Press, 2016.
Naismith, James. *Basketball: Its Origin and Development*. Bison Books, 1996.
Nelson, Murry. *The National Basketball League: A History 1935 to 1949*. McFarland, 2009.
Nelson, Murry. *The Originals: The New York Celtics Invent Modern Basketball*. Bowling Green State University Popular Press, 1999.
O'Connor, Gerry. *Don Newcombe Drills a Millionaire*. Haunted House Press, 2016.
Peterson, Robert. *Cages to Jumpshots: Pro Basketball's Early Years*. Oxford University Press, 1990.
Peterson, Robert. *Only the Ball Was White: A History of Legendary Black Players and All-Black Professional Teams*. Oxford University Press, 1992.
Rice, Ed. *Baseball's First Indian: Louis Sockalexis: Penobscot Legend, Cleveland Indian*. Tide-Mark, 2003.
Ritchie, Andrew. *Major Taylor: The Extraordinary Career of a Champion Bicycle Racer*. Johns Hopkins University Press, 1988
Ross, Charles. *Mavericks, Money, and Men: The AFL, Black Players, and the Evolution of Modern Football*. Temple University Press, 2016.
Scoggins, Charles. *Bricks and Bats*. Lowell Historical Society, 2002.
Southern, Eileen. *The Music of Black Americans: A History*. W.W. Norton, 1997.
Stark, Douglas. *Breaking Barriers: A History of the Integration of Basketball*. Rowman & Littlefield, 2019.
Stark, Douglas. *The SPHAs: The Life and Times of Basketball's Greatest Jewish Team*. Temple University Press, 2011.
Stout, Glenn, and Johnson, Richard. *The Pats: An Illustrated History of the New England Patriots*. Houghton Mifflin Harcourt, 2018.
Thomas, Ron. *They Cleared the Lane: The NBA's Black Pioneers*. Bison Books, 2004.
Vermette, David. *A Distinct Alien Race: The Untold Story of Franco-Americans: Industrialization, Immigration, Religious Strife*. Baraka Books, 2018.

Index

Allen, Phog 117
Amateur Athletic Union (AAU), segregation 36
attempted boycott of Lew 102–4

baseball, institution of color line 30–32
basketball: and dancing 120; invention 35–36
Basloe, Frank 50
Bavasi, Buzz 177
Birth of a Nation (film) 138
Boston College basketball team 152–53, 156
Boston Patriots 179
Brattleboro, VT, basketball 122–27
Bristol, PA, basketball 67, 96, 111
Brooklyn Dodgers, integration 173–78
Brown, Walter 4, 179
Burke Temperance Institute 48, 80
Burkes basketball team 38, 48–50, 52–58, 73, 75, 80–88, 92, 97, 121, 152
Burton, Ron 179
Butler, Benjamin 20
Butler, John 23

Campanella, Roy 6, 176–78
Catholic Young Men's Lyceum (CYML) 158
Chollet, Leroy 179
Church, Charles 124–26
Clifton, Nat 179
Cooper, Chuck 4, 179
Cummings, Fred 103
Cushing, Lester 157

dead ball era of basketball 64–65
decline of pro basketball 131
Dion, John 10
Dobens, Fred 4, 5, 134, 173–77
Douglas, Bob 3, 148, 178

Driscoll, Connie 95, 99, 100–2, 105–6, 108

early basketball: ball 64–65; court conditions 68–69, 85; defensive strategy 70, 108–9; Lew's philosophy 153–54; pros 50–52; rules 66–68; shooting 66–67; violence 10, 81, 113

family history 14–19, 21, 120–22, 128, 129–30, 133, 170–172
Field, Skip 59–60, 73, 84, 94, 98
Finn, Gerry 1, 4, 58–59, 62
Foster, Rube 4
Fowler, Bud 4

gambling 28, 53, 88, 159
Gardner, George 23
Gray, James 41, 62, 91, 104–6, 111
Green, Pumpsie 1
Gulick, Lester 35

Harrison, Bob 179
Hart, Frank 2
Haverhill, MA, basketball 39–40, 91–118, 131, 134, 167
Henderson, Edwin 3, 147–48
Hepbron, George 10, 169
Holman, Nat 158
Hough, Harry 74–75, 78, 91, 96, 99, 102–3, 111, 117

immigration 7, 17, 136–37, 143
Indian Town, ME 32
indignities: called "colored valet" 85; called "coon" 104; denied shelter 122–23, 143
injuries: broken leg 134; closed eye 86; gashed hand 69, 85; kicked in stomach 87; shoulder dislocations 97, 101, 109
integration firsts: college coach 89,

203

Index

149–50; franchise owner 136–45; official 40, 163–65; pro coach 132, 163–65, 170; pro player 50–52

Jennings, Thomas 130
Jim Crow 21, 132
Johnson, Frenchy 2
Johnson, Wendy (Lew's granddaughter) 6, 161, 180

Kelliher, William 10
Knox, Kittie 3
Ku Klux Klan 20, 136–37, 143–44, 166

Lake, Fred 11, 41
Lapchick, Joe 178
Lawrence, MA, basketball 39, 56, 132, 146, 165
League sides with Lew over boycott 103–4
Lewis, William Henry 3
Lew's Lowell Five basketball team 132, 145, 160, 165
Lloyd, Earl 179
Lowell Burkes *see* Burkes basketball team
Lowell city championship 86–88
Lowell Commercial College 149
Lowell Lowells basketball team 91, 94, 104–6, 110–13
Lowell PAC *see* Pawtucketville Athletic Club (PAC)
Lowell Textile School 89, 147–61
Lowell Tigers baseball team 12, 41
Lowell, MA, basketball *see* Lew's Lowell Five; Lowell Burkes; Lowell Lowells; Pawtucketville Athletic Club
Lowell, MA, history: abolitionists 17–19; birth 16; decline 167; integration 21; and slavery 16–19
Lynch, Dan 8, 9, 29, 49–50, 97

Manchester, NH, basketball 39–40, 53, 67, 74–76, 78–80, 83, 94
Marlboro, MA, basketball 2, 9, 57–61, 72–73, 76, 82–84, 88, 96, 100, 139, 141–142
Martens, Charley 67, 114–15
Massachusetts Institute of Technology basketball team 9
Massachusetts League 52
Matthews, Clarence 3
Maynard, MA, basketball 53, 56, 71–72, 76, 144, 167

Meister, Victor 39
Misaka, Wat 179

Naismith, James 7, 35, 89, 118
Naismith Hall of Fame acknowledgement of Lew 63
Nashua, NH: baseball 4–6, 12, 173, 175–77; basketball 39, 53, 74, 77, 90, 95–95, 121, 132, 137, 158, 160, 163, 165, 173–75
Natick, MA, basketball 100, 102–5, 106–7, 109–18
National Basketball Association, integration 179
New England Basketball League championship, 1905 110–11, 113–16
Newburyport, MA, basketball 100, 110, 114–15
Newcombe, Don 6, 176–78

O'Connor, Dan 73, 133–34
O'Ree, Willie 1, 179
Original Celtics 174–75

Pawtucketville Athletic Club (PAC) 48–50, 52, 54, 60, 61, 71–88, 91, 98
Pollard, Fritz 4
Portsmouth, NH, basketball 110, 132
Posey, Cumberland 4
pro basketball, integration 59–63, 178–79

Redmond, James 50, 52, 54, 77
Renaissance basketball club 178–79
Rickey, Branch 173
Robinson, Jackie 5, 59, 173
Rockne, Knute 159
Roosevelt, Theodore 27
Rose, Irving 178
Ross, Howard 178
Russell, Bill 1

Saint Johnsbury, VT, basketball 123–25, 132
Sanford, ME, basketball 132
Smith, Florence (Lew) 121–22, 170, 171, 172
Smith, John 80
Sockalexis, Louis 3, 10–15, 32, 33, 42–44, 45, 46–47
South Framingham, MA, basketball 53, 72, 85–86, 96, 98–99, 109, 139
Springfield, VT, basketball 123–26, 127, 132
Stagg, Alonzo 159

204

Index

Starlight, Young 23
Sullivan, Joseph 163, 168
Sullivan, William, Jr. 179
Sullivan, William, Sr. 162, 163, 166

Taylor, Major 3, 25–27
Taylorville college football scandal 159
Textile School Championship, 1922 157
Tischinsky, Abraham 178
Trenton, NJ, basketball 51, 67, 111

Underground Railroad 18
University of Massachusetts Lowell 89

Vermont State Championship, 1907 123–27

Wachter, Ed 95, 108, 113, 117–18, 158, 167
wedding 121–22
Williams, Hank 178
Williamson, Jimmy 100, 108, 109
Wilson, Dido 132, 178
Worcester, MA, basketball 71–72, 139, 145
World Championship, 1905 117–18
World Professional Basketball Tournament, integration 178

YMCA of Lowell, MA, basketball team 7, 8, 40
YMCA Triangle League Championship, 1902 7

www.ingramcontent.com/pod-product-compliance
Lightning Source LLC
Chambersburg PA
CBHW020411030326
40554CB00026B/146